UNDERCOVER

Second Edition

Carmine J. Motto
Dale L. June

CRC Press
Taylor & Francis Group
Boca Raton London New York

CRC Press is an imprint of the
Taylor & Francis Group, an **informa** business

First published 2000 by CRC Press
Taylor & Francis Group
6000 Broken Sound Parkway NW, Suite 300
Boca Raton, FL 33487-2742

Reissued 2018 by CRC Press

Library of Congress Cataloging-in-Publication Data

Catalog record is available from the Library of Congress

A Library of Congress record exists under LC control number: 99462595

ISBN 13: 978-1-315-89833-9 (hbk)
ISBN 13: 978-1-351-07743-9 (ebk)

Visit the Taylor & Francis Web site at http://www.taylorandfrancis.com and the
CRC Press Web site at http://www.crcpress.com

Table of Contents

Preface

The crime of counterfeiting is one of the oldest criminal professions in the world. The Roman Emperor Nero is said to have been the first coin counterfeiter, although many European rulers of the past are known to have debased the coinage of their countries, and it is possible that Nero was merely following a pattern that had originated before his time. When the Colonists settled in the New World it was not long before they were making counterfeit wampum to fleece the native Indians. During the Revolutionary War, the British dumped so much counterfeit money into the country that the Continental currency soon became worthless. Even today the expression, "Not worth a continental" can still be encountered to express worthlessness.

Early in the Civil War it was estimated that about one-third of all currency in circulation was counterfeit. At that time our money was printed in hundreds of different designs by various banks. In 1863, the United States adopted a national currency and issued United States Notes, commonly called "greenbacks". This national currency was quickly counterfeited, and the counterfeits circulated so extensively that the Government was compelled to take steps to protect its money. Accordingly, The United States Secret Service was established July 5, 1865, as a bureau of the Treasury Department to suppress the counterfeiting which threatened to undermine the economic strength of the nation...

Money, designer clothing, computer parts and software; if it can be produced, it can be counterfeited. Drugs, corruption, industrial internal theft; the economic integrity and strength of the nation are being sapped by those who are only concerned about personal wealth and power. The most effective weapon against them are those who would work undercover...

The Authors

Carmine J. Motto retired for the third time in 1996 concluding a a career in law enforcement that spanned sixty years. He served in the New York State Police, the U. S. Secret Service, the U. S. Treasury Office of Law Enforcement, (where he was appointed to the staff inquiring into the original investigation of the Attica Prison riots), Deputy Commissioner of Public Safety for the City of White Plains, New York, and he served three years as police commissioner of Harrison, N.Y.

Carmine Motto at the conclusion of an undercover case. It became necessary to arrest Agent Motto to prevent his undercover identity from becoming known.

Mr. Motto was the recognized expert in undercover operations for the Secret Service. He was assigned to undercover work with a Special undercover detail during the very early years of his tenure with the Service. When the third special undercover unit was organized in 1962, Mr. Motto was assigned as the Assistant Special Agent in Charge. He was soon promoted to the top position as the Special Agent in Charge, which he held until his first retirement.

Mr. Motto literally wrote the book on undercover work for the Secret Service. His first book *Undercover* became a classic among a generation of Secret Service agents. *Undercover, Second Edition* is the updated and expanded of his original book. He is still occasionally called upon to instruct and lecture the new agents and police officers in the finer points of undercover work. He remains actively interested in law enforcement.

Mr. Motto has been featured in several news articles about counterfeiting and undercover work. He has also been a consultant for numerous television programs and movies. He was a case agent in the counterfeit case involving the notorious "Mr. 880" which became a movie starring Burt Lancaster. The true story of Mr. 880 appears in Mr. Motto's latest book, *In Crime's Way*, in which he recounts his undercover experiences dealing with counterfeiters and conspirators.

Dale L. June displays part of a $1 million seizure of counterfeit notes.

Dale L. June split his Secret Service career between protective assignments with the President and other high-ranking officials and dignitaries and investigative work, including undercover assignments. His law enforcement career included working as a police officer in Northern California, a Special Agent in the U.S. Secret Service, and an Intelligence Specialist (organized crime and terrorism)in the U. S. Customs Service. He also has worked as a private investigator and executive protection/security specialist. He teaches part-time in the criminal justice and social sciences/humanities fields.

Undercover, Second Edition Dale June's second book. He is also the author of *Introduction to Executive Protection* published by CRC Press in 1998

Acknowledgments

Attempting to dedicate a book after over sixty years of experience in police-related work becomes extremely difficult. The man who gave you your first break; the informant who helped give you a reputation; the teachers in the various schools; the men you worked with; the men who worked for you; your family who had to put up with your continual and extended absences and the telephone calls that took you away in the middle of the night; the district attorneys who successfully prosecuted your cases; all your brother officers and fellow agents, city, state, and federal, who cooperated with you even though they knew the case was not theirs; the unsung witnesses who gave testimony in spite of the fact they might later be in some danger — all these people, and many others, should be given the credit, because without them, there can be no truly successful police officer and no successful fight against crime.

I would like to single out the late-Director of the U.S. Secret Service, James J. Rowley. I am proud to call this man a friend and contemporary. He was the inspiration and role model for a whole generation of Secret Service agents. He had the foresight over the years to see the need for advanced training that would result in better qualified men and women in the field of undercover work and thereby keep a stranglehold on the modern-day counterfeiter. The U. S. Secret Service Training Center near Washington, D.C. has been named in honor of this dedicated individual.

Carmine J. Motto
New York City, 1999

Working on this second edition of Carmine Motto's classic book, *Undercover,* has been a labor of pride and privilege. It is a special honor to have had the opportunity to work with Mr. Motto and to have my name linked with his in this way. Mr. Motto is a legend in the Secret Service and his positive influence has been felt, and continues to be felt, by many thousands of others who came into contact with him either as a victim, witness, informant, suspect, co-worker, and acquaintance. I was never fortunate enough to have the pleasure of working with him as a Secret Service agent, but his book was never far from my reach. It is people like Mr. Motto who selflessly give of themselves, often sacrificing their personal life and family time to advance the cause of justice, who are truly the heroes we so desperately seek. When Mr. Motto finally retired from law enforcement after over sixty years in the trenches, he said that although he often worked alone, he always had a close partner. He pointed to his beloved wife, Flora. I wish to thank them both for this very special opportunity to lend my small contribution to his legacy.

Dale L. June
Los Angeles, 1999

In remembrance of all who went before
Dedicated...loyal...brave
In support of those who continue
Courage...confidence...trust

Introduction

1

In the late 1950s, there was a popular television program called *Tightrope*. The premise of this police drama was very simple: an undercover operative, working for an unnamed law-enforcement agency, would travel the land infiltrating criminal organizations (sometimes even corrupt police departments), and at the conclusion, would expose the criminal element to arrest. When the lead character (played by Mike Connors) was caught in a tight situation, or if his cover was about to be exposed, he would surprise his captors by "getting the drop on" them by whipping out the gun he kept tucked in the small of his back (he was always searched, but no one ever found the gun!) or he would be rescued by another agent who was also in on the undercover operation, unbeknownst to the main character. The program concluded with a statement similar to "…and in the excitement and confusion of the arrest, one man escaped…" Of course we all knew that one person was — the undercover agent, who walked the tightrope between the law and the lawbreakers.

They were exciting stories, even in their simplicity. Today's television fare has similar offerings, albeit more sophisticated. Some electronic gadget, computer, or untimely recognition by one of the "bad guys" usually exposes the undercover operative. But the basic formula is the same — exposure, threat, capture, and a heart-pounding last-minute rescue. And that's how it is in the real world, except there may not always be a life-saving recovery.

In today's society, suspects, undercover agents, and just plain citizens alike have access to modern means of communication and carry them as they attend to their daily business routines. An undercover operative must be able to explain to the suspect why he needs to carry a gun, a pager (or two), a recording device, a cellular telephone, an electronic organizer, or a hand-held computer, for example. Even before the case gets underway, this is one of the many problems that an undercover agent must face. He must rely on his own wit, skill, and luck to convince the criminal that this equipment is necessary and important for the conduct of his business. There is a tenant of real life that will never change — skill and daring get you close, but wit and luck get you in and out, and make the case a success. The four words that best describe an undercover agent they are "wit," "skill," "courage," and "luck." A modern undercover agent cannot expect to have a team of rescuers come storming through the door with guns blazing to save him; he is for the most part alone, with only his skill with words and a quick mind to get out of a tough spot.

Governments, armies, and the police have long-used undercover agents and informants. They are often referred to as "spies" or "secret agents." Their nececcity in government and military matters is obvious. The agents infiltrate the governments or military structures of less-than-friendly nations to learn secrets that are transmitted back to their controller for analysis and strategic planning. In the private sector, undercover investigators are frequently found on company payrolls. They are used to root out employee drug abuse, employee theft, on-site prostitution, and in other areas as diverse as "mystery-shopper" services and monitoring employee morale. In the high-stakes corporate world, operatives are useful in situations involving industrial espionage, safety, and security concerns. Police undercover work, on the other hand, is more focused on uncovering crimes that are normally unknown to police agencies or are seldom reported, such as white-collar crime, corruption, and possession of contraband.

Contraband is generally defined as any material that is prohibited by law and whose mere possession is a violation of the law. Falling into this category are such items as drugs, narcotics, and "bootlegged"items — computer software, videos, untaxed alcohol and cigarettes, phony credit cards, and counterfeit money to name just a few of the things that can be classified as illegally retained.

The public's perception of police undercover work is one of working in disguise — of officers pretending to be a taxi drivers to combat robberies of cab drivers; of officers dressed as little old ladies or homeless people, derelicts, or even prostitutes, in order to deter muggings, rapes, robberies, and, on occassion, to apprehend a serial killer. This type of police undercover work is actually a form of decoy and not to be confused with the higher echelon of genuine undercover work. Undercover work involves the agent masquerading as an underworld figure or an authority official that can be "bought." The purpose of undercover work is to obtain evidence, locate the source of contraband, or catch a public official in an act of corruption. In other words, the intent of undercover work is to gain knowledge of the criminal and the crime, and to gather enough evidence against the suspect for a conviction. Because of the nature of the crimes and the secretive manipulations of the principals, undercover operations are often the only means of developing intelligence data, securing evidence, and seizing the contraband.

Undercover work as we know it today had its genesis in the 1920s and 1930s. Illegal alcohol was the big-ticket item during the years of the Prohibition, and covert investigation (undercover work) became the best means by which to obtain information about the "bootleggers." After World War II, counterfeiting and narcotics became the major items of concern to federal crimebusters. It was at this time that federal, state, and big-city law-enforcement agencies began to use their own personnel to perform undercover work. Many years ago (even up to and through the 1970s) most agencies used informants to do undercover work. Informants generally didn't (and still don't) get respect, especially when testifying in court, that police officers or special agents do in an undercover capacity. Many informants have criminal records and lifestyles that don't favorably impress juries. Cross-examination of an informant is a defense attorney's delight. It was found, sometimes with dire consequences, that informants couldn't always be relied upon to be trustworthy or that they had the government's best interests at heart. During the Viet Nam War and "flower power" decades of the 1960s and 1970s, drugs became the major focus of many undercover operations. This has continued through the 1980s, the 1990s, will, most likely, continue to be the hot-button items that will require intensive undercover work into the 21st century.

Today, undercover work is a recognized and accepted law enforcement tool. Most of the agencies choose experienced agents or officers to become undercover agents and provide them with specific undercover training. Many agents are selected directly from their respective training academies because of certain distinctive characteristics they display. It may be personality, skills in specific areas, or just an aptitude for dangerous and challenging work. Many large police departments have three levels of undercover assignments:

1. The first level is the operative who makes drug (or other contraband) buys on the street. This agent observes a person making a sale and approaches him, negotiates a deal, makes the buy, and moves on. Surveillance and covering officers then move in to effect the arrest or attempt to follow the seller to his source.
2. The mid-level agent is the one who usually comes to mind when undercover work is discussed. An informant either introduces the agent to the violators or he manages to meet the people of interest through his own devices, luck, and skill. At this level there is more caution shown by the "dealers." They will usually work and make sales from a secured environment or compound and will discuss the illegal activity only with people they have previously done business with in the past, people who are well known to them, or who can be vouched for as being trustworthy.

3. The top level of undercover work is the most sophisticated and dangerous. This is really the "major leagues" of undercover work. The operative manages somehow to work his way into an organization, becoming a trusted ally, living and sharing common experiences with the different echelons of the targeted association. This operation or "deep cover" is similar to government spying or "moles" who sometimes lead a double life for years before the business is completed.

The United States Secret Service was founded in 1865 to combat counterfeiting. A special undercover unit was formed in November, 1934 to thwart counterfeiting operations anywhere in the United States. The second unit (or detail) was formed in July 1938. It consisted of an agent in charge and about 12 to 15 special agents who operated as a team. A third similar squad was formed in 1962. Not all agencies had the personnel or budgets to form these types of special details. However, over the years they justified the personnel commitment and budget expenditures by proving themselves capable of successfully fighting crime on all levels.

Since the original publication of this book, the U.S. Secret Service has had to deal with tremendous advances in technology. Sophisticated computers and copy machines, capable of producing nearly detection-proof counterfeit money, credit cards, and identity documents, are now widely accessible — they can be found in virtually every office, business, and home. In addition to the contraband produced by the illegitimate print shop operating in some clandestine location, anyone with a mind to making counterfeit money can instantly be in the counterfeit business.

Printing counterfeit notes has become as simple as putting the note to be copied into the machine, feeding in the paper, and out comes a nearly perfect color copy. One high-tech manufacturer boasts in their advertisement that their commercially available digital camera, with a 1600x zoom lens attachment, can capture intricate details that are invisible to the naked eye and make them fully visible without any loss of detail. The ad features a an enlargement of a section of a $50 bill (the area just below President Grant's beard). The enlarged photograph is flawless — unbelieveably sharp and detailed. It doesn't take any stretch of the imagination to understand how this equipment could be misused.

Plates, inks, residue, and ruined negatives are a thing of the past. With the new technology, once the counterfeits have been made, there isn't any telltale evidence that the machine was ever used for any illegal purposes. In 1995, less than 1% of the counterfeit money seized nationally was computer generated; however, by the end of 1998 this figure had jumped to over 40%.* In one computer-generated counterfeiting case, the defendant's attorney was quoted by the *Los Angeles Times* as saying, "The penalties for counterfeiting are substantially less than for bank robbery. You'd have to be a fool on drugs to go rob a bank — it's a lot easier to manufacture money than it is to steal it." *

The "back-room printers" are history; the Secret Service now has the enormous task of combating these modern-day counterfeiters and their high-tech equipment and distribution networks. One resulting consequence has been the introduction of a new currency with added security features that, at least for the present, cannot be exactly duplicated. In spite of the expected and well-documented rise in counterfeiting, the principles of working undercover remain the same. Sooner or later, the counterfeit will find its way into the hands of the underworld and into public circulation and it will be the responsibility of the undercover agent to break the case.

The goal of the undercover agent will vary depending on the department he is working for. In a counterfeiting case, for example, he is endeavoring to locate the plant — the printer or reproduction equipment. But, counterfeiting is no longer confined to money. Nearly any commercial item is subject to counterfeiting — designer clothing, videos, CDs, and documents such as driver's licenses, "green cards," and passports. In the alcohol case, the agent must locate the still; in drug and narcotic cases he attempts to locate the person or persons (usually an organization) responsible for bringing the drugs into the country or locality. Regardless of the contraband involved in the case, the goal is usually achieved by the undercover agent gaining introduction to those responsible and making a "buy" directly from the suspect or source. The secondary intention of the undercover operative is to convince the suspect to cooperate with the agency, after he has been caught in the act of committing a crime and learns he has been dealing with a government agent or police official. Modern undercover work and "sting" operations as employed by the various agencies, in addition to the introduction of more complex electronic devices, will undoubtedly be the ultimate weapon to combat sophisticated crime which, more and more, is run like a legitimate business.

"Sting" operations (so-called confidence games, popularized and named after the successful 1970s Robert Redford and Paul Newman movie, "The Sting") are hybrid forms of undercover work. Stings differ from the conventional uncover methods in that they are usually elaborate schemes to entice the target of the investigation to a particular location through his own free will to engage in the unlawful activity where the transaction is videotaped

* U..S. Secret Service; *Los Angeles Times,* Nov. 5, 1998.
* Ibid.

and recorded. The role of the undercover agent in a sting operation is usually limited to that of pretending to be a conduit for the contraband or activity.

Undercover work is best described as a drama involving three main participants: (1) the informant, (2) the suspect, and (3) the undercover agent. Regardless of the type of operation, sting, or undercover case, the drama will always involve interaction among these three key participants. In this book, we will focus on the roles of these three main characters in the undercover theater and explore the near-symbiotic relationship between the informant and the undercover agent as they match wits with the suspect and play out the drama to its conclusion.

Undercover agents are dedicated, intelligent, and hard-working individuals. Their role is to counter the moves and intentions of the suspect. Undercover work, or to use a slang term of a bygone era, "roping," is probably the most fascinating phase of all police work. It is also the most inexact as there aren't any standardized procedures to follow. There is no guarantee that what works for one agent, case, or situation will work again in another case. The basic rules have been written by experience, and for very good reason — *safety.* It is essential to be mindful of the "do's and dont's" and pay attention to "red flags." Don't do anything contrary to good common sense that will intensify an already dangerous situation. When the situation just doesn't seem right or when a "red flag" is raised, learn to recognize it and heed the warning. The cardinal rule is "safety first and no deviations from the plan." If something does go wrong or if it just doesn't feel right — stop the operation. There are some things that an undercover agent should never do and at the top of the list is never take unnecessary risks. No amount of contraband is worth the life of an agent.

Undercover work isn't for everyone. Not everyone aspires to or even likes working undercover, but it seems like those who do work undercover tend to remain in the specialization for as long as they are needed or until they "burn out." For many undercover agents, undercover work becomes a way of life that challenges the deepest emotions and resources of their existence. It becomes a challenge to the undercover operative to use his capabilities to the maximum in order to match wits with the denizens of the underworld. The undercover agent finds that he must rely on his intelligence and resourcefulness to deflect any question regarding his personal life, professional business, and involvement in illegal activities. "Street-wise" individuals, ex-cons, and the entire cast of characters engaged in unlawful pursuits are usually suspicious of dealing with any unknown factors. They are especially suspicious of buyers or contacts to whom they have been introduced via a third party, but with whom they have no proven track record for engaging in their specific contraband or activity. They will be slow to trust the outsider and will often devise ways to see if they can trip him up. The popular media has exposed nearly every undercover ploy developed through the years making the undercover operative's position more dangerous and precarious than ever.

Undercover work and handling informants is, at best, a hit-and-miss affair. It can never become an exact science because of the one variable that cannot be altered — the human element. Every informant, every undercover agent, and certainly every suspect is different; therefore, every case will present a new scenario. People's actions and reactions cannot be predicted or prescripted. It is the ability to convincingly "role play" and quickly adapt to unplanned and unforeseen changes (including threatening situations) that marks a successful undercover agent.

The experienced officer who has handled many informants and the officer who has been extensively involved in undercover work are soon recognized as experts in their field. It is individuals of this caliber that are expected to train the new officers,who are anxious to become proficient in all phases of police work. We have always felt that the experiences of the "old-timers" such as the agents who worked to arrest the "coniackers"* are invaluable and their expertise is sorely needed by the young upcoming agents and officers of today. These experiences shouldn't be laid to rest with the men who made them. Future undercover operatives can gain valuable learning experience and benefit from the cases that have been successful in the past. Some of the famous police textbooks of the past have been in print for over 35 years and are as useful to new recruits today, as they were when they were written. The only things that really change are the faces of the agents and the suspects and their level of technical sophistication — investigative techniques remain, for the most part, unchanged.

The rules, methods, and the procedures of undercover work were developed and refined through trial-and-error by agents who received no formal training in undercover techniques. They were the pioneers, men who relied on their natural abilities and intelligence to successfully engage the lawbreaker in his own element. Every day and every case is a learning experience. Today's undercover operative would do well to listen to the voices of past experience. A common criticism of rookie undercover operatives by veteran officers is that they tend to be careless, reckless, and foolhardy and won't listen to common sense or those who have gone before. No amount of experience, however, can eliminate the unknown variables. After all, we are dealing with the vagaries of human nature and questions posed by the role of the target(s) of the investigation and the informant (a very necessary component to the successful operation, though his trust cannot always be relied upon.)

A Vermont philosopher and co-founder of a successful business, Mr. Lyman Wood, frequently said of his enterprise, "You know, this business is

* Coniackers: an old-time slang term (1900s–1940s) used by Secret Service Special Agents to describe counterfeiters; no longer used.

pretty simple. All you have to do is more of what works and less of what doesn't!" That simple business philosophy is just as relevant to working undercover. It is the intent of this book to address and share our experiences using actual case examples. Hopefully, it will result in fewer mistakes by future undercover operatives by having them do more of what works and less of what doesn't as they are confronted by the unexpected twists and turns of the case in the pursuit of their mark — the suspect.

We have attempted to prevent this book from becoming a step-by-step "how to beat the law" book because we know that the readership cannot be limited to law enforcement. But we stress that the principles discussed here should be the foundation for innovation and discovery that will keep the undercover agent one step ahead. It will soon become obvious to the reader of this book that most of the experiences related here were successful. It is not to be construed that all undercover cases end in success, on the contrary, most cases end in failure. That is, for some reason or another the case doesn't result in the arrest of the criminal suspect or the seizure of the contraband. A 30 to 35% average would be considered excellent. We usually know why we have been successful; it is more difficult to learn why we fail. Our failures could fill volumes while the successes might barely fill a book. In the long run, however, no case should be considered a total failure because much is gained from every venture. Experience is gained and knowledge is developed that could be useful in future cases.

While no two cases are exactly the same, there are certain common elements that are in each case: (1) the introduction, (2) the acceptance, (3) the buy, (4) the arrest, (5) covering the informant, and (6) the "after action."

The introduction of the undercover operative to the suspect is made by the informant and this is the beginning of the case. From this point on, the undercover agent is either accepted or not. In the event the suspect does not accept the agent, it might be necessary for the informant to meet the suspect at a later time without the undercover agent to determine why the suspect didn't accept the agent at the time of the introduction. In the event the agent is not accepted, it is very easy for the informant to bring in another agent with a different cover story. This time, both the agent and informant will try to overcome the difficulties the first agent had.

After the introduction of the undercover agent to the suspect, there is a short period of (in boxing terms) bobbing, weaving, and circling. The suspect gets to know or feel if he can trust the prospective buyer. If a feeling of trust is established, conversation will quickly turn to the contraband that is to be purchased. This conversation will generally result in the undercover agent asking for or obtaining samples and the suspect will present the purchase price. After the samples have been delivered and the undercover agent has an opportunity to examine them, he then informs the suspect how much of the product he wants to purchase. This purchase may or may not go through. In other words, a decision must be made whether or not to arrest the suspect when he delivers the contraband (a "buy-bust" scenario) or to take that action after subsequent deliveries. This is decided before the undercover agent gives the suspect the figures regarding the purchase and price he is willing to pay. If it is decided that this buy will go through, no arrests should be made and nothing should be done to arouse the suspect's suspicion.

The first buy is usually a small one and the agency doesn't mind losing this "seed"money in order that the undercover agent can at a later time make a larger purchase. Generally, the second purchase, or if necessary several subsequent purchases, is large enough to warrant not only the appearance of the suspect, but also some of the people connected with him. These people could be present in several capacities, counter-surveillance, protection, main participants or equal partners, perhaps even "higher ups." Sometimes it is necessary because of the development of circumstances surrounding the case to arrest the suspect when he makes an initial delivery. The decision to make an arrest at the time of the delivery is called a "buy-bust."

As previously mentioned, there comes a question of payments. Most suspects cannot handle very large buys, especially if it is necessary for them to purchase the merchandise in advance from a third party. Because the first buy may proceed smoothly, the suspect sometimes oversells the undercover agent to his connection and insists that the larger buy will be just as trouble free. Usually, the suspect will get delivery, but the people who delivered the contraband to him will be in the vicinity to make certain that they receive their money after the purchase.

At the scene of the second or subsequent purchase, a signal is made at the appropriate time, and arrests are made including the undercover agent and the informant, if they are present. This is a very crucial aspect of the undercover operation. It is at this point that the informant has to be covered up and the actions taken by the arresting agents will dictate whether or not his cover is successful. It is very important at the scene of the arrest for the arresting agents to separate the undercover agent and the informant from the rest of the group. It is also advisable to separate all the rest of the arrestees. This will prevent them from trying to fabricate a story and/or it could result in the quick cooperation of one of them. In one scenario, as the arrest was occurring, the undercover agent in carrying on with his role snarled to the suspect that he had better keep his mouth shut. The suspect followed that advice and later mentioned to the arresting agency that he had wanted to cooperate but had been afraid to do so because of the implied threat by the other person who had also been arrested at that same time. The suspect still wasn't aware that the other person was an undercover agent and not a "connected" tough-guy.

The undercover agent will usually have been in contact with the suspect for several hours prior to the arrest(s) and will undoubtedly have more information to give to the arresting agents. If he is in the company of the other arrestees, it is very difficult for him to give this information. At the time he is separated, he should be interviewed immediately. He may be in a position to give information regarding other individuals who may be involved, where additional merchandise is kept, the location of the plant or manufacturing site, individuals who may be waiting for the payoff money, and many other important pieces of information that he has picked up during his conversations with the suspect.

This also applies to the informant who undoubtedly has been listening and talking to the suspects prior to the delivery. If there have been any prearranged ideas on how the informant is to be covered, this is the time to put them into effect. Some suspects can be fooled and will believe almost anything that is told to them, while others who have been engaged in criminal activities for a long time will not be easily fooled. However, some effort should be made to attempt to cover the informant.

There are informants who do not object to being exposed. There can be a number of reasons why an informant feels this way. He may be leaving the area and has no intention of returning. He may feel he is as tough as any of the people he is informing on and is not afraid of retaliation. He may have just met the suspect and does not plan to see him again. He may be a professional informant who testifies at trials and does not care what happens as long as he is paid for his services.

In cases where we are dealing with this type of informant, it is still a good idea to arrest him and the undercover agent at the scene. If after questioning, the defendants will not cooperate, the exposure of the informant and undercover agent will generally have a psychological effect on the defendants. After learning they have been doing business with an undercover agent, they may be in a position and mental disposition to fully cooperate. Before a situation like this can be worked out, all phases of the case must be explored to be certain that exposure will not jeopardize either the informant or the usefulness of the undercover agent.

After the arrests have been made, the prisoners, the undercover agent and the informant separated, the prisoners should be searched immediately for weapons and contraband. Any vehicles that the suspects have on the scene should likewise be searched and seized, if the circumstances warrant it.

There are some cases that are accomplished very quickly, sometimes in the space of an hour or less. A quick undercover case is not unusual and sometimes fast-moving events make it important that the case is moved along as quickly as possible. This is necessary when certain information about an arrest is going to appear in an early edition of a newspaper, broadcast "with film at eleven" on television or an "all-news" radio update. There are occasions when the news media learns of an arrest of a violator and just before the story is published, the violator decides to cooperate, perhaps by introducing an undercover agent to another suspect. It becomes necessary to effect this introduction and sale before the news reaches the public and announces that an arrest has been made. On the other hand, some undercover cases can last for days, weeks, and even months. In the case of an undercover agent who is gathering intelligence or subversive information from foreign sources, he can be undercover perhaps for as long as several years or for as long as his identity remains secret.

After-action reviews must be conducted after every undercover operation. It is through such reviews that reasons for the success or failure of an operation become apparent — why did the informant double-cross us, why or how was the agent's cover revealed, and how was surveillance detected? For a variety of reasons, the suspect may not be able to produce, sometimes he has no intention of producing, he is merely trying to pull off a swindle, a scam, a "rip-off." There are times when there is no apparent reason for the failure and we can only guess what went wrong. We can't learn from our mistakes unless we recognize that we made a mistake and take the necessary and appropriate steps to prevent it from happening again. Often, we have to wait weeks and even months before the informant can learn through his sources just what went wrong in the case; sometimes we learn through other non-related cases or sources and sometimes we will never know.

The stories and incidents related in this book are not told merely for the sake of spinning a yarn. We sincerely hope they are illustrative of the principles that are outlined and that they provide the reader with a better understanding of the concepts of undercover work that have been developed over time. These experiences worked for us. Perhaps another agent working the same cases would have been just as successful using a different approach. We don't expect that everyone will agree with all that is written here. That is understandable. Because there are so many factors that cannot be prescripted, we can only rely on past experience and provide generic instruction. Yet past personal experience and the experiences of others form the basis to find a working formula in similar circumstances.

Most of the cases discussed in this book are Secret Service cases because that is our background. For the purpose of this book, the cases of Carmine Motto are told in the first-person singular. Other stories relating to Dale June, or another agent, are told in the third person "an agent" or "an officer." The techniques to ascribe to, the principles to adhere to, and the procedures to follow are the same and will work as well in a narcotics case as in a counterfeiting case. We think it would be presumptuous for us to cite cases of other agencies or departments. However, we strongly feel that the principles are sound and remain the same regardless of the contraband involved. The lion's share of our experience in undercover work involved counterfeiting of currency, stolen government checks, bonds and other types of government obligations including counterfeit U.S. postage stamps. There was also a major case involving counterfeit gold nuggets. However, in doing undercover work, an agent sometimes has to make purchases of contraband or obtain intelligence data that belong under the jurisdiction of another agency. The splendid cooperation between agencies over the years should continue into the future and that is what is needed to wage a successful war against the underworld dealers in contraband and other black-market items.

Indeed the mentioned cooperation extended to the preparation of the material in this book. The personal feelings, the thoughts, anxieties and fears were gathered from conversations with several active undercover officers who were willing to speak candidly about their private concerns relating to undercover work. It is important that these feelings, including the misgivings, be expressed freely, because dealing with the fear and anxiety and knowing they are shared by one's colleagues may help another undercover operative get beyond the scope of personal paranoia and deal with his private apprehensions. It is interesting to note that some undercover agents are reluctant to discuss their private thoughts and anxieties and refuse to share their experiences, knowledge, and thoughts for fear they could be turned against them. Thus reinforcing the undercover agent's concern for safety and never knowing what or who will expose them.

A purposeful attempt was made in narrating actual cases in this book to omit times, dates, real places, and true names of people involved. This was done with the intent to not disclose the identities or circumstances that would lead to the exposure of any informant or person who violated the law, yet has paid his debt to society. In rare instances where a true name is used it is because the person has passed away or has publicly told the story to the news media and does not wish to remain anonymous.

In the course of preparing the material for this book we sometimes found that we had to revert to police vernacular or street slang. To assist the reader who comes across a word or term that they are unfamiliar with, we have attempted to identify those words and define them in the Glossary at the end of the book. The words "undercover agent," "operative," and "officer" as used in this text are interchangeable and are meant to be all-inclusive. They refer to the undercover federal agent, the state policeman, deputy sheriff, or city police officer working in an undercover capacity. In other words, any law enforcement person, walking the thin tightrope between law and the law breakers and the one of whom hopefully it can be said, "In the excitement and confusion of the arrest, one person escaped…"

The Informant

2

An undercover operation usually begins with an informant. An infromant is defined as "one who gives information." Informants are a very necessary part of police work and most agencies would be at a loss to operate without them. Many names have been give to informants, most of which are are offensive and have no place in modern-day police work. "Rat," "squeal," "stool," " canary," "fink," "snitch," "narc," and variations of these words are only a few of the less-than respectful terms that have been used to designate one who gives information to enforcement or investigative agencies. Generally accepted deferential words today are "source," "asset," "contact," and "C.I." (f short for "confidential informant"). For the purposes of clarity and uniformity there should be one definitive word: informant.

Informants are one of the principal tools of the police. Like all journeymen who must use tools, the police too must realize the importance of the informant when there is a job to be done. There is a saying in police circles, "A good officer or agent can be measured by his number of informants." In fact many agencies, rightly or wrongly, use the number of informants an agent has as a criterion in job evaluations and promotions. Contacts with informants are made, and developed in as many ways as there are reasons for the person to want to provide information. Developing an informant begins with knowing what it is that would induce them to share the knowledge they have about the topic of investigative interest.

Anyone can be an informant. It is important that the agent or officer making contact with a potential source recognize their possibilities and make every effort to learn what information the contact has and how it might be of value. Every contact an agent makes in the course of his regular duties, or may learn about from others in his nonpolice-related activities, should be considered as a candidate to be a source of information. It is incumbent upon the agent to obtain information by asking the right questions. It's common for an informant to have information pertinent to other subjects that the contacting agent may want to know about and all it takes to get the information is asking the right questions. Informants must be cultivated, rewarded, respected, cajoled, and re-interviewed often. Recognize them for what they are and treat them accordingly. An informant may be a prostitute, a homeless street person, a "junkie," a "druggie" or dealer, or they may be a housewife, a well-respected businessman, or possibly a co-defendant. It is often very difficult to work with informants. Most frequently the undercover agent must trust the informant, but he should always be alert to the possibility of an informant "going sideways." In other words, an informant is only as good as his motivation.

Motivation

Motivation is that "something" that prompts a person to take a certain action. Always remember that an informant has his own reason or motive for informing and it is imperative for the agent to deduce exactly what that motive is. Without knowing his motive, it would be virtually impossible to work with him; his monetary expectations may far exceed what the agency is prepared to impart. It would be beneficial to look into some of the reasons *why* a person informs.

Profit

Some people inform for profit – money is a great motivator. There are people who make their livelihood by entering into the underworld to learn information that they can sell to interested agencies for money. They are professional informants. They will always have information for sale and will, naturally, seek to get the highest price for it.This usually creates a problem; one that needs to be addressed "up-front" as soon as possible after the informant has made his overtures. The supervisor, the case agent, or the undercover agent must work out an agreeable arrangement with the informant before committing to the case. Some professional informers, even some novices, will have preconceived notions of how much money their information is worth. They will either ask for a percentage of the recovery or will place a flat fee amount on their services. This amount in most cases is far more than the agency is willing to pay.

It is common in counterfeit money cases for the informant to ask for a fee amounting to 10% of the recovery. While that 10% doesn't sound like much, in a case involving a $1million dollar seizure of counterfeit notes, it will net the informant $100,000 – a very sizable amount of money. Even a 1% reward would be very costly at $10,000. In cmost ases of counterfeit seizures, a percentage generally cannot be worked out because the informant doesn't know how much fake money there is in the plant and a percentage would be far more than common sense and appropriate responsibility can allow. There is also the possibility that the informant could be working with the counterfeiters and would intentionally run off an extra million or more just to increase the size of his payoff.

In smuggling cases or in cases where the government recovers something of value, 10% would probably be a fair amount. Here, it must be kept in mind that the government actually receives something of value, but in a case involving counterfeit money, the government gets nothing but worthless printed paper.

In counterfeiting and credit card cases, the informant's fee for services rendered is usually agreed upon before the case is undertaken.This amount could generally be increased if a larger seizure is made than had originally been anticipated. Of course, the informant should not be told in advance about the possibility of a "bonus" if the seizure is larger than the agent expected. If a counterfeiting plant is seized with a large amount of counterfeit money, a considerable amount can be paid to the informant.

In attempting to arrive at a fair amount, the supervisor must take into account the following: How long has the plant been operating? Who are the people behind the plant? What is the amount of the seizure? How good and or deceptive is the product? How much of it has been successfully passed? How many investigators is this note tying up on the street? How much money is available for rewards before the end of the fiscal year? By considering the responses to these questions, a supervisor or agent can arrive at a figure to pay the informant. The money is generally paid out immediately after the case is made. It isn't practical in this type of case to wait until the case has been successfully prosecuted — it could take years.

Some agencies find it profitable to keep informants on the payroll, giving them money on a regular basis. The informant in turn supplies the agency with a steady flow of information. This arrangement works out very well where the department involved, such as the local or state police, or the FBI,.is interested in all types of crime. However, for organizations whose work is specialized, the Secret Service, Alcohol, Tobacco and Firearms Division (ATF), and the U.S. Customs Service, for example, the informant is a "one-shotter." He is someone who stumbles upon the information and reports it and may never have another opportunity to bring a case to those agencies. Some informants have given the Secret Service counterfeiting information and have never again run into another counterfeiting case, not because they weren't looking for it, but because the crime is not as prevalent as say, drugs, for example. The same could be said of the other crimes under Secret Service jurisdiction. Federal crimes such as check and/or bond forgery rings, bank fraud, telecommunications and computer crimes, fraudulent identification, and government and commercial securities fraud, and electronic funds transfer fraud are crimes that informants will not have continuing knowledge about. Narcotics cases and dealing in stolen property are ongoing investigations and a professional informant will have ample opportunity to develop worthy information to sell to the appropriate agency.

Some professional informants will actually mimic law enforcement tactics to obtain their information. They will actively seek to penetrate an organization, sometimes even having their own contacts introduce them to the principals. They will develop information that they either sell to the agency having jurisdiction or shop it around to the highest bidder.

> One such informant was "Danny the Driver." Dsnny came ino a southern California Secret Service office with information regarding a family of gangsters having counterfeit money for sale. The family consisted of two brothers (one of whom had done time murder); the mother (the mastermind of the organization) who didn't trust anyone, including her husband; and the father (the "front-person") who did all the negotiating. Except for the father, who was a white Anglo, the family was of Oriental/Mexican background and would only deal with people they had known personally for a long time and who had a similar ethnicity. Because of a favor Danny had done for the family through his connections, they accepted him, and allowed him to become their "contact man" for their counterfeit. The family's real business was drugs. They had recently concluded a sale to an organized crime family on the East Coast and had been ripped-off by being paid in counterfeit money. Now they were stuck with the bogus money and had no way to recoup their losses except to sell it to some unwitting outsider.
>
> Danny was a "weasel" of a guy. He was six-foot tall, but didn't weigh a pound over 130. He was in his mid-30s and had been a cross-country truck driver but had given up driving the big rigs when he found out he could make a living brokering information and wouldn't have to work as hard. He wore thick glasses and had a shock of unruly hair, held in place with what looked and smelled like motor oil. He always wore a cap that was as dirty and greasy as his unkempt hair. He was a working man, a "red-neck" who always wore western shirts and boot-cut jeans. He gave the appearance of being more at home discussing cars and motorcycles over alongneck bottle of beer than he was with arranging the sale of contraband. However, that was just his public persona. He actually was a very sly person who had a knack for getting into and out of closed groups such as the "family" who trusted him to find a potential buyer for their money.

According to Danny, the family was suspicious of any strangers who would knowingly want to buy counterfeit money with real cash. So it was at Danny's suggestion (after verifiing that he did indeed have serviceable information and after he had received some $50 in"walking-around cash") that the case agent and his supervisors decided to barter some other illegal object for the counterfeit. The undercover agent would offer to trade a shipment of new semi-automatic/automatic modified (short-barrel) Uzi assault weapons for the counterfeit. Of course, the guns would never leave the agent's possession. It was planned that the arrests would be made immediately upon exchange of the guns/counterfeit in a "buy-bust."

Arrangements were made to meet the father and one brother in a conveniently located restaurant. The undercover agent and the informant arrived early and took a booth away from the most crowded area. A few minutes before the scheduled meeting time, the suspects arrived. They looked the patrons over to satisfy themselves that there weren't any police in the place before approaching the informant and undercover agent. Following introductions, the suspects questioned the undercover agent about his background and what he had to sell. They were given a pre-scripted story that as far as his business and background were concerned, all they needed to know was that they had a product they wanted to unload and he had some merchandise they might be interested in. In no time at all (which is unusual in most similar cases) the suspects agreed to look at the merchandise and if they liked what they saw, perhaps a bargain could be struck. The four men proceeded to the parking lot where the agent removed new Uzi from the trunk of his car. It was still in the original wrapping and covered with creosote preservative. The agent told the men that the gun was part of a shipment stolen from a midwestern national guard armory. The suspects liked what they saw and expressed the thought they could get a very good price for it in Mexico. They displayed a single $100 counterfeit bill and saying it was all they had with them, but that they had a total of several thousand dollars worth they would trade at another meeting. An argument ensued. The agent expressed disappointment that they didn't have the money with them and said that they wouldn't get any guns until they had what the gun was worth. Before the meeting broke up, it was agreed they would get back to the informant with the time and place an exchange could be made. An attempt was made at this point to get the infomant out of the negotiations, but the suspects insisted that all contacts be made through him.

For his assistance, and as an additional incentive, the informant, who said he desperately needed money because his family was being evicted from the low-rent motel they were staying in, was paid an another $200.

About a week later, the agent learned from casual conversation with an agent in the ATF that an individual whose description matched that of Danny, had contacted his agency with information concerning some people who were interested in buying some Uzis. According to the informant, these people had seen one of the weapons and thought it had possibly been stolen or lost from the government. According to the ATF agent, this individual wouldn't give any specifics until he was paid in advance for the information. The ATF agent had refused to pay for the information and hadn't heard from the informant since and had no way to contact him. At about the same time, but unfortunately it was before the conversation with the ATF agent, the informant reported back to the Secret Service by telephone that the family had disposed of the counterfeit and was no longer interested in buying any automatic weapons. That should have been the end of the story because no more of those particular counterfeit notes were passed and we were unable to contact Danny. But there was more to the story.

A few weeks after the meeting with the suspects in the restaurant parking lot, the undercover agent was at his home in an upscale neighborhood. The off-duty agent was mowing the lawn and just happened to look up as a car came to a halt at the corner of his street, a cul-de-sac. He instantly recognized the driver as the informant — someone who had no business in the neighborhood. Quickly, before the informant could see him, the agent ducked down in the driveway behind his car and watched as the informant drove away. The agent surmised (and correctly so) that Danny would have sold the information of where the agent lived to the suspects in the case or to others. That was the last time Danny the Driver was ever seen by the agent.

Based on the showing of a single counterfeit note with the intent to sell and distribute, a grand jury returned an indictment charging the suspects with possession of counterfeit money. They were convicted and sentenced to six months in prison. After the suspects were convicted of the one-note possession, they let it be known that the informant had sold them information that the person they had met in the restaurant was an undercover agent. As a result, they had burned the remaining notes. They also revealed that before Danny brought the undercover agent to the meeting, he had introduced them to other interested persons who had expressed a desire to buy the counterfeit, but the family decided against selling to people they didn't know. The last we heard about the informant was that he was a suspect in a truck hijacking in northern California.

Revenge

Some informants inform because they want revenge. For reasons best known only to them, they want to see the violators arrested because it suites their particular purpose or because of something that the violator did to the informant for which he wants revenge. The spirit of revenge that motivates this type of informant is very strong and generally the informant will overextend himself to see that the case is made.

> A few years ago, the Secret Service was plagued with counterfeit government checks in and around the Southwest. One local Secret Service agent developed information from an informant that a local prostitute was handling the counterfeit government checks for a group that "controlled" prostitution in the area.
>
> I was assigned to work on this case and I proceeded to the small southwestern town to meet with the informant. The informant agreed to introduce me to the girl handling the counterfeit checks and to help me make a purchase from her.
>
> I spent several hours with the informant and couldn't make up my mind why he was informing. Several more meetings with the informant were necessary before I finally found out what motivated him. It was learned that he was a "talent agent for professional women," otherwise known as a "pimp." At one time, he had controlled all the prostitution in the area. The people who were responsible for the counterfeit checks had, through "strong-arm" techniques, convinced all the local professional talent to join their booking agency, thus taking away control (and profits) from the informant. The informant knew if he could have the opposition arrested on counterfeiting charges, he could regain control of the prostiution.
>
> The introduction was made a short time later and I was able to buy 50 checks from the prostitute. I then put in an order for 1,000 checks and she explained that it would take up to three weeks before a delivery could be made. She wouldn't explain why it would take that long except to say that the checks came from a far away location.
>
> I made several meetings with the girl and on each occasion she asked me a lot of questions about myself. I explained to her that I had found there was too much "heat" in New York and I was on an

"extended vacation" and couldn't return until my people advised me that it would be safe to do so. The purchase of 1,000 checks involved a considerable amount of money and some of her delaying actions couldn't be explained.

Several days after my last meeting with her, the sheriff of the county told other agents he had received information from one of his confidential sources that a gangster from New York was in town with a lot of money and a group of people were going to sell him some counterfeit government checks. Instead of turning the checks over to him, they were going to murder him and take his money. The sheriff didn't know how reliable his information was, but it tied in perfectly with the case I was working on and it was decided that this would be a good time for me to leave the area because of the stalling tactics of the group.

I had a final meeting with the girl and I made sure she had an undercover telephone number where I could be reached. Then I told her I was going back to New York because I didn't think her group could produce the checks I had requested. She tried hard to get me to stay, but I insisted that I couldn't stay any longer, as my services were needed in New York, and my people wanted me to return.

Several days later, I received a telephone call from a man who identified himself as a friend of the prostitute. He said that the checks were ready and suggested that I come get them immediately. I told him my people weren't interested any more and didn't trust his group. He explained that there had been a lot of trouble producing the checks, but now they were ready and the whole deal could be final within 24 hours. I again told him our deal was dead.

Then I told him I knew a wealthy Chinese merchant, who was leaving for the Philippines, who might well be interested in purchasing the checks. I stated, however, that this man wouldn't budge from his own home to make the deal because he was be afraid of being ripped-off or robbed. The man was insistent and suggested that we meet somewhere halfway, perhaps in Cleveland or Chicago. I suggested he bring the checks to New York, but he was reluctant because he didn't know New York and would be uncomfortable there. After several telephone calls, Washington, D.C. was agreed upon as the place of delivery.

We all met at National Airport (Ronald Reagan National Airport) near downtown Washington, D.C. The suspects were arrested after turning the checks over to me. They were armed and also had samples of bank checks, driver's licenses, and Social Security cards to show me for future sales.

After the arrest, one of the men decided to cooperate with the prosecution and stated that the counterfeit checks were made in Durango, Mexico. A detail was sent to Mexico to work with the Mexican police. In a short time, the printer was identified, the plant was seized and all who were involved in the operation were arrested.

This case is a classic example of an informant giving good information because it suited his purpose to have the opposition taken out of circulation. In an interesting aside to the case, I had misgivings about dealing with the informant because of his bragging that he controlled all the "professional night-time female talent" in his county. I felt I had to do something with the information. I contacted the informant and told him I was honor-bound to let the local sheriff know that he was the man running all the prostitution in his county. I expected that the informant would be outraged about my ungrateful concern. His simple reply surprised me, " You do what you have to do, and don't worry about me." I then notified the sheriff who appeared rather philosophical about the information. He said, "Prostitution is always going to be with us; arrest one man and another will just take his place."

Concealment of a Crime

Many people become informants after they have committed a crime and fear that the police are in the process of having them arrested. They think that if they inform, the police will either forget the violation or have it reduced because of the information that they give. This type of informant is hard to identify because he generally won't admit that he committed a crime or that he is trying to conceal it. One of the better cases broken by the Secret Service was accomplished because of an informant who fitted in this category.

One day a man whom we will call Pele came into the New York office with a package containing $75,000 in counterfeit $20 bills. These counterfeits originated in Chicago, Illinois, and were being circulated nationally in large amounts. The informant told the agent in charge that he was given this package to take overseas to exchange for drugs and then to return to the United States with the drugs and relinquish them to the man who had given him the counterfeit.

The informant had a responsible position aboard a U.S. merchant vessel. He told the agent in charge that he couldn't go through with the deal and wanted to bow out. He stated he would surrender the counterfeits, but wounldn't give any further information.

While Pele was still in the office, I received a telephone call from a woman who said a man had victimized her by paying her with cash that she had since learned was counterfeit money. The victim came to the office and it soon became apparent that she was a prostitute. She provided a description of the previous night's "client". She said the person was a seaman on a U.S merchant ship and she could recognize him if she ever saw him again. Her description of the passer of the counterfeit notes was identical to Pele, who was still in the office insisting that he couldn't help the Service any further. The "business woman" was allowed to see Pele and it became necessary to physically restrain her after she identified him as the "lover" who had given her the counterfeit money. This of course shed different light on him and he instantly fell into another category of informant. He was no longer a willing informant, but rather, a potential defendant.

After the informant was told he was going to be arrested for possessing and passing counterfeit, he quickly decided to cooperate with us. He stated that a man he knew from Chicago, named Luis, was involved in illegal enterprises in Savannah, Georgia. Luis was able to obtain counterfeit notes from a contact in Chicago and that he wanted the informant to take the notes overseas and return with drugs which Luis would sell to his own connections.

Luis had a reputation as a violent person. The informant was afraid of him and refused to introduce an undercover agent to him, nor would he agree to testifyagainst him. We prevailed upon the informant to make a telephone call to Luis and to advise him that there was a "lot of heat" in New York because of tighter Customs searches in the port and that it was prudent not to take chances with the counterfeit and drugs at this time. We had Pele tell Luis that he was going to return the counterfeit to Luis by a trusted confidant. The conversation between Pele and Luis was monitored and recorded. Luis warned Pele that he would be killed if he tried to return the money to Savannah. He repeated it several times to make sure Pele understood. Finally, he told the informant that if he didn't want to purchase drugs overseas and if he wanted to dispose of the counterfeits, he should send them to a man named Kulik in Chicago.

A check on Kulik revealed that he worked as a taxi driver in Chicago and was apparently a good family man with no police record. Sending the notes to Kulik wouldn't make a case. The agent in charge, after a conversation with the informant, told me to take the notes to Savannah to return them to Luis and then place him under arrest when he accepted them.

I left for Savannah immediately. After checking into the hotel, I placed the package of counterfeit notes into a safe-deposit box in the hotel. I then proceeded to a local tavern where Luis was known to hang out. After several hours of waiting and sharing conversation with the bartender and patrons, Luis showed up at the bar and when he heard that a man from New York wanted to see him, he immediately went into a rage surmising (correctly) that this had something to do with the counterfeit money. Upon meeting me, he angrily demanded to know who I was and who sent me. I told him I was from New York and because I owed Pele a favor for taking a "rap" for me on the West Coast a few years earlier, I was simply doing Pele a favor in repayment. I explained that Pele had asked me to take a very important package to Luis and that Luis would reimburse me for all my expenses.

There was a lengthy conversation between Luis and me about the package. It was apparent that he didn't want to take the package. I finally told him I'd take the package and keep it myself. The package represented at least a $10,000 investment for Luis and he wasn't anxious to lose his money. He finally agreed to take the package and pay me my expenses. He accompanied me to the hotel, where I picked up the package, and handed it to him. He accepted it and was immediately arrested. True to his promise, Luis didn't cooperate and remained close-lipped throughout the questioning. His defense was to be that he accepted the package from me thinking it was a gift from a seaman and fellow countryman.

While we were still in Savannah, we decided to interview a friend of Luis' named Fred who we had reason to believe, from other investigative information, was involved. Fred ran a local aviation service and school and we also knew that on several occasions he flew Luis to Chicago. Fred proved to be very cooperative and helpful. He led us to a place in the woods where he had buried over $100,000 worth of counterfeit notes. When he read in the papers that Luis had been arrested for possessing counterfeit money, Fred had a suspicion that he would be questioned and his premises searched. He lost no time in hidding the notes, but when he saw the futility in lying he decided to cooperate. Fred admitted flying Luis to Chicago when Luis picked up the counterfeit money. Fred also accompanied Luis to the house where the source of the notes lived. From the description given by Fred, the unknown man could be none other than "Satan."

Satan had been a painful thornin the side of the Secret Service for many years and everyone was anxious to make a case against him. We flew to Chicago in one of Fred's planes and while we were there we arranged to have Fred surreptitiously view Satan. Fred identified

> Satan as the source of the notes. We decided to wait until the grand jury convened in Savannah and to attempt to have him indicted and then arrest him there. That was possibly a serious mistake because of the tragic consequences.
>
> On the morning that the grand jury met, I was instructed by the United States Attorney to determine what was keeping Fred, our lead-off witness. I walked the few blocks to where Fred maintained an electrical shop, but I arrived just a few minutes too late. Just moments before my arrival, Fred shot himself in the head. It was a fatal shot and he was dead. The case against Satan was blown for now. It was several years later that he was finally arrested. (His life came to a violent end also, but more about that later.)
>
> Eventually, Luis went to trial for possession of the counterfeit notes. His lawyers fought hard to get the jury to believe that Luis was "set up" and was the victim of government entrapment. The lawyers pulled no punches and left no bars undone as they attempted to smear me by making references to my Italian background. They boldly suggested to the jury that perhaps I had received the counterfeits from some of my "relatives" in New York. The trial was bitter from start to finish. when it was finally over and went to the jury, they didn't even take time for lunch. Instead, they returned with a verdict of guilty as charged within seven minutes. Luis was immediately sentenced to serve a term of 15 years in federal prison. He came out of jail some years later, a broken man, whose family had left him, and with a terminal illness to which he succumbed shortly after his release.

This case probably could never have been made if the informant hadn't become greedy and started passing counterfeit notes before departing the United States aboard his ship. He had committed a crime and he realized the prostitute might have recognized him and knew enough about him to identify him. He decided to cooperate and become an informant, hoping that he wouldn't be arrested for the passing of the notes. However, it probably also prevented him from becoming involved in the drug trade which could have had disastrous consequences for him if he had been found buying drugs with phony money.

Pele was charged with possession and passing counterfeit money. He was sentenced to serve 5 years in prison with imposition of the sentence suspended. He also lost his maritime license. Pele's arrest was simple enough, but who could have guessed and known that before the case was closed it would include 2 murders, a suicide, the arrest of 11 defendants, and the seizure of millions of dollars in counterfeit currency?

Assistance in Another Criminal Matter

A percentage of informants are motivated to inform in order to help themselves in another criminal matter. This form of motivation is often called "working off a beef." The informants believe that by informing they can make a deal with the appropriate agency to help them either in another court case or to have their cooperation brought before the sentencing judge on another matter.

One of the largest counterfeiting cases ever made in New York was made because a man, needed help in a criminal matter, not for himself, but for his brother, who had been arrested with him. The Esposito brothers were arrested when they were caught in the act of selling counterfeit money to an undercover agent. The buy itself was rather inconsequential being only for several thousand dollars, but the interesting fact was that one brother immediately wanted to make a deal if something could be done for the other brother. Sal, the older brother, explained that his younger brother, Frank, was addicted to heroin and that he had a related narcotic matter pending in another court. He asked that his brother be released and if this were done, he would take the agents to a spot where there was more counterfeit money than any of us had ever seen in our lives. I explained to him that something could be done the following day, but for the night his brother had to go to jail. Sal pleaded that Frank would need a "fix" or "booster shot" during the night or by morning he would be experiencing painful withdrawal symtoms. I told Sal that Detention Headquarters would undoubtedly give Frank something to help him make it through the night.

The following morning, both brothers were ready for arraignment. As predicted,the night had been very uncomfortable and Frank didn't look too good. This was of great concern to Sal, who was ready to do almost anything to help his brother. We received permission to postpone the arraignment until we could check out Sal's information. His first story was that he had purchased the counterfeit notes from an unknown person at $2 per hundred. I knew that Sal had been selling the notes for as cheap as $5 per hundred and it just didn't make sense — the market was much higher. I insisted that he be straightforward with me or that all deals would be off. It took some convincing, but finally, Sal was ready to tell us how he got the notes.

He spoke of a distant relative who was holding a large sum of counterfeits for a group of "connected" people who had been desperate to find an safe hiding place for their notes as they were experiencing a lot of law enforcement interest as the result of friends who had been arrested with the notes. They had prevailed upon Sal's relative to keep the money in a storage bin in his cellar. He lived in a four-family building and was a hard-working family man without a criminal record so the "organization" thought he would be a safe person to trust to hold the money. Sal's relative, Pepe, kept the money as requested except he made one mistake; he took Sal into his confidence.

Sal was adept as a burglar. When Pepe and his wife went to work, Sal went into the cellar and examined all the storage bins until he found the one containing the cartons and suitcases full of counterfeit money. Being small in stature, Sal was able to squeeze through an opening at the top of the bin and helped himself to some of the money. Sal didn't know anything about counterfeit money and was happy to sell it at $5 a hundred. Naturally, at that price, the customers were plentiful and his trips to the cellar became more frequent. Sal made out well with a little profit until he had the misfortune of selling to an undercover agent. That is what led to his present predicament.

It was obvious that neither Sal nor his brother could afford to cooperate any further. The only thing Sal could do was to identify the spot where the money was located and identify his relative. He did this within minutes of the beginning of his cooperation. It was necessary for us to move as quickly as possible. We knew that as soon as the news of Sal and Frank's arrest became known, the money would undoubtedly be moved. We applied for a search warrant on the basis of confidential information we had received. The warrant was issued by a United States Commissioner for the search of the storage bin in Pepe's apartment building.

The warrant was served shortly after Pepe arrived home from work. I told Pepe I had a warrant for the search of his cellar. He asked what I was looking for and I said counterfeit money. He said, " Well, I guess you know all about it, so follow me." He let two other agents and me down into the cellar. He opened the storage bin and led us to over $1 million dollars that was packed in cartons and suitcases. Pepe was immediately placed under arrest. He was questioned and he stated that he had stolen the notes from the basement of a home where he was doing some work.

He said he was a plumber and when he worked in this particular cellar, he saw some cartons. Being alone, he looked in the cartons and found they contained a large amount of what looked like money. He determined it was counterfeit and when the people were out, he went down into the cellar and stole the cartons of notes.

He claimed he couldn't remember exactly where the home was located. He recalled it was somewhere in New Jersey but he was sure he wouldn't be able to find the place again. I asked him when this occurred and he answered sometime in July or August. He insisted that he placed the notes in his cellar and never went near them again. I told him he was lying. He insisted he wasn't. I asked him to explain how it was that the notes were wrapped in newspaper that was dated six months after he put them in the cellar. He asked for a few minutes and stated he would think of an answer. We were sure he would. Sure enough, he did. He said on one occasion he went to the cellar, took some notes out, wrapped them in newspaper, and then in a gift box. He put the box under the Christmas tree as his wife's present. He claimed he did this on a lark. Well, we had asked the question and we got an answer.

It looked like we had a perfect case against Pepe. He hired an expensive lawyer who immediately made a motion to suppress the evidence as the search warrant was illegal. A hearing was held before a federal judge. He heard the facts of the case and ruled there was insufficient probable cause to obtain the warrant. He castigated the agents and the United States Attorney for moving too fast and not taking enough time to properly prepare the case. The fact that the press was about to go public with the news of the brothers' arrest and that the money could be easily and quickly moved, didn't phase the good judge. We couldn't argue with his prerogative to throw out the search, but to chastise the investigators was almost too much to swallow. After it was over, we were thankful that the judge didn't go one step further and make us return the money to Pepe — with interest. Even though we had received a bad break, there wasn't any doubt that taking over a $1 million of counterfeit money out of circulation was a great help to the merchants around the area who could have been victimized with these counterfeits.

The Service brought Sal's cooperation to the attention of the judge and both Sal and Frank were given short prison terms. Frank was sent to a federal institution where he received treatment and was able to kick his drug habit.

This is just one example of how violators will cooperate fully with authorities when they feel they will be helped in another criminal matter. In these cases, it is very important to find out in advance how serious their problems are. Some informants have a habit of telling only part of the story and when the time comes to help them, it is learned that their violations were far more serious than originally believed. In one case, a man stated that he needed help because he assaulted another man. It developed that the victim died and the charge against the informant was manslaughter for which he was to serve 20 years. He was out of jail on bond pending an appeal when he came to us. It was originally thought that an assault would be a relatively simple matter to assist him with. Needless to say, nothing could be done for him and he was not used.

An accomplice-defendant could also be put into this category. The accomplice could have endless information not only of the pending case, but of other criminal matters that he may have been involved in. Attempting to help an accomplice requires the combined efforts and cooperation of the agency, the District Attorney's office, or the U.S. Attorney's office prosecuting the matter as well as the accomplice's defense council. If the subject agrees to testify, his cooperation is noted for consideration by the sentencing judge and ther is the possibility of a reduced or suspended sentence and/or he can be placed in the witness protection program. The break-up of traditional organized crime (the Mafia) is generally credited to the testimony of Sammy (the Bull) Gravano. He admitted to being involved in 19 murders while he was a high-ranking underboss. However, the government felt that using him as a star witness against many of his former associates, solved and prevented many more murders and other criminal activities that were attributed to the Mafia or its affiliates.

Good Citizenship

There comes a time in an investigator's life when a good citizen approaches him with important criminal information. Unless the investigator is experienced or perceptive to the informant, he might not handle this person properly. The informant comes to him in an awkward manner. He generally does not speak in the vernacular of the underworld and at times appears naïve. It may be painful for the good citizen to come forward because the information could involve a close friend or relative. This type of informant is a gem and must be recognized and handled carefully. All efforts must be made to see that he is not exposed and everything possible must be done to make him feel that he is appreciated for the good citizen that he is.

> Jim Thompson, was one such good citizen. Jim was responsible for breaking one of the largest counterfeiting cases in the South. He had no other angle than to report what he had seen and heard to the proper authorities. Jim owned a small jewelry store in a midsized city in the South. One night, just before closing time, a man entered the store and engaged Jim in a conversation. After a short time, the man, Billy Joe Addams, showed Jim a $20 bill and asked Jim what

he thought of it. Jim said it looked all right to him. Addams said it was counterfeit and that it was just printed and he could get all he wanted. He asked Jim if he knew any people up north he could contact and maybe set up a sale Addams left the sample note with Jim and said he would be back the following Monday to find out if they could do business.

Jim immediately reported the matter to the local FBI office who in turn notified our local office. An examination of the note revealed it to be a new counterfeit that as yet had not been put into circulation.

I was given the assignment of going down to meet Jim Thompson with a view to making a purchase of the counterfeit currency from Billy Joe Addams. I arrived in the city early on Monday morning and after arranging for several rooms at a nearby hotel and obtaining the necessary coverage from the local police and our people, I went to the jewelry store and introduced myself to Jim. Jim just started to explain what had happened the previous Friday night when in the middle of the conversation Billy Joe Addams walked in. I hurriedly told Jim to introduce me to him and say that I was his friend from New York. Jim played his part to perfection and after the introductions, he left the two of us in the back of the store and went about his business as usual.

Addams took several of the counterfeits from his pocket and showed them to me. He stated he could get them in any amounts and he quoted a very reasonable price per hundred. I told Addams that I only had $1,500 in cash with me, so I could do a small deal and would return in a few days to make a large purchase. I asked Addams how much of the stuff he had and he replied that he had $100,000 in the trunk of his car and over $900,000 at his home. It sounded like a far- fetched story, but Addams was convincing and I half believed him.

He agreed to deliver a package containing $10,000 to my hotel room. I went to my room and he went to a parking lot where his car was parked. He was observed by the covering agents to take a package from the trunk and then proceed to the hotel. I admitted him to my room and after the exchange, the covering team entered and placed us both under arrest. In front of Addams, the arresting officer and agents accused me of being wanted for a bank robbery in New York. I immediately told the agents that the counterfeit money was owned by Addams and that he also had more in his car and at his home. Addams didn't appreciate my giving him up and volunteering the information, but he eventually shrugged his shoulders and decided to cooperate with the officers. He then became a cooperative defendant-informant. He took the agents and officers to his car where $90,000 were recovered and his car was seized; then to his house where had almost a million dollars hidden under his bed. Further questioning of Addams resulted in his identification of the print shop where the notes were made. The shop was raided and the printer and several of his associates were arrested. When the last of the local arrests were made, I looked at my watch, shook my headin disbelief that the case only took about three hours to complete. I had time to catch an early plane and was home that night for dinner.

There isn't any doubt that the only reason this case was wrapped up so swiftly was because a good citizen had the guts to come forward with the valuable information that he possessed. The counterfeit in this particular case was of excellent quality and had it been distributed in the proper manner, it would have tied up many investigators for a long period of time. The loss to the public could also have been great.

It appeared to the defendants that I had been returned to New York to face bank robbery charges. They pled guilty and the informant had no problems with Addams or anyone else. This is the type of ending we all strive for, especially when it involves the good citizen.

We must always keep in mind that a good citizen must be handled with the utmost care. He should be advised that the Service (or appropriate agency) will keep his identity a secret for as long as possible. If a trial will expose the informant against his wishes or if exposing him would place him in potential harm, then the U.S. Attorney must be appraised of this fact. Sometimes it might be necessary to abandon the prosecution of the case and let the defendant go free. There will always be another time to catch and prosecute him.

In today's judicial and criminal justice climate the federal authorities have many ways to protect an informant. They can give him a new identity, move him to another part of the country, get him a job, and support him for a reasonable time (the witness protection program). It may sometimes be possible to remove the informant from the case (as illustrated above) thus never exposing him to the suspicions of the arrested defendants.

This system serves many informants very well, but the informant who doesn't want to be moved nor does he want a reward must be considered. He merely supplies information and hopes the government won't disclose him. Many informants believe that federal agents can accomplish anything. They seem to be unaware that all law enforcement personnel must obey the restrictions that protect all citizens.

I recall at a trial in which I refused to name the informant. The judge ordered me to name the informant and again I refused. The judge said he would find me in contempt of court if I continued to refuse to name my source of information. At that moment the deputy U.S. Attorney prosecuting the case interjected and asked to speak to the judge privately in chambers. Accompanied by the defense counsel the judge and attorneys were in chamber for about 25 minutes. When they returned, the defendant pled guilty and was sentenced to one year and one day in prison with the imposition of the sentence suspended. I was quite relieved because I didn't relish the idea of spending even one hour in a jail 1,000 miles away from home (or any jail as far as that goes).

The deputy U.S. Attorney assessed the situation and made a deal with the judge and defense although he knew he had a winning case and could have succeeded in getting the defendant a longer prison term. Sometimes it is better to compromise than risk the life of a good citizen who came forward with a sense of duty.

Inadvertent Informing

There is a type of an informant who is an unwitting informant. He may be someone who is in possession of some valuable information, and after a few drinks begins to talk aloud in a public place where anyone can hear, sometimes even a police officer. This informant is giving information, but unwittingly so. This information might be exaggerated, but on closer scrutiny, it is learned that some part of it is true. If, during the time the person is talking freely, he is identified and is later approached by an officer, he generally will give information but will pass from an unwitting informant into another category, depending upon what motivates him.

> One evening, our office received an anonymous phone call concerning a woman in a local bar called "E.J.'s." The woman's name was Esther and she was telling everyone who would stop to listen that she was buying counterfeit money for 20 cents on the hundred. The bar patrons weren't taking her talk seriously, but the caller believed she was telling the truth. Before he could be questioned, he hung up. EJ's wasn't difficult to locate. After making several inquiries, I learned that Esther was a ditzy blond in her 40s who usually came to the bar alone on Tuesday nights. We conducted surveillance in the bar for the next few Tuesdays. One night she showed up. She bought a drink and gave the bartender a $10 bill. The bartender examined it and was satisfied that it was a genuine note. I immediately ordered a drink and paid for it with a $20 bill. In making change, the bartender gave me the $10 that Esther had given him. I went to the men's room and examined the bill and found it to be genuine.

Rather than prolonging a case that appeared to be simply bar talk, I waited until Esther left the bar. I followed her for a block or so and then I stopped her, identified myself, and showed her my credentials. I asked her to tell me what she knew about counterfeit money. She assured me she had just been bragging to get attention and that she really didn't have any information. I gave her a card with my name and telephone number. She showed me her driver's license, but resisted when I asked for her telephone number. I told her that an assistant U.S. Attorney would probably want to talk to her about counterfeit money and her role and knowledge about it. She became alarmed at that and said she didn't want to talk to any U. S. attorney, district attorney, the FBI, or anyone else about counterfeit money. After some more conversation, she said, "Listen, if I tell you the truth do I still have to see the D.A.?" I said, "Why don't you leave it up to me. I'll see that you get the best deal possible." After thinking about it for a few minutes, she decided to tell me all that she knew.

Esther said she had been living with a man named "Ace" for the last few years. He was an inveterate gambler (hence the nickname), an alcoholic, and a dealer in counterfeit money. To top it all, he was a womanizer. About a month ago he had moved in with another woman named Linda. Esther was certain Linda was passing counterfeit money for Ace. She had noticed them exchanging bills when they were together. Esther said she would get more information and would get back to me. Within a week she telephoned me and was able to tell me two places where Linda had passed counterfeit bills. We checked out the information and were able to have Linda identified as the passer. We obtained a search warrant for Linda's apartment and found fifteen hundred more in counterfeit notes. Linda readily gave up Ace and he in turn provided the name and information about his supplier.

This is a good example of an unwitting informant who tried to make an impression in a bar. She then became an informant for the purpose of gaining revenge on Linda for stealing her boyfriend. We never had any more information about Esther. If she was in fact a counterfeit passer she must have given it up as a bad idea.

Repentance

There is a rare breed of informant called the repenter. This person is generally an older person who has spent many years in jail and was either doublecrossed by his associates or has "seen the error of his ways."

"Sammy the Flopper" had been released from New York's notorious Sing-Sing prison for the third time over 20 years ago. He had spent most of his life in prison for various and sundry crimes. One day I had reason to interview Sammy about a stolen and forged government check. Sammy was anxious to talk and while he didn't have anything to offer about the stolen check, he gave me a complete rundown on all the "bad apples" in the neighborhood. I realized that Sammy would make a good informant. He said I looked like a good honest cop and if I wouldn't expose him, he'd give me any information he came across that would help arrest criminals. He requested that when I came to visit him, I should dress casually as to avoid arousing any suspicion. He suggested that I wear jeans and a sweater.

Sammy was a product of the Lower East Side and grew up in a cold-water tenement in a neighborhood that was formerly known as the "ghetto." During his youth, he made his money by his wits and various illegal enterprises. He was a burglar, a drug distributor, and a "flopper."

I would call on Sammy at least once or twice a month just to keep up on the crime in the neighborhood. I asked him to tell me why they called him "the Flopper" and what a "flopper" was. Sammy explained that a flopper was someone who was experienced in falling in front of a slowly moving vehicle without getting hurt. He would fall in front of an automobile that was just beginning to accelerate or was slowly turning a corner. Two of his friends were posted nearby and would be witnesses to the fact that the driver of the car had knocked him down. A dishonest doctor and lawyer were also part of the team who saw to it that the victim recovered a substantial sum from the driver or insurance company.

Eventually the time came when Sammy's activities were brought to the attention of the District Attorney. The group was arrested. His friends cautioned Sammy to keep his mouth shut, which he did. At the trial, all of Sammy's co-defendant friends testified against him. They were given suspended sentences while Sammy was sentenced to serve a sentence of 7 to 15 years in the state pen.

This wasn't Sammy's first experience with friends who gave him up. After this prison hitch, he made up his mind that when he got out of prison he was going to live a law-abiding life and would provide the police with any information he learned about regarding crime in the neighborhood. He became a repenter. He was genuinely sorry and remorseful for all the crimes he had committed and he was now against crime and criminals in every phase and form.

I knew Sammy for many years and I feel we were friends. Not many weeks would go by that he didn't call me and we would get together for lunch and some conversation. He operated a pushcart just outside the entrance to the building where he lived. He worked when he pleased as he didn't have a family and was quite satisfied with his lifestyle. My visits to Sammy became a weekly routine. He furnished me with information about murders, robberies, and narcotics peddlers. After talking with Sammy, it became necessary to determine and locate the appropriate agency handling a particular crime. Many of the agencies became irritated with me when I refused to let them speak with directly with him., but I was sure that if I allowed another agency to talk with him, Sammy would very soon become another casualty of the underworld. It took almost two years before Sammy came up with a good counterfeiting case. When he did, it was a very good one. He told me where the money was hidden and furnished me with he names of the printer and distributors.

One Christmas I gave Sammy a small radio for old time's sake to replace the old one he had in his apartment; he never did have a television set. It took hours of explaining before Sammy was convinced that the radio was just a present and not a reward for anything he had done for me. I told him I was just sick of the poor reception of this old radio and was replacing it so I could hear some good music for a change. Over the years, Sammy was responsible for giving me excellent intelligence and for making many good cases for the Federal Government and the State. It was necessary in one counterfeiting case to dismiss the complaint when it appeared that Sammy might have to be called as a witness. Sammy died in a city hospital. I saw him the day before his passing. He jokingly said, "Carmine, watch the pushcart, there's some bad apples on my street and some worse ones in the cart."

This is another example of a case where the informant has to be handled very delicately inasmuch as this man had no other angle except to see violators arrested. Many investigators would have been tempted to pass Sammy off as just another street vendor and not recognize the potential wealth of information he just wanted to give away. I found him to be true to his word and he never seemed happier than when he would read about people being arrested as a result of his information. For a man who spent over half of his life in prison, he never expected, nor did he ever receive, anything for his information. It would take a lot of experience or understanding to accept Sammy's story that he honestly would help the police in a criminal matter

Carmine Motto and friend.

and would not expect anything in return. He differed from the good citizen in that he was a man with a long criminal record and felt that informing was the best method to pay back to the State and Government for the wrongs he had done in the past. Sammy fits into one of three informant categories. Some would say he was a good citizen, others would say he was getting revenge. I prefer to believe Sammy was a repenter.

Eccentricity

Probably the hardest type of informant to deal with is the eccentric, the mentally ill, the demented, or the person who is known in police jargon as the "mental" or "psycho." Most officers believe that categorizing a man as a "mental case" is a good enough excuse to do nothing further on the case or the information he is supplying. There are many people who have mental problems yet have good information and are good informants. True, they are hard to handle, but nevertheless, they sometimes have excellent information and are willing to impart it.

> Big Bill had just been discharged from a mental hospital and had returned to his old neighborhood. He had only been home for a short time when he learned that some of his old friends were engaged in a counterfeiting scheme. For some undetermined reason, he decided to report the matter to the local police. Unfortunately, the police knew he had just been discharged from a mental hospital and didn't pay any attention to him. In desperation, Big Bill went to the FBI and finally was directed to the Secret Service. I interviewed Big Bill and he told me that he had just been discharged from a state institution after having spent 7 years there. There were times during the interview that he appeared perfectly normal; at other times, he appeared to be out of touch with reality.
>
> After interviewing him for some time, it certainly appeared he knew some of the violators that were involved in this counterfeiting ring. We researched far back into Big Bill's background and found that he had served many prison sentences and had been in jail with some of the people he was informing on. Big Bill agreed to introduce an undercover agent to one of his friends. I worked the case and I had no trouble in making a purchase of counterfeit notes after Big Bill gave me a big build-up.
>
> While we were working this case, Bill tried to kill his wife and was returned to the mental hospital. We felt that we had gone as far as we were able in investigating the case. We made several arrests on the strength of the purchases I had made and one of the defendants turned out to be the printer. He worked for a fairly large printing business. He managed to get a key to the premises. On weekends, he would enter the shop and use their facilities to make the counterfeit money. The plates, negatives and paraphernalia were found in his locker and the case was wrapped up in a very short time.

I hate to think of what might have happened if Big Bill would have called on the telephone in one of his less lucid moments. He could have easily been brushed off for the mentally ill person that he was. Officers must take their information from wherever they can get it and run it out before deciding that they are wasting their time on a sick person or other type of mental case.

Until increased security at government buildings restricted the free flow of pedestrian traffic into the building, it wasn't uncommon for demented persons to go from one agency office to another claiming to have confidential information about criminal conspiracies and people dealing in contraband. It would usually tie-up an agent for a while until the person was interviewed and an evaluation could be made of his information in spite of his obvious mental instability. No one who claimed to have information was dismissed out of hand. There were regulars, however, who would be given a few minutes of an agents time then they would move on to the next agency with other fanciful tales.

The Stool Pigeon

A term commonly used for an informant is a stool pigeon. This derogatory term usually connotes contempt and disrespect. Stool pigeons are a special category of informants. All stools are informants but all informants are not stools. A "stool pigeon" is a pigeon usually tethered to a bench or "stool" to decoy other pigeons, or others of his kind, into a net or pigeon coop. Thus the term stool pigeon refers to an informant who decoys others into a trap. However, he often plays the violators and police against one another. He gives information to both sides in an attempt to keep good relations with both the police and the violators and he tries to profit from both. This type of informant is very dangerous and shouldn't be trusted; he would even get an undercover agent injured, or worse, if it suited his purpose. The case of "Danny the Driver" is a perfect example of this type of informant. As mentioned earlier, Danny was a professional informant who sought information and sold it for a profit to anyone having an interest. In that particular case, Danny was working both sides and even attempted to bring in another agency and there was no doubt in the undercover agents mind that when he saw Danny in his neighborhood that Danny would have sold the information of where the agent lived to his underworld connections.

Sometimes these professional stool pigeons have good information; other times they invent the information because it suits their particular need at the time. It is very important for the undercover agent or the interviewing agent to recognize a stool pigeon immediately. Working a case with a stool pigeon is difficult and he should be given as little information as possible while the case is progressing. Sometimes it is necessary to give him false information or "misinformation" to see if he uses it against the police. The danger posed from a professional stool pigeon is mitigated if he is recognized and placed in the proper category in the beginning of the case. As it was demonstrated in the case of "Danny the Driver," an agent should be alert for the possibility the informant is a "double informant" or stool pigeon.

Certain informants have to be tested in order to find out whether or not the information they are giving is genuine. In Secret Service work, it is generally not necessary to test the informant because the types of crimes they investigate are unique. In most cases, the evidence disappears after it leaves the violators hands. In the case of drugs, the user ingests the product. In the case of illicit alcohol, the consumer disposes of it. However, in counterfeiting cases or other Secret Services cases, such as bank fraud or access device fraud involving credit and debit cards, there is usually a "paper trail" that verifies the validity of the informant's information. In counterfeiting cases, the evidence is always returned to the government through banking sources. The Secret Service knows each day how much counterfeit money is being passed in every locality in the world. If an informant says he was out with a group passing counterfeit notes in a certain area the previous week, these notes must come in to the local Secret Service office. If, in a reasonable time, the notes do not come in, it can be assumed that the informant is lying.

In the case of "Danny the Driver" all the previous activity involving that particular counterfeit note was on the East Coast and it was known by the Secret Service that those responsible for the notes were associated with an organized crime family. Danny appeared to be knowledgeable about the notes and those involved. He was doubly dangerous to the agents because he had enough verifiable information to lend credibility to his stories.

The "Bon-Vivant" or the Man about Town

Another type of informant is the rare one that doesn't care. He has been informing for a number of years and takes a philosophical attitude about his work. He doesn't particularly care whether he is exposed. As a matter of fact, this type of informant will take the stand if he is called to testify and will generally make a good witness. He is egotistical and will make cases for the sake of showing he can do it. This person may be a police "wannabe" or views himself as a one-person crime stopper. He may even have a Bruce Wayne–Batman complex. He needs to be carefully handled and controlled because his supercharged ego and enthusiasm can lead to dangerous situations that he never considered or he may jeopardize the case by committing illegal procedures.

> Chris was an informant I had met several years before. At the time, he was doing very well. He stayed at the best hotels and moved in the inner circles. He could easily have made a very good living legitimately; however, he chose to hang out in the gray and black area. He was the type that liked to report to just one person and would go out of his way to help make a case. If he was doing well financially, he wouldn't take any remuneration. There were times where he spent a considerable amount of his own money to make the case. He was meticulous and articulate and had a charming personality. Most people who dealt with him knew he was an informant, but for some strange reason, they took a chance with him, hoping that this one time he was playing it straight and not bringing in the police.
>
> One day Chris came to me because he needed help with a little problem he had with another agency. I interceded for him and obtained the desired results. Before long he had made some friends

with the other agency and was doing a lot of work with good results for them.

On one occasion, he was out of town purchasing a load of stolen stocks and bonds. He was working closely with the authorities. Due to no fault of his own, the securities were delivered prematurely to his hotel room. Chris took the securities and told the person delivering them to immediately leave the room, and that he wasn't going to get paid. Chris also mentioned that the police would soon arrive and arrest them and take the securities. The delivery person went back to his connection, Jack, who was waiting in the lobby and told him what had happened. Jack became outraged and proceeded to Chris' room. Chris wouldn't open the door. Jack swore and said he was going to kill Chris and began kicking the door down. When it became apparent the door was coming down, Chris calmly picked up his gun and fired a round through the door. The bullet struck Jack in the head, killing him instantly. Shortly thereafter, Chris was arrested for homicide.

I had arrived in the same town a few days following his arrest. While there wasn't any doubt that he would win the case, he still needed a little help, someone to speak to the judge and mention that he had been working for various agencies in the past and was reliable.

I went to the jail to see Chris. I expected to see him depressed and concerned. True to form, he was in the squad room talking with a group of detectives. When I came in, he asked to be excused and we were shown to an anteroom where we could talk in private. I told him what I was planning to do and said I would see him in court the next day.

Later, a detective was showing me out of the jail mentioned to me that Chris was a great guy. I asked him what he meant. He stated that his squad was preparing a raid on a large prostitution operation that had been giving them a lot of trouble. It was important that the raid should occur in the next few hours. Somehow, Chris had gotten word of the impending raid while he was in jail and asked to see the officer in charge. Chris told them they were preparing to raid the wrong premises because the operation had been moved and they were going to a decoy location. He then gave them the actual address. The raid was made and was extremely successful. Needless to say, Chris was very well treated during his short stay at the jail. The homicide charges were dropped and he was released.

A few months after the shooting, Chris returned to New York. He told me that several of his friends were distributing counterfeit money. He said he would try to get them to stop their activities, because he didn't want to see them get arrested. He explained that they were semi-legitimate businessmen and were just peddling the counterfeit as a sideline. I told Chris that his feeling for his friends was commendable, but that it didn't particularly interest me. If they were selling counterfeit money, I wanted him to introduce me to them and I wanted to try to make a purchase. Chris objected for a while but later told me that he would see what he could do.

By this time, he was no longer "Dapper Chris," because of the shooting out of town. He was now referred to as "Killer Chris" and was feared by many people in the underworld. Why they continued to do business with him still remains a mystery.

One day Chris called me and told me that he had an appointment with two of his friends in the dining room of a high-class New York hotel. I told Chris that I'd go to the hotel dining room just to get a look at his friends so we would know them for future reference. Chris met his friends in the dining room as he had planned. At this point, I thought it would be the ideal time to force an introduction. I had several agents in the vicinity covering me and I walked over to the table where Chris and his friends were seated. I shook hands with Chris and acted as though we were old friends. Chris had no alternative but to introduce me to his friends. They were introduced as Merlyn and Maylan. There was no doubt they were businessmen. The conversation for the next hour was buying and selling, selling and buying. If they were involved in counterfeiting, they certainly were the most unlikely counterfeiters that I had ever met.

Chris excused himself to make a telephone call and left me with the "twins" as they became known to us. Merlyn asked me what I did for a living. I gave him the stock answer of "I buy and sell." He asked, "Buy and sell what?" I said "anything I can buy low and sell high." He chuckled and looked at his partner then reached into his inside jacket pocket and pulled a $20 bill from his wallet. I could tell it was a counterfeit. He asked me if I liked it. I said I always liked $20 bills. He said he could get me all I wanted at a discount price. I asked why a discount and he said that they were, "funny money." I wanted to know how much of a discount he was talking about. He replied, "20 cents on the dollar in amounts of $25,000." We bargained for a while and it was agreed they would sell me $50,000 in counterfeit notes for $7,500 in genuine money. Maylyn said it would take a few hours to get the stuff. I said it would take half that to get my money. We agreed to meet back at the dining room in two hours.

When Chris returned to the table, Merlyn and Maylyn told him we had just concluded plans for a delivery of counterfeit notes. They asked Chris if I was all right. Chris said I could be trusted. Maylyn asked Chris not to set them up. Chris laughed and said he would never do anything like that. We parted company and Chris and I left together. He said he should be angry because of the way I operated, but he couldn't forgive Merlyn and Maylyn for being so greedy and trying to make a sale when he wasn't around. I asked Chris to lose himself for the rest of the afternoon, at least until the deal was made. He insisted on being there and so he joined me later when I met the twins again.

Merlyn stated they were ready to do business and asked for my $7,500. I showed them my package of money and told them that I'd pay them as soon as the counterfeits were delivered. Maylyn insisted that I pay for them in advance. I refused, saying the money wasn't mine and I wouldn't gamble with someone else's money. They then asked me to put up half the money to show good will. Again I refused. We negotiated this matter for about an hour. Finally, Maylyn made a few telephone calls and asked me to wait until he returned. He said he'd be back in an hour.

When he returned, he took a small package from his pocket and asked me to open it. I did and the box contained two beautiful diamonds. He then showed me a memo slip from a jeweler in the neighborhood. This slip indicated the diamonds were worth $5,000 each and Maylyn had received them "on memo" from the jeweler. Maylyn told me to hold the diamonds and give him $5,000 so he could get the counterfeit delivered. I told him I wasn't in the jewelry business and couldn't tell whether the diamonds were real or phony. Merlyn and Maylyn, having seen my money, were becoming quite frustrated as they knew they couldn't get the counterfeits without paying for them in advance.

Finally, Merlyn made a telephone call. A few minutes later he met a man and had a quiet conversation with him. The covering agents saw this and followed the man to New Jersey. Merlyn returned to the table and told me that he had given the unknown man the two diamonds as collateral on the counterfeit note deal and he expected to get delivery within the hour.

The unknown man was seen contacting a known distributor in New Jersey and getting a package delivered to his car. The car returned to New York and the man came into the dining room of the hotel. He contacted Merlyn. I then suggested that we all go to a room that I had in the hotel. On our way out of the restaurant, we were all arrested and taken to the room. Merlyn and Maylyn insisted they were itinerant jewelers. I insisted I was a businessman. The arresting agents wanted to know what I was doing with the large amount of money in my pocket. The unknown man, Tom, found it very hard to explain the package of counterfeit money that was in his possession. Chris pleaded that he was an innocent victim of the whole affair.

The connection in New Jersey was picked up later in the day and the case was wrapped up. Chris later arranged bail for Merlyn and Maylyn and the deal didn't hurt their friendship in the least.

Female Informants

Female informants are generally very good informants. Men will confide in them and they will usually have a great deal of information about the people they are associating with. As a gross generalization, the motive for female informants is most often emotional and at the time they give the information it is generally reliable. They sometimes inform to seek revenge on a lover, a husband, or a boyfriend. The agency should move as quickly as possible upon receipt of their information. There is always the possibility that the informant will settle her differences with her "significant other" and will change her mind about informing. There have been innumerable cases where they will go out of their way to prevent their loved one from going to jail after having given information against them.

Female informants present many problems not normally associated with male informants and they should never be interviewed by only one agent or a female agent should interview them. If possible, the interviews or meetings should take place in the office or in a public place like a restaurant or similar setting to preclude the possibility of the informant making charges against the agent at a future date.

The majority of female informants don't have the best reputations in the world. Many are prostitutes, some are "strung-out" on drugs, and some are police "junkies" who like the idea of being involved with police officers and in police matters. Police officers and agents must be very careful about their relationships with these informants and should be careful not to put themselves in a position that could cause them embarrassment or to lose their jobs or worse, such as being accused of a crime or moral turpitude. Every contact and everything said and accomplished should be well documented as soon as possible.

One day a young lady was arrested for passing a counterfeit $20 bill. After the arrest she was found to be in possession of several more.

I interviewed her while she was still incarcerated in the women's house of detention. She told me her name was Phyllis, she was 22 years old, she lived alone in Manhattan, and was currently unemployed. She stated she wasn't going to answer any more questions. She refused to discuss the counterfeit money or anything further about her background.

I was able to locate her mother and father and found them to be honorable people. They said Phyllis had always been a problem child and it seemed no matter how hard they tried, they just couldn't keep her from getting into trouble. Phyllis finally left home when she was 19 years old and lived with various boyfriends. She rarely came home except when she needed some money. Her family was very sorry to hear about her arrest, but under the circumstances there was nothing that they could do. They weren't in a financial position to provide the $10,000 bail, however, they said they would visit her and perhaps they could change her mind about cooperating with the government.

A few days later her father called me and said that he had visited his daughter and she had given him the keys to her room and if I wanted to, I could join him in removing her belongings. I said I would be happy to assist him. As her father removed her personal belongings from her room, I was on the look-out for any information I could see. There were no counterfeits on the premises, but there was a small telephone address book her father gave me for the time being and I could return it later. The book had many names and addresses, but one name was very important to me. On the back cover of the book the name "Elmer Coy" was neatly printed. There was no address or telephone number. Elmer was of record in our files as a suspected distributor of counterfeit money. He was never arrested for dealing in counterfeit money, but it appeared he might be Phyllis' supplier. Several days later the father called again. He said that Phyllis was ready to be interviewed. She had been in jail for over a week and no one except her father and mother had paid her a visit. She was angry and was ready to talk.

I spoke with Phyllis the next day and she confirmed that Elmer was the man responsible for the counterfeit notes she had been arrested with. She also told me that she had since learned she was pregnant and wanted to be released from jail. She said she would be an informant and even testify against Elmer just so she could return to her mother's home and eventually have the baby. I managed to get the bail reduced to $500. Her father provided the bail and made sure she had a room at his home. I told Phyllis that it would suit me best if she would keep me informed on the activities of Elmer.

Phyllis contacted me on a weekly basis. She stated that no one in Elmer's circle of friends wanted to become involved in counterfeiting as they believed things were getting too hot. One night she called me and said that Elmer and his group were planning to hijack a truck. She mentioned a truck stop in New Jersey, but they hadn't decided on a date. There were three men involved in the proposed hijacking and they were going to use a stolen car. They were going to hijack a liquor truck and they already had ar garage where they would store the cargo after it was hijacked. She said she would call back when she learned the date, time, and place of the hijacking. Two days later she called back and gave me the information. I immediately called the State Police and gave them all the information. The group followed their plan. They hijacked the truck, put the driver in the stolen car, and were about to depart the scene when the State Police arrested them all.

The following day I met Phyllis and the first words out of her mouth were "I guess we're even now." I said, " I guess so, I still would have liked to have made a counterfeiting case but I guess we'll have to try another angle." She asked me if I would take care of the charges against her. I told her it was arranged to have her plead guilty and she would receive a suspended sentence. I then asked her what her plans were. She said she would move back home to have her baby and wait for Elmer to serve his sentence. She said she would then join Elmer and try to have a good family life. I didn't say anything, but I sure had a lot of misgivings about her future plans.

All in all, she was a good informant; she could be trusted and probably could have made a good counterfeiting case if the suspects continued to deal in counterfeit money.

Keeping the Bargain

A time comes in every interview with the police officer and the informant when the officer has determined what motivates the informant and why he is giving information. At this point, the officer and his organization enter into another phase of the case with the informant. That is the negotiation and meeting the price or the conditions that have been set, either directly or indirectly, by the informant. If the informant is motivated only by a monetary reward and he is a professional, he will probably tell the officer exactly how much money he wants. Very often, it is too high and it will be necessary for the officer or a representative of the department to hash it out with the informant.

There are many informants who think they should get a percentage of what is seized or recovered. Sometimes, this can be worked out with companies that have insured the stolen merchandise or with the agency for which the seizure is being made. After some discussion, reasoning, and negotiating, a price will be agreed upon. This phase of working out the expectations of both sides may involve serious bartering and compromise. But the informant must be made aware there are certain compromises that cannot be made and there are specific guidelines that must be followed. Once an agreement is reached and both sides understand the positioning and requirements of the other, it is of the utmost importance that the officer and the agency live up to the terms of the bargain. No officer should agree to a price and/or conditions unless he is absolutely positive that his agency will, in fact, pay that much money or meet the stipulated conditions. The officer should have an approval from a supervisor or person authorized and responsible to make those decisions before he even proceeds with the case.

If an informant needs help in another criminal matter, it is important that inquiries be made to see if he can be helped, that is, a call to the district attorney who is handling the case to see if a reduced charge or a suspended sentence can be worked out. Here again, it is very important that the officer live up to the terms of the bargain he has made. A police agency will quickly get a bad reputation if the officers or agents continually make promises they cannot or will not keep. Sometimes it is better to say something along the line, "I can guarantee nothing except that I will personally make a visit to the district attorney and discuss this with him and you have to be guided by what he says." Most informants who need help will be satisfied if someone makes a good faith effort in their behalf, while the results might not be what they expected; they will generally be mollified. It is also necessary for the officer to weigh what he expects to recover against what the informant wants. It is very common for the informant to want to give the police officer information regarding a misdemeanor and expect the officer to help him with a felony. It can be explained very easily to the informant at the time of the interview that the information must be at least on the same level or greater than the help he is seeking.

Usually, it is a wise suggestion to get the informant out of an official office and into less formal circumstances. It is a good idea for the officer assigned to the informant to take him to lunch or have a cup of coffee with him. It is during this time, that an officer can learn a lot about the informant without making it appear that he is questioning him. The range of topics discussed need not be limited to the case at hand. Most informants have a story to tell; many times it is a tale of pathos and they just need someone to listen. The informant will be grateful to have someone listen with a sympathetic ear and a little understanding of why he is informing.

I can recall a time when a man came to me and related that he knew a very important counterfeit distributor. He said the man had disappeared and wanted to know if I could help him locate the man. He guaranteed that if I found the man I would also find a large amount of counterfeit money. I asked him why he was anxious to locate this man. He replied that his wife had been having an affair with the counterfeiter and about six months ago she had moved away with him. I asked him if his wife was implicated in the counterfeit operation. He said he didn't think so. He added that his wife wasn't important, but she had his four-year-old son with her and he was anxious to get his son back. He assured me that was the only reason.

He told me the counterfeiter's name was Ronnie and that he came from the Midwest but had lived in New York City for the last 5 years. The informant said he had appealed to the court and had been awarded custody of his son. According to the informant, he didn't believe any agency, including child welfare and other social services, were actively searching for the child but if the child could be located he would have no trouble raising him.

I told him that I was certainly interested in the counterfeiter and that I didn't want to interfere in his family life. However, I would try to locate his wife and Ronnie. I spent several days making futile inquiries and looking for Ronnie. I ran out every lead the informant had given to me and wasn't getting any closer. Of course there were several problems with this case. Even if we located Ronnie we would still have to make a case against him. We'd have to get probable cause for a search warrant, develop witnesses, or attempt to make a buy from him. No matter how it was sliced and how you looked at it, it was going to be a difficult case.

One night I received a call from a local detective. He said there was a serious accident on the highway. The driver had hit a telephone pole, his car was totalled, and he was in the hospital with a fractured skull. In examining the car, the accident investigators found $22,000 in $10 bills. They didn't know if the notes were counterfeit or genuine, but because of the amount and denomination they were questionable. I immediately went to the precinct station and examined the money. It was all counterfeit. The police advised that the car had been previously reported as stolen and the driver was under arrest. The detective gave me the name and address of the injured driver. He was Ronnie West from Brooklyn, New York. The detective and I went to the address to inform West's family of the accident. At the home we found the informant's wife and child.

> She alleged to have no knowledge of the counterfeit money and gave a consent search of the apartment. We didn't find any more counterfeit money or leads that would help us find the source. When Ronnie recovered sufficiently to be interviewed, he refused to cooperate or provide any information about the counterfeit. An arrest warrant hold was placed against him for possession of counterfeit money. The informant was delighted to regain custody of his son; his wife went to live with another man.

While this case appeared to be very complex, everything worked out by accident. It is not unusual for an informant to seek assistance in personal matters. If assistance can be given and if assurance is made that help will be given, the bargain must be honored.

Whose Informant Is It?

An eternal controversy always arises in police circles as to whose informant is it anyway? This is a question that has several arguable points. Some police officers feel that an informant is their own personal property. The officer may feel this way because he developed the informant, he is the only person the informant will work with, there has been a type of bonding, closeness and trust with the informant that no other officer has comparatively experienced. Furthermore, in many agencies and departments, the officer may pay, or advance fees, to the informant out of his own pocket. In some agencies the officer's professional evaluation report and promotions are partially contingent on the number of informants he has developed and who provide him with reliable information for the successful conclusion to important cases. Some agencies have been known to establish a quota system for the number of informants developed by the officer each month. If these criteria are sanctioned in a police agency, it is a logical assumption that the informant belongs to the officer.

If the agency assumes the responsibility (as it should) of maintaining payments to the informant for his services then it should be that the informant belongs to the agency and the agency merely assigns an agent to work with the informant. The primary responsibility of working with an informant should fall to the case agent who is actively working a particular case, though the organization maintains overall control of the informant.

Remarkable as it may seem, some organizations limit by definition or regulation, the people who can have informants. In those agencies only a sworn police officer or agent may have access to an informant. In such an agency one non-sworn employee received, through his personal social contacts and associates confidential information pertaining to local political corruption, public construction contract irregularities, and other potentially sensitive white collar crime areas. The informants adamantly insisted that no one except the person who received the information was to know their identity. They absolutely refused to be interviewed by a sworn officer because they didn't trust any one except the non-sworn employee whom they had known as a friend and colleague for many years. The informants provided the information only as good citizens who came into possession of the information through their own employment and felt any type of disclosure would jeopardize their job and position. When the non-sworn employee refused to name his sources after preparing a memorandum containing the sensitive information, the agency informed him that he could not have informants and suspended him. The employee argued that the information was actually available through public sources and records and the informants had merely brought the information to the attention of the agency through him, someone they knew and trusted. He also pointed out that it was not necessary to interview the informants. An investigator merely had to look at official records where the informants had found the information. The agency's stance was that all informants belong to the agency for control purposes and that no one employee could claim an informant as his own. By that reckoning the agency was correct in its policy.

By control of the informant it is meant that for administrative purposes there must be documentation of the informant, payments (including expenses) made to him, and the results of his information. When preparing an affidavit for an arrest or search warrant based on information provided by an informant, the preparing officer must be able to articulate the informant's reliability. If proper records have been maintained by the organization, it should be an easy task to satisfy the requirement to even the most skeptical judge.

Informant Identification

In agency records and case files the informant should be designated by a number or code name. The personal information of the informant should be maintained somewhere in the department in a locked and secured confidential receptacle and made available to officers only on a "need-to-know" basis. All efforts should be made to keep the identity of the informant confidential. In writing reports the informant should be referred to by only his number or code name. It is usually sufficient to say the "information was obtained from a reliable confidential source." When preparing an arrest or search warrant affidavit based on information from a "reliable confidential informant (or source)," it is usually necessary to articulate a number of past instances when the reliability of the informant was proven. Any reference to activities involving the informant should be couched in terms that would provide no clue to his identity.

Through the rules of discovery, defense attorneys are entitled to copies of all reports, recordings, etc. in the possession of the prosecution. Consequently, it has become more important than ever to exercise care and caution when alluding to the informant. Very often, a judge will order the prosecution to name the informant. At this point, a decision has to be made whether to expose the informant or to refuse and have the case thrown out. Each case has to be weighed on its own merits. Is the case important enough to warrant possible corruption of or risk potential, very likely, harm to the informant? At the very least, the informant's future usefulness will be destroyed, as will the officers credibility with other informants. This decision must be addressed early in the case and discussed with the prosecuting attorney. Also. bear in mind that some informants don't care whether they are exposed. This must also be worked out far in advance with the informant. The informant should know the likelihood of his possibly being unprotected and named in court. Surprisingly, there are a good many informants who don't care if their name is mentioned in open court or not.

When working with an informant, the officer or agent assigned to him should endeavor to get the informant's photograph and criminal record and any other pertinent information. That is not to suggest that the informant should be sat down and photographed, but, through conversation, an officer can learn about any criminal history, driver's license, etc., and a photograph can later be obtained from that record. The photograph should be placed in the informant's confidential file. The purpose of the photograph is to serve to identify him later during a raid, or to recognize him in the future when any officer who may know him has been transferred or moved on. Sometimes an officer is asked to meet the informant during late night hours at a designated location. If he hasn't ever seen the informant before, the photograph in the file will serve to help identify him.

Developing Informants

Developing informants is the responsibility of everyone involved in police work — all the way from the top-level supervisor to the newest "I'm not even sure I know what an informant is" recruit. Informants approach the police in many different ways. Sometimes, they simply walk through the office door and announce they need to talk to someone about information they have. Sometimes they call on the telephone. Sometimes an agent will be assisting a citizen in another matter or engaged in a social function when in the course of conversation, it is discovered that the contact will possess information relative to police interest.

All possible information regarding criminal activities should be obtained from the informant when he is being interviewed. More often then not, agencies will only question the informant about information that is of possible interest only to their particular service. This is wrong, because it is often very likely that an informant will have information about some other very serious crimes and won't volunteer this information unless he is asked. It is typical that an officer or agent engaged in the investigation of one case will be given information in a completely unrelated case.

Obtaining information on a crime that is of interest to another service is one of the more important aspects of police work. The easy exchange of information between departments builds up confidence and trust in one another. In some instances, it is beneficial for departments to exchange informants when the informant has information for another jurisdiction. Not many people will subscribe to this but we have seen it work over the years with great success. The department that originally developed the informant can maintain a hold on him, even though the informant is cooperating with another agency.

> An agent was investigating a rather complex check forgery case involving payroll checks stolen from a payroll officer's office aboard a U. S. Navy vessel. The checks were stolen from the officer's supply of checks so that he didn't even know they were missing until the checks suddenly began appearing at local banks as naval re-enlistment bonuses. The investigating agent quickly developed a suspect, a sailor aboard the ship who had access to the payroll officer's safe and records. It was found that among his civilian circle of friends, were several people who worked for a local television cable company as cable installers. One of the friends was arrested for possessing one of the stolen checks. He (and it was later confirmed) said he had no knowledge of the source of the check, he was merely holding it for a co-worker who had asked him to keep it for him. Interviewing him further about his co-workers and his own habits it was soon learned that many of the people working to install cable television in homes for that particular company were heroin and crack cocaine users and they "dabbled" in other lucrative activities such as burglary after business hours. This information was passed along to the local police who used the arrested suspect as an informant to solve several burglaries and to begin a rather extensive drug investigation. The check thief and his check passers were soon arrested and convicted. The two primary witnesses against them were neglected girlfriends who

decided to come forward and give all the information they had and to testify in court after they were arrested by the police for cocaine possession and were asked about the check thief.

The check forger, who was also the primary passer, took a special trust in the investigating agent and over the course of the next few years help solved many cases including a homicide. He never asked for anything in return except an occasional visit while he was serving his jail term and to have someone occasionally check on his mother. A good informant was developed and the police cases were made as the result of an agent, who while investigating a check theft and forgery, decided to ask other questions leading to the information about the drugs and burglaries. The police, in turn, returned the favor by asking two drug abusers about any knowledge they might have about the check thief and forgers. The case in point here is that several cases were made as a result of an agent (then later the police) asking an extra question beyond their own jurisdictional interests and recognizing the value of the information of people who quickly went from arrested suspects to helpful informants.

There are times when an undercover agent starts on one case and stumbles onto something more important and then pursues that case even though it might not be in his own jurisdiction.

Cody was an outstanding undercover narcotics agent working in and around the Chicago area, making substantial cases against narcotics violators. One day, while still working under- cover, Cody met Pete, a big-time hoodlum from a small suburban town and who was known to handle drugs and other contraband.

Pete apparently didn't have any drugs to sell at that time, but in conversations with Cody he proposed selling him some counterfeit money. Cody felt sure the Secret Service would be interested in sending a man to work undercover with him. He took it upon himself to tell Pete that he had a friend from back East whom he was sure would make a purchase. He promised to get in touch with his friend and would contact Pete as soon as the friend came to the Chicago area. Cody then notified his supervisor about the counterfeiting proposition and the Secret Service was notified. I was assigned to work with Cody and a few days later we proceeded to a private club owned by Pete, outside of Chicago.

Pete showed me some sample counterfeit notes, which at that time were receiving national distribution and were being passed in large quantities. We knew the source was in Chicago. We knew the suspect was a man who had been arrested many times previously for counterfeiting and was known in his own circles as Satan. All attempts to make a case against Satan had been futile. There was no one, that we knew, willing to effect an introduction to this man.

After the second meeting with Pete, I arranged to purchase $5,000 dollars worth of counterfeit notes from him. I told him I was returning to New York and then would undoubtedly call him in a few days with a much larger order. I indicated to him that I represented a consortium or a syndicate who were anxious to make contacts in the Midwest for various kinds of contraband. Pete jumped at this opportunity to break into what he thought was the "big time" in New York. He suggested that in the event I wanted a large amount of counterfeit notes, he would personally deliver them to New York in company with Cody and hoped that at that time he would be introduced to members of the syndicate.

About 10 days later, I called Pete and told him that I needed a quarter of a $1 million dollars worth of these counterfeits. Pete assured me that he would have no trouble obtaining the notes and asked me for a telephone number where I could be contacted. I gave him a number and the following day he called me and told me that he would be in New York the next day and supplied me with the name of the airline and flight number. After his original call to me, Pete was observed on two or three occasions in the company of Satan who was undoubtedly making the arrangements to get the notes to Pete for his trip to New York.

I met Pete and Cody at the airport at the given time. Pete was impressed with the limousine that we used for this occasion and the fact that I had my own chauffeur. Pete told me that he was being very careful, that he had come armed and he had to be sure that nothing could happen to these notes because he had mortgaged everything he owned in order to make partial payment on the notes he brought to New York, without getting payment in advance.

We went to a large downtown hotel where we had made arrangements to have Pete have his own suite of rooms. While in his suite, we counted the stacks of notes and found that he had close to a quarter of a million dollars. We received several telephone calls at his room and we assured Pete that the syndicate was getting together to pay him a visit. Although Pete was completely satisfied with all the arrangements, he was very nervous and insisted upon carrying his fully loaded gun in a shoulder holster. Just before the agents arrived to make the arrest in the hotel room, I convinced Pete that it didn't look good for him to be wearing his gun. He relented and and I hid it in a closet.

The arrest was made without incident and Pete was lodged at the Federal House of Detention in New York City. It was important that we made some sort of move before the newspapers printed the story that Pete had been arrested.

The following morning, we were able to delay his arraignment. Pete was brought to the Secret Service Office. Cody and I both identified ourselves as Federal Agents, which was quite a shock to Pete. He needed time to think and we were pressuring him for an introduction to Satan. He assured us that nothing could be done as far as an introduction because the notes had to paid for first and he doubted whether Satan would talk to any strangers. He admitted that Satan was the source of the counterfeit notes and agreed to cooperate, even if it were necessary to testify against Satan. In order to corroborate his testimony, we had him make a telephone call to Satan and discuss the sale of the quarter million dollars. Satan was quite evasive over the telephone. However, enough information was recorded to convince anyone that Satan was the source of the notes.

Pete was held in lieu of a very high bail that he couldn't afford to meet. During his absence, his personal life began to unravel. His common-law wife left him for another man, he lost his private club for non-payment of debts, and all his personal belongings were stolen by another girlfriend he was keeping in an apartment. All these events depressed Pete and had a tremendous psychological impact on him. He lost interest in making bail, he just wanted to dispose of his case as quickly as possible, serve his time, and be done with the whole mess.

As a result of the information supplied by Pete, a warrant was obtained for the arrest of Satan. Satan was arrested at his home, which was thoroughly searched, but no contraband was found.

Satan knew that he had been a target of the Secret Service for quite a number of years. He also knew he'd had a close call several years earlier when an excellent witness against him committed suicide. He knew a long imprisonment would separate him from his young daughter who was the apple of his eye. All these things were on Satan's mind when Cody and I questioned him. In a surprisingly short time, Satan decided he would throw his lot with the government and cooperate. He said he wasn't responsible for the manufacturing of the counterfeit money, but he could arrange to set up his source. He agreed to introduce me to his connection and he felt that he could arrange for a half-million dollar delivery. The astonishing thing was he was certain he could arrange this without any "front" money. He further stated that the counterfeits wouldn't have to be paid for until I had disposed of them.

Satan eventually introduced me to a man called "Frisco." Frisco looked like your stereotypical movie hood. The conversation was completely dominated by Satan and in no time Frisco agreed to let me have a half million dollars to take to Europe. It was agreed that I would pay for it after I returned to the United States. Frisco agreed to these terms and indicated he would wait two months for the payment. We later talked this deal over at the office and all agreed Satan was up to something. It certainly looked like the deal was all his and that Frisco was someone who took orders from him. Nevertheless, Fricso went through with his part.

About a week later, he arranged to leave a half million dollars in my car, which he had borrowed for the transaction. About a month later, my brother, Bob, working in another undercover capacity, contacted Frisco and told him I was ready to dispose of the notes in France but I needed another $100,000. The whole deal had to be completed at once. We knew that Frisco had to contact Satan, which he did and Satan approved the deal. It was clear to us that Satan was still the boss. We confronted him with our suspicions. He vehemently denied any connection with the plant.

We then set Frisco up with another $50,000 order and placed him under arrest. He refused to cooperate and after several days, made bail and was back on the street.

Satan had not been officially arraigned up to this time and he pleaded for more time and agreed to work for other agencies so he could square himself with the government. It was pointed out to him that it was "sheer madness" and suicidal on his part to stay on the street without being arrested (officially) on the counterfeit charges. He still pleaded for more time and it was granted. Satan went on to make more cases for other agencies. It soon become apparent to the underworld that Satan was miraculously staying out of jail while everyone else was being arrested. Satan's double-dealings came to a sudden a halt one morning. He was found slumped over the steering wheel of his car with six bullets in his head. His car was in the school parking lot of the school his daughter attended.

Frisco later went to trial and stated that he was merely a delivery boy of Satan. He said his every action was dictated by Satan who controlled the whole counterfeiting plant. Frisco served a short term and later met the same end as Satan for his part in the "Satan conspiracy."

It is refreshing to know that this whole case was made because a brother agent investigating another crime saw fit to pursue information given to him by a suspect, even though it meant nothing to his Service. It is cooperation of this type from various agencies that make police work the rewarding job it is.

It is important when developing informants in any case, that the person handling the informant do so in an intelligent and respectful manner. Informants can be very sensitive and may even be reluctantly providing the information. The informant and his information should be treated in such a manner that the information is not demeaned nor the informant offended. When a telephone call is received from an informant, the officer should try to arrange a meeting. In the beginning the informant is very wary of meeting a law enforcement officer and sometimes it takes an officer with a lot of personality and convincing attitude to have the informant agree to meet him. No police officer should simply dismiss a telephone call from an informant as a crank call. It must be born in mind that no one calls the police unless they need help or they have something to report. The officer receiving the call should make every effort to attempt to meet the calling person and find out for sure whether or not it is a crank call.

Sometimes, very important information comes over the telephone, often by people who don't want to become involved. It may be easy to dismiss the call as a hoax if the information is so outrageous that it seems hard to believe it's true. We have discussed earlier that even though a person may be a mental patient or a genuine "crackpot," it is still possible that he can have information which could be used by the police. The only sure way to determine that is to see the person and interview him personally.

Sometimes, an informant is referred by another agency. The agency generally will give an evaluation of the informant before the meeting with the informant. At this time, it is important to ask the other agency what the informant wants and why is he informing. The agency introducing the informant will usually provide a full briefing about the informant's reliability, any past criminal record and any other information that would be of significance, such as character idiosyncrasies. It is imperative to never expose the identity of an informant, especially if he is given to you by another agency. This would certainly result in hard feelings, not only between the agents, but also between the organizations. Disclosing the informant's identity would also result in a loss of credibility of the agent and his organization with the informant.

Sometimes because of developments in the case it may become necessary to divulge the existence and identity of the informant. In those instances, the introducing officer from the other agency must be informed. If he or his organization disapproves, the informant cannot be unveiled and the prosecuting attorney must consider dismissing the case.

At the time of the informant's introduction by the cooperating officer and in his presence, is the desirable time to have a discussion with the informant about the ground rules of the new relationship. The representative of the other agency would then be informed of exactly what his informant is to get and what promises are made. Unless they are professional informants or have worked as informants in prior cases, very often they don't realize the importance of the information or the role they are about to play and don't realize the consequences in the event they are exposed.

> James Tomack was a young employee for a local bank in a run-down section of Queens, New York. James was a product of the neighborhood and he knew almost everyone in the neighborhood: the good and the bad. He lived with his widowed mother in the same house in which he was born and was her sole support. While he knew many people who were dishonest, cheats, and thieves, he managed to keep out of trouble and established a reputation as an honest hardworking person who would make a success of himself.
>
> One day, James was approached by "The Hornet" (also known as Cato Green) who was the leader of a neighborhood street gang. The Hornet and his followers had come into the possession of many thousands of dollars in United States Treasury securities. The Hornet, knowing James' reputation for honesty and trust at the bank, approached him and asked if he would filter the securities through the bank or other financial institution. If not, perhaps James could find a buyer who would purchase the securities without asking too many questions. Hornet promised James a portion of the profits if he were successful.
>
> The day after the offer, James came to my office where I interviewed him. He wanted to report the matter and said he would be willing to do anything we suggested. He would even introduce an undercover agent to the Hornet. I knew the background of Cato "The Hornet" Green. He was allegedly responsible for at least three murders and was considered a very dangerous person. I knew that regardless of the outcome of the case, James would find himself in the middle and would be dangerously exposed. He couldn't afford to move because of his elderly mother and wouldn't be a likely candidate for the witness protection program. I told him that we couldn't use his services, but we would appreciate his giving us information on the activities of the Hornet and his gang whenever he could.
>
> It was difficult for James to understand why we didn't go ahead with the case at that time. As a matter of justice running its course, the case against Cato Green was made later with great success through

> the efforts of another informant who wasn't as vulnerable as James. Before the Hornet was sent away to begin serving a 7-year sentence for the stolen securities, he became involved in another murder and was sent away for good. It was shortly after the last murder that James came into the office and said he now fully realized why we didn't want to use his services.

In analyzing the case, much thought went into what could happen to James in the event his services were used to effect an introduction to the Hornet and his gang of murderers, thieves, and swindlers. No matter how we approached it, it always came out the same — James would invariably be exposed and killed. The entire case revolved around him at the time, but it just wasn't worth the danger to him and no one wanted him to risk his life for some worthless paper.

Cooperation by the Informant

In working with the informant before beginning a case, it must be learned how far the informant is willing to go. In other words, would he be willing to introduce an undercover agent to the suspect. As far as the agency is concerned this would be the ideal condition for working the case and meeting the target of the investigation. The percentages of successfully working a case and obtaining a conviction are greatly enhanced through undercover techniques. If the informant will not, or cannot because of circumstances such as the one involving James Tomack above, will he make a purchase of the contraband by himself and be covered by agents? This isn't a very desirable situation and it can become very complex. First, in order to make the arrest, the informant has to agree to testify and his testimony has to be corroborated by the covering agents. The informant must be carefully and thoroughly searched to ascertain and be able to testify he had no contraband when he went to meet the suspect and he had the illegal substance upon his return. If the suspect is going to be immediately arrested, a "buy-bust," the money paid to him should also be identified in some manner. Sometimes, an informant, for whatever his particular personal reasons, desires this situation and is not concerned about the possibilities and consequences of testifying in court. If the informant is willing to testify, then the case can go forward. If he is not willing to do any of the above, then he will usually agree to give information from time to time. While this situation is highly desirable, it generally doesn't help too much in an undercover case. The important thing in any of the above situations is to find out from the informant if he is willing to testify at a trial and have his identity become known. It is of the utmost importance to find out how far the informant will go as the entire undercover operation depends upon it.

Sometimes it takes many interviews and meetings with the informant to find out how far he wants to go. Sometimes his fears are unfounded and can be overcome. Other times he is sufficiently far-enough removed from the suspect, even if his identity does become known, that no actual danger to him exists. Again, each case has to be handled as an individual case on its own merits as no two cases or scenarios are exactly alike. Many possibilities have to be explored with the informant until he sees a situation that suits both the agency and himself. This can only be done by frankly discussing all the possibilities with the informant.

A case may present unusual challenges that must be met with imagination to protect the informant. An informant knew a certain person had access to a large amount of counterfeit money. Only the informant and the holder of the counterfeit knew of its whereabouts. The informant could not think of any situation where the government could seize this money without him being exposed. Many situations and possibilities were discussed and rejected by the informant. Finally, out of desperation, I suggested that under the guise of a routine investigation, I would stop at the home of the suspect and make innocuous inquiries and leave. I suggested that the time be arranged when the informant would be visiting at the suspect's house. The informant would tell the suspect that the visit was obviously a phony or that the Secret Service was on to something. He would then suggest that the suspect change the location of the counterfeit money as quickly as possible. The suspect would be followed to the new hiding place and arrested.

To my complete surprise, the informant listened to the proposal and stated that he thought it would work. He made a few revisions in the plan and we proceeded to implement it. The amount of counterfeit money involved was in excess of $100,000. The suspect didn't want to be caught with it in his house, and at the informant's suggestion, had it moved. We followed him when he left his house with the contraband and arrested him at the time he was depositing it in a second hiding place. The suspect eventually pleaded guilty and the informant was never suspected of being involved. It is interesting to note that it took over fourteen hours of talking with the informant before this plan was agreed upon.

Handling Informants

It has been said a thousand ways. Police officers should handle informants with respect and refrain from using the word "informer", "squeal", "rat", "narc", "stool" or other similar derogatory descriptions. We have seen instances where an informant was in a room and a police officer referred to another person as a "squeal." This of course didn't sit well with the informant who was in the room. In one particular instance, the informant, who was volunteering his services, took such offence that he changed his mind about helping and walked out of the office. Even though the officers are talking about someone else, the informant feels that he will be referred to in the same manner when he is out of earshot. Over the years we have found that using the term or euphemism "friend" when talking to an informant or referring to someone else giving information is a very effective, non-derogatory, even respectful, description.

Police officers and agents must learn to speak on the proper level with an informant. There are too many officers who look down upon informants and make it very obvious during the interview. There is nothing that will freeze the informant quicker than an interview with an officer who appears to be talking down or patronizingly to him. There are times when the informant obviously has more education than the police officer and it is important that an officer with more experience and education handle this type. Here you have a situation in reverse, where an informant talks down to a police officer because he feels superior to him. The ideal situation is to have the informant and the officer speaking on the same level.

In handling an informant, do not let him overestimate his importance or go beyond his role of informant. Some informants, especially those who are a "wannabe" officer or those with an authoritative personality will try to manipulate the officer and attempt to run the case. They will want to dictate where and when meetings will be conducted and the circumstances. Some have been known to attempt to control the briefings regarding raids, surveillance, agent manpower assignments, and any other aspect of the operation. Some will even attempt to direct the officer in other duties important to the case, such as telling the officer to obtain copies of the suspect's driver's license, criminal record, etc. This type of informant must be firmly, yet with all due respect, rebuked and reminded that the case agent is running the case. Never leave reports, notes, pictures or other relevant documents where an informant can see them. In discussing the case with an informant give him information on a "need-to-know" basis. It is a sorry state with possible dangerous or embarrassing consequences when an informant is privy to the same information that only a case agent should have.

An informant should never be given a license or free reign to violate the law. This is a problem some police agencies have experienced. There are some police officers, for example, who will overlook informants handling stolen property and selling it at a profit. The informants will then inform on their source, enabling the police to arrest the burglars or receivers of the stolen goods. This usually develops into a situation where the informant feels he has a license to operate illegally and he "gives the police crumbs while he keeps the loaf." Police officers should exert every effort to make it clear to the informant that he has no right to violate the law because he is working with the police and violations will not be tolerated.

"Tommy the Tote" was a street-wise, racetrack hustler who stumbled onto some counterfeiting information. He was willing to give me this information for $200. The information was certainly worth the price and we worked with Tommy in trying to make the case. In the middle of the case, Tommy said he had to go out of town. I asked him why. He said he and two of his friends were going to rob a motel in a nearby town. Before I could talk him out of it, he left the office. I called the State Police at the nearby town and they kept the motel under surveillance over the weekend. Sure enough, at about 3:00 A,M. on Sunday, Tommy and his two friends attempted to hold up the motel night clerk. They were arrested by the Sate Police officers who were stationed at strategic vantage points.

I later had an opportunity to talk to Tommy at the local jail. He couldn't believe that I was the one responsible for his arrest. He stated that he felt as long as he was cooperating with the Federal authorities, we could at least give him a chance to make a living. Needless to say, Tommy the Tote went away for a long time as a very bitter man stating that the Secret Service had double-crossed him.

We have previously discussed the fact that in most cases we felt that informants belong to the department and not to the individual officer. However, this does not preclude the fact that some informants will only work with one man. This might be for a number of reasons: they are compatible, they speak the same language, the officer might have gone out of his way in the past to help this informant and so on. When an informant expresses a desire to work with a particular officer or agent, this request should be honored unless there is some strong reasons to do otherwise. If an agent and an informant have worked together successfully in the past, that is all the more reason that the informant's desire to work with this particular officer in another case be fulfilled.

I had worked in the past with an informant named Fred Graymoney. He was a fairly successful businessman and money was the one thing he didn't need. His business operations were always in the shadowland between being lawful and not quite legal and he always had his share of trouble with the police. Fred, however, couldn't walk away from the opportunity of setting up a good deal. I hadn't seen Fred in some time. As a matter of fact, I was working several hundred miles from him and had been promoted to a supervisory position. This never stopped Fred from calling whenever he had what he thought was something I might be interested in. Knowing that Fred never exaggerated or built up a case, I always managed to find the time to listen to him when he called.

On this particular occasion, he called me and left word that he had some information on Treasury checks. This could have meant anything, stolen checks, forged or even counterfeit checks. I was not too inclined to travel a great distance to discuss the forgery of a check with him. This was a routine matter that could have been handled by anyone. Knowing full well that Fred would be disturbed if I sent someone else to interview him, I made arrangements to see him the day after he called.

When we met, he explained that a day or so before, a man had come into his place of business and wanted to sell him a U. S. treasury check for 50% of the face value of the check. He further stated that the man told him he was in a position to get unlimited numbers of treasury checks and he could supply them with whatever amount the purchaser wanted. The informant stated that he did not know the man very well. However, the man was well dressed, drove a luxury car and looked fairly prosperous. Fred could not supply very much more information but suggested that I hang around his place of business for a few days. He felt that the subject would come back and he would introduce me to him. I wasn't too inclined to spend the time there. Certain administrative duties were pressing and I felt that I should return to my office and assign a man to work with Fred. Fred wouldn't hear of it and insisted that I spend at least a few days there as he felt that this would turn out to be something big.

In my mind, it added up to someone who had found a way to steal government checks out of the mail or was pulling some sort of fraud on the Internal Revenue Service and was able to obtain large refund checks. I suggested to Fred that if the suspect came into his shop, he should introduce me as a friend from New York who had a check cashing agency there and was interested in obtaining some Treasury checks. He could indicate that he had discussed the proposition with me and I was interested.

On the second day, the suspect came into the store and he was introduced to me as "Cal." After some general conversation, he confided that he was in a position to supply unlimited numbers of United States Treasury checks and could have them made out in any amount. He stated that they would be sent through the mail and he would see to it that they were sent to any address that I supplied to him.

Once Cal learned that I had my own check-cashing agency, he was very anxious to do business with me. I suggested that he and I go somewhere to talk in private. He suggested that we go for a drive in his car. That was all right with me and off we went.

I was able to learn that Cal was some kind of a United States Government employee, that he was a supervisor in some unit and that he was responsible in some way for sending out government checks to individuals. He had found a way to arrange to have checks sent to anyone he wished. He had to use a certain name; the address could be supplied by the purchaser. The purchaser had to give Cal one-half the face value of the check. Cal went on to say that it took him 18 years to figure out how to beat the government. He knew that his system was foolproof and that no one could get into trouble for cashing the check. I told him the whole scheme sounded incredible. However, I was willing to take a chance with one or two checks to see how they went. Cal stated that he had a check in the trunk of his car. He stopped the car, gave me the keys, and told me to open the trunk, that the check would be in an envelope in the trunk. Opening the trunk gave me an excellent opportunity to get his license number and find out who he was. I found the check and went back into the car. The check was made out to Ambrose Fieler in the amount of $420. I examined the check. There was no doubt that it was genuine and it was drawn payable by the Veterans Administration.

Continuing the conversation with Cal revealed that he would let me have that particular check and after I cashed it, I would call and arrange to pay him. He then wanted to be supplied with a list of addresses anywhere in the country. He stated that he would arrange to send a check to each of these addresses in any amount I wanted. His only caution was to make sure that I could get these checks out of the mail. He didn't want the checks returned to sender as undeliverable. I assured Cal that I could handle it and told him that I would return to New York and contact him in a day or so and supply him with the necessary address list. We parted company. He again assured me that there never could be a complaint on the checks because the payees would never know that they had been issued. He gave me his home telephone number and two days later I called him and made an appointment to see him at a local hotel.

In the meantime, an exhaustive check revealed that Cal was indeed a government employee. He was a supervisor in the Veterans Administration handling the dormant accounts of military veterans. There were hundreds of accounts in the names of veterans who were due large sums of money. However, for one reason or another, these veterans couldn't be located and the money was lying in a dormant account and could be activated any time the veteran contacted the Veterans Administration.

The check that I had obtained from Cal was in the name of a real veteran. However, the address on the check was not his. Mr. Fieler was unknown at that address. Cal had arranged to send the check to that address and then was able to intercept it. It was agreed that I would pay Cal for the check he gave me. Then I would supply him with 15 addresses in the New York area. These addresses were actually the addresses of our own Secret Services agents who would be expecting the checks. Arrangements were made to place surveillance equipment in my hotel room and have officials of the Veterans Administration auditing department and General Accounting Office listen to our conversation in order to determine how Cal was able to perpetrate the fraud.

Cal came to my hotel room and we immediately got into a conversation about the checks. I paid him for the check he had given me and supplied him with the list of addresses he wanted. He was still very concerned that I understood that the checks had to be received and not returned to the government. He explained that it would not be a disaster if a check were returned but it could cause suspicion in the department. I assured him that I had arranged to get the checks and they would not be returned. He emphasized again to me that there was no risk or chance of getting caught and that I could be comfortable putting the checks through my personal account as none of the payees would ever complain and the government had no way of checking without a payee complaint. He said he would explain the entire process to me but he was sure it was too complicated and involved. I told him to go ahead as I had plenty of time to waste and beating the government intrigued me as it had him.

He then explained a very sophisticated system whereby he would activate a dormant account belonging to an actual person who was either not aware of the VA account or was unable to access it. He would then arrange to have a check payable to the veteran sent by the U.S. Treasury Department to whatever address he wanted to use. He was also able to keep the account from having the money deducted from it. This literally gave him an inexhaustible supply of money. It was like going to Uncle Sam's well, helping himself to as much as he wanted as often as he wanted and there was no way for anyone to even know the money was missing. The auditors in the next room listened carefully and were able to follow him easier than

I could. They later admitted that he had found a flaw in the system and exploited it and potentially could have raided those accounts for untold thousands of dollars with minimum risk of exposure.

Cal told me to carefully watch the mail at those addresses I had given him for the next ten days as the checks would be in the mail within the week. As he departed the room, I promised to call him as soon as the checks began to arrive. The initial checks I had ordered were to be in amounts in the vicinity of one thousand dollars each.

About a week later, various agents in the office began to receive the checks at their homes. Within ten days, just as Cal had promised, all the checks were accounted for. It was planned that I would call Cal and tell him that most of the checks had arrived and I had people looking out for the remaining ones. I would then meet him at the hotel and tell him that I had cashed the checks that had been received. I would have further discussion with him about the rest of the checks and supply him with a new list of addresses. Then I would give a prearranged signal for the arrest.

Everything went along just as we had planned. I met Cal in the same local hotel as before. We went to my room where I told Cal I was waiting for a courier to bring me the money for the checks. We had a further conversation about how long it would take for a new batch of checks to begin arriving. I gave him a list of about thirty more addresses. A knock came at the door. I opened it and a group of men entered. One man announced that he was my parole officer and that I had violated my parole by leaving the state of New York without permission of the court. He immediately searched me and found a dozen government checks in my possession. Cal almost fainted when he saw them take the checks from my pocket. The men asked Cal who he was and what he was doing in my hotel room. Cal stated he was a federal government employee and a friend of mine and he hadn't done anything wrong. My "parole officer" said I was being returned to New York for parole violation and would also be charged with theft of government checks. At this point, I turned to Cal and told him that I was going to cooperate with the agents and confess. I explained to him that I owed the state seven and a half years and I couldn't afford to be charged with the theft of the government checks. I then turned to the police and stated that I had received these checks from Cal who was a government employee and he had devised a way of getting checks issued in any numbers and amounts. I told them that we were going to cash these checks and split the money. Cal turned pale and after some questioning, finally told the whole story. I was removed from Cal's presence and was quickly taken out of the picture and was supposedly returned to New York to face parole violation.

Further questioning of Cal revealed that there were several other people employed by the government who were involved with him. They were identified and arrested. After an exhaustive auditing, it appeared that Cal had actually recently started on his fraud scheme and not too many checks were sent out. The system of controlling and issuing checks was revised and further thefts were prevented. It was estimated that Cal could have swindled the veteran's dormant VA accounts out of millions of dollars if the scheme had lasted for any length of time.

Because of his cooperation and the fact that he had no prior criminal record, Cal received a comparatively light sentence and within a year and a half, he was back on the street. He stopped in to see Fred, the informant, and asked about me. Fred stated that I was still in jail. Cal felt sorry for me and periodically called at the informant's place of business and left a carton of cigarettes for me.

Fred called me on many other occasions, and needless to say, I always responded, even though he was not in my district. I always took the time to see him and made another attempt to make an undercover case. Here was an excellent informant who actually belonged to the agency but would only work with one agent. Whose informant was he any way?

Maintain contact with informants, see them regularly. It isn't enough to develop and use informants — they need to be maintained. As they learn about other criminal activity, they will be willing to share it. Informants are human beings and many of them are fine persons. Police and Federal officers are always anxious to obtain any information they have. Sometimes an informant gives information, he is paid and no one from the agency ever sees him again. The informant perhaps does not come around to give new information because he may not believe that the particular agency with which he is familiar can use the information. An informant may think that because his information does not involve the jurisdictional concerns of that organization that if he were to reestablish contact he would be needlessly bothering a busy agent. During the course of closely working a case together, bonds of friendship often develop. Unfortunately, when the case is completed the informant resumes his life and the agent returns to more pressing matters and in no time at all, a valuable contact (and possibly a friend) has been lost. Experienced agents have made it a practice over the years to visit many informants who have been of service to them. It is surprising (and rewarding) how pleased many of them are to have an agent take time to call at their home or meet them somewhere just to pass some time with them over a cup of coffee or a sandwich.

An informant sometimes can recall something that can be very useful to the Service, especially if the agent has no motive other than to renew old acquaintances. This is very good for the informant's ego and self-image and he will double his efforts to be of assistance, especially if his previous experience with the agency had been favorable.

> I had heard that an informant whom I had known for 20 years was ill and alone at home. One night, I decided to go visit him. I took a carton of his favorite cigarettes and spent an hour talking with him. It had been a long time since he had given me any information and I was sure that he didn't have any and I told him so. He was so happy to see me and pleased that I would take the time to share with him and relieve his loneliness and discomfort.
>
> Throughout our conversation and the hour we spent together, we had been discussing some of the people in the neighborhood. He brought me up-to-date on what each was doing and mentioned that one, Jack Little (we knew him as Little Jack) was living in a rooming house nearby. The informant had reason to believe Jack was trying to avoid the law and was possibly hiding out but he didn't know what agency was looking for him. I told the informant that we had been looking for Jack for the past year and had a warrant for his arrest. The informant opened the window of his apartment and to pointed to the building where Little Jack lived. Needless to say, within two hours, Jack was apprehended and in custody. He couldn't understand how he was found, living in this remote neighborhood.
>
> The evening had a three-point reward. I felt good about visiting a long-time friend and seeing his happiness to think I would go out of my way with no singular purpose than to visit with him. He was pleased that someone was concerned enough about him to bring him cigarettes and to check on his condition. And Little Jack was surprised to be visited by the Secret Service and be taken to a new home.

Use all legitimate means to develop informants. This is a never-ending task for all law enforcement officers. Having defendants cooperate; the police officer making friends with various people that he comes in contact with develops informants; sometimes relatives have information which is useful. There is a never-ending source for information as long as the police officer will take the time to try to develop the source.

> An agent had arrested Manny Estabez for stealing his brother-in-law's government tax refund check. Manny's wife was pregnant and this case at first appeared as though it could be handled as a family matter. So it was surprising when the the Assistant U. S. Attorney, decided to charge Manny with forgery.
>
> Manny pleaded that his wife was alone at home; that he had no money for bail and that he would positively appear if he were released on his own recognizance. The agent was instrumental in having Manny released. Manny was very grateful and told the agent that someday he would like to repay the favor. The agent knew that Manny was probably only expressing his thankfulness but for the lack of anything else to say, replied that the Secret Service was interested in counterfeit currency in addition to stolen and forged income tax and social security check payments. It appeared unlikely that a man in Manny's position would ever have any information about counterfeiting.
>
> The next day, Manny called the agent and told him that he knew of an acquaintance that was printing something illegal in his cellar. The information appeared consistent with a counterfeiting operation. A surveillance was maintained at the given address and after five days, a complete counterfeiting plant was seized. The counterfeits involved had been plaguing the New York area for approximately seven months. Until the time Manny came forward with his information, there had been very little intelligence obtained on the source of this particular note, as it was a one-man affair, and he only dealt with people he personally knew from his particular ethnic group.

It was obvious that this case was made because the agent had a little compassion for the defendant and went out of his way to see that the man was released on his own recognizance at a time when his wife needed him.

Forcing an Introduction

In working an undercover case, it is not always possible to gain entrance to the subject of the investigation through the efforts of the informant. The circumstances may be such that the informant will refuse to make an introduction or there are times when the agency knows all about the background of the suspect and feels there is too great a risk of danger to the informant. Sometimes informants are reluctant to introduce an agent because the suspect has stated that he did not want to meet any strangers. Sometimes a suspect will live in a "compound" type setting, i.e. in a cul-de-sac, where any strangers could be spotted and reported to the suspect, thus ruling out surveillance. These are times when an agent has to force an introduction. Forcing an introducing simply means meeting the suspect and being brought into his confidence by bypassing or cutting out the informant.

Hank, a "knockaround" kid from New York's East Side had lunch in a local pizzeria every day. The owner of the pizzeria, Salvatore , didn't have a criminal record, but he did have many contacts in the underworld. There came a time when Salvatore made a connection to purchase narcotics and counterfeit money. One day when Hank came into the pizzeria, Salvatore showed him sample $10 and $20 counterfeit notes. He told Hank that he could get them in any quantity and was also able to obtain heroin and cocaine. Hank, a basically honest kid, reported this offer to the Secret Service and I had an opportunity to interview him.

I asked Hank if he would take me into the pizzeria to meet Salvatore. He said "absolutely not." Salvatore wouldn't meet any strangers nor would he do business with anyone he didn't know . I asked Hank if he was afraid of Salvatore and he said he wasn't, but he was just as positive that Salvatore would freeze up if a stranger came into the establishment. I tried many possibilities out on Hank, but he always came to the same conclusion that the plan would fail if anyone other than himself attempted to purchase the counterfeits or narcotics. Finally, in desperation, I said to Hank, "Let's go up to the pizzeria and get some lunch. Certainly, Salvatore can't object to that."

Hank and I walked into the pizzeria and Salvatore greeted Hank with, "Didn't I tell you not to bring any strangers into this place?" I immediately cut in and said, "Look, I don't know you and I don't know what your problem is, but I came in here to eat. This is a restaurant isn't it? I don't care if you talk to me or not, but I want some pizza and a beer." Hank and I sat at a table and ordered something to eat and drink. About 20 minutes later, after our pizza arrived, Salvatore came over to our table and stared at me for a couple of minutes, then stuck out his hand and said, "My name's Salvatore. I can tell you are an okay guy. No hard feelings?" A short while later, I managed to have the informant leave and I sat with Salvatore for about an hour.

I told Salvatore that I was "shuffling" used cars up from Florida and would take anything down there that I could make a dollar on. Salvatore asked me if I ever handled "junk." I told him I didn't know anything about it. He immediately gave me a 10-minute discourse on the difference between cocaine and heroin, the difference in price and the proper method in testing the product to determine its purity. He also showed me two counterfeit notes and stated that I could purchase them in any amounts at $15 on the hundred.

I ordered $10,000 worth of counterfeit notes and an ounce of heroin. Salvatore told me to come back in an hour. I was able to leave, contact the covering agents, and they were able to identify the person who made the delivery to the pizzeria and arrest him as he and Salvatore made the sale to me.

Salvatore and the delivery person pled guilty to the possession and sale of counterfeit currency and heroin. They each received a prison sentence. Salvatore hung himself shortly after he arrived at the Federal prison. The informant, Hank, is still working in the same neighborhood. Apparently, no one suspected he was the informant in the case.

Summary

Even though some informants try to drive hard bargains, it doesn't mean that they won't listen to the problems that the investigators have. Sometimes, the informants ask for too much money, sometimes they ask the police to do something that is illegal or impossible. If the officer will take the time to explain to the informant step-by-step why his bargain is impossible, some informants will then remove the obstacles that make it impossible for the informant and police to get together. It takes an experienced officer to handle informants and it would be well for the younger officer to observe the methods and listen to the experience whenever possible.

After all the details are worked out with the informant, the officer should be sure that he lives up to his part of the bargain. If it becomes necessary because of fast-moving events to make certain promises to an informant, the officer should explain that the bargain is contingent upon a final decision by a higher authority. The informant will appreciate this, especially if he can see that the officer cannot check with anyone because of the time factor.

Some informants are unique and it is very difficult to put them in any category. "Jimmy C" was unique, to say the least, and to this day, his motive remains a mystery. Jimmy called the office late one night and an appointment was made to meet him. Jimmy had considerable information about counterfeiting and some samples of counterfeit notes that were being passed around in the mid-town New York City area. He was agreeable to introducing an agent to the source of the counterfeit notes and he appeared very anxious to help make a case.

Jimmy had plenty of money and there was no apparent indication that profit was his motive. The agent handling Jimmy took him aside and went out for a cup of coffee and a sandwich. When they came beck, the agent advised me that Jimmy C had a problem that he wanted us to help him with. Jimmy stated that his driver's license had been revoked some time ago and that he had over 200 parking tickets pending against him.

Before he would proceed with the case, he wanted our okay that the tickets would be taken care of and his license restored. This was practically an impossibility, as 200 parking tickets would have made him the king of the "scofflaws" and no judge would go along with our request. Nevertheless, the following day, I made inquiries and after searching all the records, I couldn't find any indication that there were any parking tickets pending against Jimmy under his true name or any of the aliases he had used. Neither was there any record that he ever had his license revoked.

At this point, it was very easy to go ahead and work with Jimmy. Jimmy made four good cases for us and after the cases were made, I advised him to go to the Department of Motor Vehicles and apply for a license. He did. He took the test, passed and was issued a valid license.

To this day, I cannot understand what happened to the so-called tickets and the revoked driver's' license. Nevertheless, at the end of the case, we had satisfied an informant and what appeared to be a tremendous obstacle, was, in fact, no obstacle at all. If Jimmy was an eccentric or a "mental case," he was one of the rare ones that didn't show it.

It is very important to know the complete background of the informant, whenever practical. There have been many cases where police organizations have used informants who were actually fugitives and were being sought for criminal offenses in other areas. This is very embarrassing for the police department or agency using the informant. As a matter of fact, some agencies require that an informant submit his fingerprints and he is not utilized until such time as a return is received on the prints. This is an impractical procedure, though it undoubtedly is a safe measure, because many informants would object to being fingerprinted and the waiting time for a return might jeopardize the case. Obtaining a photograph and personal data for the records sometimes involves some tricky imagination; fingerprints would be a near impossibility.

It has become obvious that developing and handling informants is an art that all officers must learn. To be successful in maintaining informants, an agency and its employees must have the respect and confidence of the informants that they meet through various sources. The agent and agency must live up to their commitments and every effort should be used to prevent the informant from being exposed.

The Suspect

3

It's clear that without a suspect or target of an investigation, there really isn't any reason for an undercover operation, unless it is merely to gather intelligence. Even though most law enforcement units seldom use undercover as a method of intelligence gathering, the same principles apply. In some instances such as the undercover investigation code named ABSCAM (Ab[dul]Enterprises, Ltd. with the suffix "scam") of 1978 to 1980, wherein FBI agents disguised as and acting the part of Arab oil merchants enticed several federal legislators into accepting cash for special favors — there was no specific target other than potentially corrupt congressmen. As an undercover operation it was extremely successful. With the assistance of informants and prior recipients of cash, word quickly spread throughout the Washington community that wealthy Arabs were freely giving cash for promises and favors. This operation was described in the news media as a "sting" that ensnared numerous U.S. Congressmen and other officials in the actual act of being offered and accepting bribes. This operation and many others since were successful; however, when it began there was no specific suspect targeted. In that instance and the ones emulating it, a large net of opportunity was cast and those with a mental predisposition to greed were lured in.

In non-law enforcement work, when a private investigator is placed in an undercover workplace setting it is usually to determine what is happening to the company product, why and how is it disappearing, who is responsible, and how can it be stopped or to resolve any number of corporate management concerns. An undercover operative also usually does not have a specific suspect. His role is to be accepted and trusted by his fellow employees and through the course of his duties will determine specific suspects; then he will proceed to establish evidence of their wrongdoing. In some circles his role is described as "an employer 'mole.'" Sometimes, the undercover investigator will be provided the name of someone who is suspected by top management as being a possible thief, drug dealer, trouble maker, etc. In those instances, the undercover operative follows the same course as an undercover law enforcement officer in getting introduced to the suspect, making a buy, establishing evidence and building a case against him.

Obtaining Background

Organizations endeavoring to work undercover cases, must get all the information possible on the suspect. In workplace undercover cases. the starting point is usually the human resources department or the top-ranking supervisor who placed the undercover investigator in the position, which of course is the same as saying the informant. In law enforcement circles, the best source of information , and the quickest, is the informant, especially if he is in a position to introduce the undercover agent to the suspect. If he can make an itroduction he has generally known the suspect for a period of time. He can give the agency background information on the suspect and answer most questions about the suspect. Following are some of the questions that need to be answered:

1. How long has the informant known the suspect?
2. How well does the informant know the suspect?
3. Does the suspect have any background or information with the agency investigating him? Is he on record with other investigative agencies?
4. Is the suspect capable of doing what the informant believes? In other words, is the suspect potentially able to produce contraband and/or is he prone to violence.
5. Is the suspect one of the top people in the operation or is he simply a "front"?
6. Can the undercover agent safely work where the suspect and his friends are likely to be?
7. Does the informant know who is behind the suspect or does he know any others in the operation?
8. How is the informant involved with the suspect?

These are important questions to be answered because in assigning an undercover agent to work with an informant, it is necessary to "know the territory" and most of the people involved so the undercover agent will not encounter a person he has previously confronted. Of course, many of the above questions are automatically answered when the suspect, or target of the investigation, has a previous record with the agency. The time must be found to answer the above questions, and related matters such as researching all the necessary supporting and peripheral information before the case proceeds. Once an operation is underway events occur with such speed there is seldom an opportunity to go back and resolve any issues that should have been addressed initially. These questions, if answered properly, will let a supervisor know the method he must use to protect the undercover operative and the informant; what agent or agents he must use for the undercover work; what places must be covered during the operation; and who are the people who might appear on the scene at the time of the "buy."

In considering the suspect, it is beneficial to know what his habits are — what time he gets up in the morning, what time he leaves the house, what route he takes, the car he drives, the people he meets and where he spends his time. Is he a good family man? Does he spend his nights at home? Does he have children, what are their ages and what school do they attend? Is he the type of person who would keep the contraband at home? Does he have a wife and/or girlfriend? Does he have another address, sort of a "home away from home"? Who are his associates and business contacts and where does he meet them? What are some of his usual routines? Does he, for example, frequent a specific restaurant for breakfast or lunch? Does he have a legitimate income? Does he "front' for anyone else, or perhaps a business? Can he or does he make decisions regarding the contraband, i.e., is he in a position to negotiate or must he defer to someone else? Are there any outstanding warrants for him or is he under investigation by any other agency? Knowing the answers to these questions in advance will make the undercover case easier to work and perhaps achieve more successful results.

There was a time when two agencies had warrants for a suspect. There was something in his background that indicated he might be armed and most likely wouldn't hesitate to use violence. Much thought was given as to where he should be arrested. At first it appeared that the best place to arrest him was at a club where he spent much of his time. It was finally decided to arrest him at his home.

A background check on this individual revealed that he had several small children at home. It was decided that the suspect wouldn't become involved in a gun battle, that would place his wife and children in jeopardy. Elaborate plans were made by the two agencies to ensure there wouldn't be any violence. The arrest at the home went smoothly and although we found he had a small arsenal, he made no attempt to use it. It was understandable; although he was a very violent and vicious man, he still didn't want to do anything that would jeopardize his children.

In researching the background of the suspect, look for evidence that will fit in with the particular crime that is being investigated. Were his previous violations the same as the one he is being investigated for? Was he previously arrested as a result of an undercover operation? Is there any indication he might cooperate? Does his previous record show any indication of a lesser sentence than his co-defendants? Is he currently on probation or parole? Does he have a reputation for being a "stand-up guy"? Does the informant's past experience with the suspect indicate that the suspect is reliable or is he noted for backing out on deals or does he make promises and commitments he either cannot or will not fill? In previous dealings with the suspect, did the informant give money in advance or was it a hand-to-hand delivery? What is the suspect's financial situation? Has he had recent arrests that required bail money and lawyer's fees?

It is very important to know the suspects' past criminal history and current financial condition because if he needs money badly, he may not take as elaborate precautions that he would normally take. Most of the answers to the questions needed to appraise the suspect can be found in probation or parole reports, past arrest records and court filings, reports from other agencies and, of course, reports from the agency making the investigation. Before working an undercover case, no detail, however slight, should be overlooked and unanticipated. By investigating the suspect and examining his lifestyle, background, record and reputation, it will be easier to predict his moves and demands. Very often, if enough is known about the suspect, many of his movements and activities can be discounted as routine and much of the surveillance could be curtailed in order to minimize suspicion.

Suspect's Problems

In working an undercover case where contraband is involved, the agency and the undercover personnel should be aware that the suspect might be having trouble in bringing everything together for the delivery. Patience is the keyword and must be exercised liberally. Several hours may spell the difference between success and failure. The suspect generally is not truthful in telling why the delivery is taking so long. Sometimes it is something as innocuous as a child's orthodontic appointment, a soccer game, or any one of a thousand other family and domestic problems. At times, he is embarrassed to admit that he is getting the merchandise third- or fourth-hand and has to wait until the others involved are ready to make the delivery. Sometimes 12 to 14 hours isn't an unreasonably long time to wait for a delivery. As long as the suspect indicates that he is expecting the merchandise, the undercover personnel and covering agents should wait. In some instances the suspect's delivery has been delayed for several days. In that instance, the undercover agent shouldn't totally give up. He should merely work with the suspect to reschedule the delivery at a more convenient time.

I can recall a case where an undercover agent was expecting a delivery of $100,000 in counterfeit money at a local diner. Originally the suspect stated that he controlled the plant and the merchandise leaving the plant. He tried to make the undercover agent believe that the operation was entirely his. This is not a rare situation, many suspects have been known to over-inflate their importance.

When the time came for delivery, the suspect had to wait for another man to come home from work and the other man had to wait for someone else to take the money from its hiding place. The covering agents in this particular case became very impatient with the delay and several times during the operation they called me and indicated that they didn't believe a delivery would be made. Each time I managed to contact the undercover agent and he believed that a delivery would be made but it might take longer than anticipated. A delivery came fourteen hours after it was expected. The suspect had to get some money in advance before a delivery would be made to him. The extra hours that we waited in this case made the difference between success and failure.

Salesmanship

The suspect will often try to impress the undercover agent that he is "Mr. Big." He will try to show that he controls the entire operation and that he does not have to answer to anyone. Common sense generally will dictate that this is not true in most cases. Seldom will the person responsible for the entire operation expose himself to a person he doesn't even know just to sell a few thousand dollars in illegal merchandise. More likely an underling will be acting as a go between and in that role he may merely be bragging that he is the top person for a couple of reasons. The first is that he may be fronting for someone else to protect or insulate that person. Then again, he may be puffing his importance to enhance his personal standing with the undercover agent. The suspect has a product to sell and like all good entrepreneurs he is a salesman and self-inflation or product aggrandizement is part and parcel of his sales pitch. Very often the undercover agent should go along with this deception (at least for a while until the appropriate opportune moment when, under some pretext, the undercover agent manages to convince the suspect to introduce him to upper echelon people). Nothing would be initially accomplished by knocking down his claim of being "The Man," or "the brains of the outfit." It is good for the suspect's ego and will establish a good relationship between the undercover agent and the suspect to accept his boasts. This also tends to make a successful case.

In a case involving the manufacture and sale of counterfeit gold nuggets in Northern California, the suspect was such an enthusiastic salesman, he invited the undercover agent into his house and showed him the entire operation he had set up in his garage. The suspect and his ring of associates were stealing gold from a mine in Nevada. They then melted it and while it was still liquid dropped it into a running cement mixer with water, trace

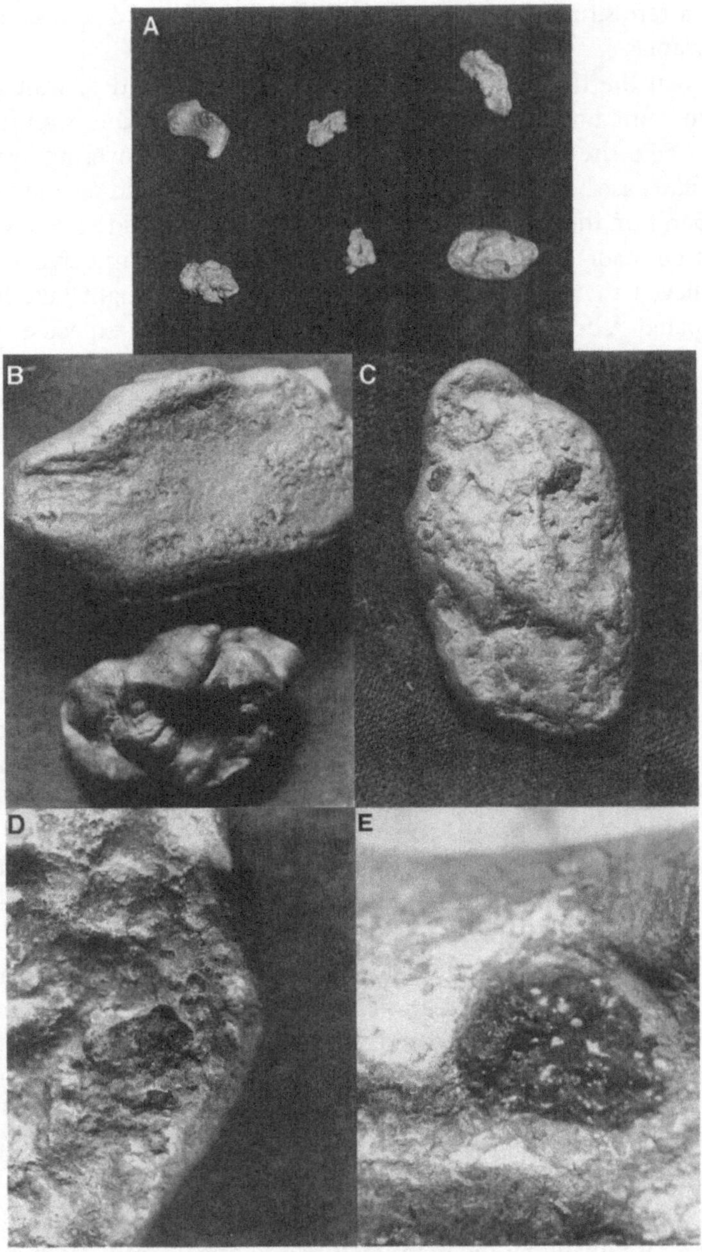

Display of counterfeit gold nuggets. (**A**) Counterfeit gold nuggets magnified 2×; (**B**) counterfeit gold nuggets magnified 5×; (**C**) counterfeit gold nuggets magnified 8× — note "slag" spots (slag is a residue left from the smelting process); (**D**) counterfeit gold nuggets magnified 18× — note the slag center; (**E**) counterfeit gold nuggets magnified 50× — note the smelted globules of gold in the slag matrix — proof that these nuggets did not occur naturally .

materials, and sand. The rotating motion of the mixer and the cold water mixed the sand and trace material into the gold, giving it a natural stream tumbled appearance. The nuggets, though containing a high percentage of gold, were then sold as natural occurring nuggets at two and a half times the current price of gold.

Stereotypical Operation by the Suspect

Some suspects have an established a routine of how they want to conduct business. It can be very difficult to get them to change their methods. These traits are usually found in more experienced and sophisticated suspects who have found that they have been successful in distributing contraband in a way that protects and insulates them from being set up. Attempting to "make a buy" from this type of suspect is very difficult because he will usually want the money in advance and he might not even be on the scene when the delivery is made. He will also refuse to be introduced to strangers and will not discuss business with people he hasn't known personally for a long time.

> Anthony lived in a midwestern city. He had been in this country for 25 years and in that time had established several successful businesses. He was also a member of an organized group who had victimized inhabitants of this city for quite a few years. Anthony made a lot of money with his legitimate businesses and he made a lot more with his underworld enterprises. He was involved in alien smuggling, handling drugs, and a complex street lottery or "numbers" bank. There came a time when he became the principle distributor of a new counterfeit note that appeared in the midwest. Anthony was very careful about who he conducted business with and because he was successful, he wouldn't change his method of delivery. The particular counterfeit note that he was handling was getting very wide distribution and the passers were quite successful in victimizing the public.
>
> An informant had purchased some counterfeit notes from Anthony and had confided in him that he had over $1 million dollars worth of these counterfeits and he was quite anxious to dispose of the whole lot. The informant reported this to the Secret Service and a decision was made to send an agent with the informant to attempt to make a purchase of counterfeit notes. This particular agent happened to be my brother, Bob Motto.
>
> Anthony had a pizzeria, a grocery store, and a bar and grill all in the same building. This building had a large cellar where Anthony stored supplies for his businesses. This, we suspected was also the storage place for the large amount of counterfeit notes we felt that Anthony possessed.

When the time was right, the informant introduced my brother Bob to Anthony. Anthony was very suspicious and immediately accused the informant of bringing the law into his place of business. This was another of Anthony's traits. Every time he met a potential customer for the first time, he would accuse the stranger of being a "cop" and would shout and threaten the informant with a beating or death if anything happened to convince him that the stranger was a "cop."

After two or three meetings, Anthony gradually accepted my brother and their meetings ended when Anthony delivered $50,000 to Bob. No arrests were made as a result of the buy. It was agreed that this buy would never be used because the informant introduced Bob to Anthony. It was decided that Bob would bring another agent in and attempt to acquire the million dollars in counterfeit notes. The arrest would be made at that time. As much denunciation and acclaim as possible would be thrown on the second agent to make it appear as though he was the informant in the case.

About three weeks after the first buy, it was decided that I would accompany my brother, Bob, to this city and he would introduce me to Anthony. He would tell Anthony that I was a bank robber and that as a result of my string of robberies, I had enough money to purchase all the counterfeit notes that Anthony had left.

One Saturday afternoon, both of us went to Anthony's bar. Anthony spoke heavily accented English and very poor Italian so communicating with him was very difficult. As soon as the introductions were made, Anthony called Bob aside and accused him of bringing a "cop" into his bar. He said he wouldn't say anything in front of this stranger because he didn't feel comfortable with him around. Bob and I sat at a table and had lunch. Shortly thereafter, Anthony joined us. His first remark was that we looked like brothers. This was very disturbing because we didn't want to give this impression to Anthony. The conversation at the table was cool, casual but almost formal, and nothing was accomplished. We told Anthony we would be back for dinner later that evening.

It didn't appear to me that anything could be done with Anthony because of his attitude and distrust. Bob reassured me and said that this was exactly the same attitude that Anthony had with him at their first meeting.

Later that night, we returned to the restaurant. Again, Anthony joined us at the table. This time, for some unknown reason, he decided not to talk to Bob and instead, directed his conversation to me. He said he knew what I was there for and he was in a position to deliver $1 million dollars, providing I could give him $100,000 in cash before the delivery. I told Anthony that I had come into the city with $100,000 and there would be no difficulty making a purchase, providing the method of delivery was satisfactory. After discussing several methods of delivery, Anthony said that he had one last method of making a delivery and this would be the only way he would handle it. He suggested that we come back to the bar at midnight with the $100,000 in genuine currency. We would all proceed to the cellar under his bar. Immediately after the bar closed, he would count the $100,000 that I had brought with me and he would let me examine and count the million dollars that he would arrange to have in the cellar.

He suggested that my brother and I carry a weapon because he would have several armed bodyguards to protect his counterfeit money. Anthony said that once the money was counted and exchanged, we would remain in the cellar until daylight. We would then go into his grocery store, put the counterfeit notes into shopping bags, walk out of the store, put the bags in the trunk of our car, and be on our way. I replied that I liked this idea very much except I didn't want to spend the whole night in his cellar because I had more important things to do. So I suggested that I would drive to his store on Sunday morning and bring the $100,000 with me. We would then go down into the basement and it would take Anthony a short time to count my money. I would take the counterfeit money and assume there was $1 million dollars there, put the money in shopping bags and leave as Anthony suggested. I reminded him that I'd be back if there were any shortages. Anthony mulled it over for quite some time and finally agreed to it. He suggested that we should be in front of his grocery store at seveno'clock sharp on Sunday morning. He said that he would be in the store preparing it for the day's business. As soon as we drove up, he'd open the door for us. He would then immediately examine my money and then take us to where the counterfeit money was located. I agreed that these arrangements would be satisfactory.

He again suggested that we arm ourselves for our own protection. We left the building and had a meeting at the office that night to make arrangements for the "buy" the next morning.

There were still many problems with the "buy" as Anthony suggested. If we weren't using the first "buy" as evidence, we would have to see counterfeit money on Anthony's property before an arrest could be made. Anthony wanted to see our money before we saw the counterfeits and this was the problem. We considered various possibilities for several hours and finally decided on a plan of action. As suggested by Anthony, I would drive up across the street from the store, brother Bob would get out of the car, and I would stay in it. Bob would cross the street and we were sure that Anthony would open the door as soon as he saw Bob and would ask him what was wrong. Bob would say, "My friend is very nervous because of all the talk about carrying guns. There are only two of us and we don't know how many people you have hidden on the premises. He's afraid that we'll be robbed as soon as we enter the store with the money." That is exactly what we did.

When Bob arrived at the store, Anthony was fuming, "Why doesn't your friend come in?" Bob said that his friend was scared to death and thought that Anthony had people on the premises ready to take his $100,000 at gunpoint and not give up the counterfeit. Just as we planned, Anthony said, "Okay, you go down into the cellar and look for yourself." Bob went into the cellar pretending to look for anyone who might pull a "rip off." Anthony had two armed bodyguards in the cellar sitting right next to several cartons full of counterfeit money. Again, just as we had planned, Bob came out of the store and shouted to me that everything was okay. "Get your money and come on in!" We had made sure that on Sunday morning there wouldn't be any unusual cars parked on the street because Anthony undoubtedly had friends checking the neighborhood. We had a surveillance/communications truck parked several blocks away from where the agents and detectives had a clear view of my car. I had made arrangements with all concerned that as soon as I opened the car trunk, everything was set for an arrest.

When Bob shouted to me that everything was okay, I left the car and opened the trunk, spending some time fumbling with a briefcase. My opening of the trunk was the signal for the men in the surveillance van and a message went out to all cars secreted on surrounding streets to immediately move in and effect the arrests. Within half a minute, several cars of officers and agents converged on the scene. Officers with shotguns leapt out of the cars and completely overwhelmed Anthony and his men so quickly, that they had no time to react — let alone protest. The counterfeit money was seized from the cellar along with some firearms and other contraband Anthony was dealing in.

Anthony and his friends were later sentenced to 10 years in prison. Anthony had been successful most of his life in making deals the safe way. However, even a man as cautious as Anthony must take some risks to expand and grow his business. Arrangements can be made to make them deviate from their own routine of operation. I doubt if Anthony was even aware of the fact that he had radically changed from the safe position that he originally took in the beginning and had practiced all his life.

Using Conversation for Corroboration

An undercover agent should never underestimate any phase of the case he is working on. The case or relationship with the suspect could conceivably end at any time during the negotiations and a prosecutable case can still be sustained. One sample can be sufficient to convict a distributor in a counterfeiting case. Even a short conversation with the suspect about a previous sale can corroborate the testimony of another witness and result in the conviction of the suspect. Many counterfeit note distributors have been sent to jail for comparatively long terms on the strength of one or two sample notes given to an undercover agent. It should be borne in mind that a conviction, even on a one-note pass, carries a very severe penalty.

One of the toughest men I ever worked on was Mario. He was a short in stature and but he was built like a fireplug. He had been a cross-country trucker he drove the big rigs — 18-wheelers and was feared by everyone he dealt with. Mario was a hard-working man with a sideline of dealing in drugs and counterfeit money. He operated successfully for quite a few years and was known for his shrewdness in making deals. If he had the slightest suspicion that something was amiss, he would indefinitely postpone or entirely cancel the delivery, if necessary, until he could test the purchaser and convince himself that the man wasn't a police officer.

In his younger years, Mario had spent considerable time in jail for vicious assaults on those he suspected of double-dealing him. He always carried some type of weapon he could use for those assaults. However, he was careful never to carry a gun or knife. He had learned at an early age that there were plenty of other weapons that could be used to assault and beat people without taking unnecessary chances of being arrested for carrying a concealed weapon.

Another suspect who didn't know my true identity introduced me to Mario. After a few meetings with Mario, he told me he could get me counterfeit money in unlimited quantities. I asked Mario for a sample note and he said he'd have one for me the following night.

He then suggested we have a drink at a nearby tavern. It was necessary to drive to the bar so Mario used the opportunity to see if we were being followed. After driving three or four blocks, Mario called my attention to a car that was obviously following us. He tested this car for about a mile and there was no doubt Mario was convinced that they were interested in him. Mario's only problem was that he wasn't sure whether they were federal agents or local police. We arrived at the tavern and after a drink, I excused myself to make a telephone call to my office and advised them to discontinue the surveillance on Mario, because he was aware he was being followed. The agents in the follow-up car immediately withdrew. Mario again asked me to join him for a ride after we left the tavern. He drove randomly for over an hour but couldn't find anyone tailing him and was convinced that perhaps it was the local police but they had no real interest in him.

I met Mario again the following night. He said he didn't have the sample as he was still testing for surveillance. It took two more weeks before he would even talk about samples again. Finally, the day came when Mario was convinced that he wasn't being followed any longer and agreed to deliver the samples on a subsequent night. I kept the appointment, but Mario didn't show up. I waited for several hours and when it became apparent that something was wrong I left our meeting place. When I returned to the office, I learned that Mario had been arrested in a small nearby town when he tried to buy a drink with a counterfeit $20 bill. The police held him for our Service and it was decided to arraign him on the charge of passing a single counterfeit bill. Mario pleaded not guilty and claimed he was an innocent victim who had received the counterfeit bill when he cashed his paycheck. He made bail and was released.

A few nights later, I met with him again and he told me of his troubles. He told me that on the night he was arrested, he had the sample counterfeit for me and stopped in a local bar for a drink. After a few drinks, he inadvertently gave the sample note to the bartender. He said he had discussed this matter with his attorney who told him that the government didn't have a case and probably wouldn't prosecute on a one-note pass. Mario told me that he wasn't going to handle any more counterfeit notes until his case was disposed of.

Not long afterward, his case came up for trial. The bartender testified about the note Mario had passed. Mario kept calm throughout the proceedings as he was certain that the jury wouldn't convict

> him. I was called as the final government witness. This was quite a shock to Mario. When I took the stand, he flew into a rage. He shouted obscenities at me and the whole judicial system. He had to be forcibly restrained during my testimony. I carefully went through our whole relationship and the conversation we had prior to his arrest and how I had waited three hours for a sample on the night he was arrested. His lawyer made a feeble attempt at a defense which wasn't too impressive. The jury was out only 15 minutes and returned with a verdict of guilty. Mario was sentenced to seven years in prison. After the sentencing, he threatened the judge, the assistant U. S. Attorney, and me. However his threats never materialized — he served his time and upon his release, slipped into obscurity.

I doubt if Mario would have received any more time even if he had made a sizeable delivery of notes. That pass, together with the conversation we had, was enough to convince the judge and jury that Mario was not an innocent victim of a counterfeit note.

Handling the Suspect after the Arrest

Unfortunately, there are some investigators who think that an undercover case ends with the arrest of the distributors after the delivery of the contraband. Undercover work is a means to get to the source of the crime. In counterfeit cases the eventual goal is to work to locate the plant where the counterfeit is produced. In drug cases the undercover agent wants to determine the network of distributors as well as those responsible for the importation or manufacture of the illegal substance. When the suspect is arrested, the arresting officers must use knowledge and psychology in attempting to get the suspect to "rollover" and name his source or to assist in locating the plant. Most people who are arrested in the act of committing a crime go into something that resembles shock, especially if it is their first arrest. The knowledgeable officer can turn this "state of shock" into an advantage. If he can interview the suspect properly, gain his confidence and show the advantages of cooperating, the defendant very often will cooperate and bring the case to a successful conclusion. Many more times than one would like to see, sources have "slipped through the fingers" of incompetent or poorly trained investigators because they didn't handle the defendant properly, immediately following the arrest. The investigators lost sight of the fact that the arrest signaled the end of a phase of the investigation and the beginning of an important new phase.

They made the mistake of playing the role of the tough cop and trying to bully admissions from the defendant. While interviewing the arrested person, some investigators have been known to place their handcuffs on the desk in full view of the subject or lean against a wall or table so their suit coat falls at an angle to expose their weapon. Some have been known to place a pad of paper on the desk beside the handcuffs and demand a written statement while indicating the handcuffs as an alternate choice. These methods have been determined by the courts as being heavyhanded and to smack of coercion which can have the effect of making the information gained as inadmissible. Yet many officers will still attempt to conduct the post-arrest interview in this manner. They completely choose to disregard the fact that the defendant has certain rights which can never be abridged or denied him. Explaining one's rights is a duty imposed upon governmental agencies and fervently guarded by the Constitution. The defendant expects to be advised of those inalienable rights every time, even though he may have heard them thousands of times by the press, television, the movies, etc. Even if a person has been arrested several times, he is still entitled to information of the rights and to be treated without coercion and disrespect. In non-law enforcement settings, such as a workplace undercover operation, the dishonest or corrupt employee should be provided an opportunity to be interviewed in the absence of bullying tactics and must be allowed to exercise all of his rights such as union representation, etc. Heavy-handed procedures are not only ill- advised, but they most probably will backfire and the cooperation of the defendant will be lost.

An arrest creates many problems for the person being arrested. Criminals don't expect to be arrested when they are in the act of committing a crime and so they usually don't plan accordingly. There are times when these problems are just as important to the defendant as the arrest itself. The wife has to be notified, a date may be waiting at some rendezvous location, the children have to be picked up at school, groceries have to be delivered, or the mother might become seriously ill if not notified properly, etc. The intelligent officer will listen to these problems and make attempts to solve them, if at all possible, and if it does not violate any departmental rules. A genuine interest in these problems will establish a rapport between the defendant and the officer. It is important to note that there is no safety in numbers when interviewing a defendant. Suspects, witnesses, and defendants are reluctant to talk before a group. They feel they can always deny a statement made before just one officer. Furthermore, several people questioning a suspect may make him feel uncomfortable to the point of feeling coerced. It should also be borne in mind that most defendants don't think too kindly of an officer who immediately takes out a pen and writing pad at the very start of an interview and attempts to record every word. Immediately after an arrest, many defendants appreciate a cigarette, a cup of coffee, or a cold soda, and a man-to-man conversation with the arresting or questioning officers. This sometimes brings far more success and cooperation than a combination of out-dated police methods. During the post-arrest shock trauma, a little understanding and genuine concern shown toward the plight of the defendant will greatly enhance the chances of moving successfully into the next phase of the investigation — the cooperation of the defendant in providing intelligence data and the location of the plant, other people involved, the criminal network, etc. It has become a trite cliché , but as the old saying goes, "You catch more flies with honey, than you do with vinegar." In police tactics that is a very profound and true statement.

Everett and his family were quite popular in the community. They had moved to a sleepy New England village and were immediately accepted by the usually cool and standoffish residents. Ev was outgoing; and his wife, a former ballet dancer, lost no time in establishing ballet classes for the children of the community. Their own children were popular with the other school-aged children in the town. Ev and his wife had purchased a large, old refurbished house and Ev ran a publishing company from there. He was extended all kinds of credit, especially when he made it known that he was related to a high-ranking government official (which wasn't true, however, he did have the same name as a Cabinet member.)

Several months later, a number of counterfeit $10 and $20 bills and some counterfeit American Telephone and Telegraph (AT&T) stock certificates began showing up in the larger cities in the area. At this time, there wasn't anything suspicious about Ev, except that the townspeople thought he was working too hard — "burning the midnight oil" in his basement office. They knew he had financial problems and thought he was working overtime to meet his obligations.

One day, an informant came into our office and told us that he had been offered counterfeit $10s and $20s by a man named Harvey who ran an auto repair shop in a nearby city. This informant had just been another customer in the auto repair shop and he had no ties with Harvey. The informant stated that he would have no objection to introducing an undercover agent to Harvey.

I accompanied the informant to Harvey's shop. After a conversation lasting about half an hour, Harvey asked me if I would be interested in purchasing some "funny money." I said that I didn't know too much about it, but I'd take a couple of hundred and see how it went. I said I'd show the money to some friends as well, and try to get some large orders. Harvey was able to immediately supply me with several hundred dollars worth, and told me he could get more in any amount as long as I gave him a few days notice. I returned to the office — the notes were examined and they matched the same notes that were being passed in that area.

Several days later, I called Harvey and told him I was interested in purchasing between $50,000 and $75,000 worth of these notes. Harvey gave me a fairly good price on them and I arranged to have another meeting with him. He told me he was very busy that day because he had to buy groceries, as his wife and family were returning from a vacation; he had a date with a girl who expected him to take her to a nightclub that night; and that he also had a date to meet the printer and turn over the money from our sale. He thought that this would keep him quite busy.

Later that evening, he came to my hotel room carrying a package. This package contained almost $75,000 in counterfeit notes. Harvey was annoyed at the fact I was examining and counting each note and he was impatient to get going. He said his girlfriend was waiting in the lobby and he still had to purchase his groceries before the stores closed. At this time, agents entered the room and placed both of us under arrest. Harvey didn't have a prior criminal record and certainly appeared as though he was in a state of shock. Agents attempted to question him, but couldn't get any coherent answers.

I told one of the more experienced agents that Harvey had a lot of problems and to try to solve them as quickly as possible because he had to meet with the printer later that night and the printer might become suspicious if Harvey didn't keep the appointment. The agent established rapport with Harvey and the first thing that was accomplished was to let Harvey go to the lobby and quickly break the date with the girlfriend. Harvey was then allowed to get the groceries before his wife and kids got home. We also agreed to let Harvey meet his wife and get her and the children home.

Harvey was immediately advised of his Constitutional rights upon his arrest He stated that would cooperate fully and that he wanted to get the whole matter off his chest He told the agent that he had to meet the printer, a man called Everett at a downtown bar and turn over the buy money to him. He verified that Everett was the printer and the plant was in Ev's basement.

Harvey was allowed to make this meeting, at which time both Everett and Harvey were taken into custody. At first, Everett denied knowing anything about counterfeiting. We let him know that a search warrant was being prepared for his residence. This upset him quite a bit because he had just finished printing several thousand in counterfeit money that morning and hadn't bothered to clean up the basement or take the plates off the press. He realized that all the necessary evidence was at his home so he decided to cooperate. He stated that before he gave any information, he wanted to know if an agent Motto was still in the Secret Service. When asked why, he said that he knew Motto as a New York State Police officer at a time when he was a county police officer and further that they had renewed their acquaintance when he and Motto both joined the Marine Corps. It wasn't made known to him immediately that I was the one doing the undercover work, but he was told that Motto was still in the Secret Service and they would bring him up at a future date.

The next day, we converged on Everett's large home. We found enough contraband to fill a truck. A printing press, plates, negatives, ink, and money were all over the cellar — it was obvious why Everett had decided to cooperate. Certain background information was obtained from town residents in connection with the understanding that after the trial was over, they fully intended to take care of Everett and his family. Immediately after his incarceration, Everett's wife went on welfare and she was paid as an instructor for the dancing lessons she gave the children of the community.

I visited Everett at the federal prison sometime later. We renewed old acquaintances, and I asked Everett if I had met him while I was working undercover, could I convince him that I was an ex-police officer gone bad. He laughed and said that I could never have convinced him in a million years that I wasn't working undercover, regardless of the circumstances under which we met. It wasn't long afterward that Everett wrote of his exploits as a counterfeiter for a national publication.

There isn't any doubt in my mind that this case was really made by an agent who was able to convince Harvey that he should cooperate with the Government. He handled Harvey decently and so was able to gain his confidence. Harvey wasn't a pushover in any sense of the word. He was a big man who had been around quite a bit, even if he didn't have a criminal record. Had he been handled improperly in the beginning, he certainly

Agent Carmine Motto examining the evidence after seizure of a counterfeiting plant. The undercover work was complete and the premises were raided.

wouldn't have taken the agents to the meeting with Everett. Up to that time, we didn't have any evidence to indicate that my old acquaintance, Ev, was a counterfeiter.

Summary

The suspect and gathering evidence against him are the primary reasons for conducting undercover operations. The investigating agent should attempt to obtain all the information possible regarding the suspect prior to commencing the undercover assignment. Ask the informant (or a knowledgeable person cooperating with the investigation) questions pertaining to the case at hand and the role of the suspect's involvement. Official records and indices including criminal records, intelligence files, civil and domestic court records, even county records are all potential sources of information. A search of the records should include a history of similar violations or activity in the past for which he is under investigation and the names of any associates and/or family. If possible photographs should be obtained in order that the undercover agent might recognize the suspect and associates.

An undercover agent might have to be patient while waiting for a delivery because the suspect may have unexpected problems arise that prevent him from making a delivery exactly at the agreed upon time. The patience on the part of the agent might additionally be an asset because he is the suspect's client, a buyer; the suspect is the salesman with a product to sell. A little conservative reticence or selective reluctance to buy the proffered contraband at appropriate times will heighten the suspect's efforts to sell his product, often leading him away from his standard procedures rendering him more vulnerable to arrest.

Braggadocio and conversation on the part of the suspect can be used to corroborate statements of witnesses and informants. An undercover agent should document all conversations with the suspect as soon as possible after the statements are made and they should be quoted as accurately as possible.

Arresting a suspect is usually the end of only a part of the investigation, as it may be the beginning of a secondary phase such as identifying and locating the source of the contraband and peripheral associates, methods, and materials. It is incumbent upon the arresting agents to handle a suspect in a manner that will establish rapport and encourage his cooperation.

The Undercover Agent

4

What does it take to become an undercover agent? A recent advertisement in *The San Diego Union* newspaper placed by a national security and intelligence agency, described it in terms that sounded like an adventure of a lifetime, "the ultimate ... experience"... "For the extraordinary individual who wants more than a job, this is a way of life that will challenge the deepest resources of your intelligence, self-reliance, and responsibility. It demands an adventurous spirit ... a forceful personality ... superior intellectual ability ... toughness of mind ... and the highest degree of integrity. It takes special skills and professional discipline to produce results. You need to deal with fast-moving, ambiguous, and unstructured situations that will test your resourcefulness to the utmost."

Working undercover will certainly test the mental agility and resourcefulness, even the courage, of the undercover agent. An undercover agent is usually an extroverted individual who makes friends easily, gets along well with people, and can blend into a crowd. Even when acting out a "tough-guy" role, the undercover agent has a way of instilling acceptance in the people he meets. He appears emotionally strong and projects an outward calm, never over-reacting to a situation. However, when the situation demands, the undercover operative can be forceful and "take charge," but in a way that allays hostility, mistrust, and suspicion.

There are two other attributes that are of the utmost importance. The first is a good memory. In addition to possessing superior mental alertness and dexterity, the undercover agent must be able to remember and report the smallest detail. It is rarely possible to record or write down everything as it happens. To properly report the activities as they occurred, the agent must be able to mentally retain conversations, instructions, and descriptions. The second attribute necessary to a successful undercover agent is common sense and judgment. He often is called upon to make on-the-spot decisions that could have a consequential impact not only on the outcome of the case but on his own safety. The agent must be alert at all times to avoid being placed in a compromising position. Common sense dictates avoiding, if at all possible, those situations wherein he could be trapped or exposed without the possibility of a safe extrication.

Popular Misconceptions

There are a number of misconceptions connected with undercover work. Many police officers and agents feel that they don't have the proper appearance or temperament to do undercover work and therefore, avoid it as much as possible. The popular image of the undercover agent is based on the belief that he must "look like a criminal." But, just what exactly does a criminal look like? Experience has shown that there is no "criminal type" outside that filmmaker's studio and sound stage. Long gone is the Hollywood movie "gangster" dressed in a black suit, dark-pink shirt, and white tie. Dealers in contraband come in all shapes, styles, and cultures, and speak everything ranging from "street slang" to foreign languages. Plainly speaking, agents should not ascribe to the belief that they don't fit the mold of an undercover agent. There is a place for everyone. Most undercover agents don't have to change their personality or looks. It's just a matter of finding the right fit. For example, if an agent is a "redneck," a "good ole boy", then that should be his undercover persona.

A major fallacy, is that an undercover agent must be a good actor. Granted he is playing a role, but it is not an acting role. Acting really isn't part of undercover work. The only acting that should be done is to act naturally. As in any other business, there should be a goal, and the officer must use all the means at his disposal to attain that goal. As previously stated, in undercover work the goal is to penetrate a certain group in order to locate the contraband and to arrest those involved in the importation, manufacture, distribution, and sale of the contraband.

Another popular misconception, perhaps perpetuated by the popular media is that an undercover officer (or person pretending to be a contraband dealer) is a big spender. You don't have to be a big spender, leaving outrageously large tips, ordering the most expensive wine on the menu, or failing to negotiate for the best bargain to impress the suspect. This is true because sometimes people will be just as suspicious of a careless or big spender as they will of one who doesn't spend. Observation and experience has taught us that there are many defendants who are quite tight with their money, even though they may gain it by easy, albeit illegal, methods. In making purchases, they drive just as hard a bargain as someone living on a legitimate salary and trying to make ends meet.

As unreal as it may seem in this highly informed and generally well-educated society, there is still the misconception that an undercover agent must be an uneducated dolt because gangsters have very little education. Of couse, this is ridiculous — even laughable. While this misconception may have been true 40 or 50 years ago, today's undercover agent can expect to encounter well-educated, well-spoken, and very well-mannered people involved in the contraband trade. This brings to mind the old nursery rhyme that seems to fit with the arrests we have made — there have been "tinkers, tailors, soldiers and sailors; rich men, poor men, beggar men and thieves." There have also been a number of doctors, lawyers, and Indians (not necessarily chiefs). Probably the only category not accounted for is the candlestick maker, which appears to be a dying art, but certainly every other type of employment, and all educational levels have been well represented in past undercover arrests.

Fitting the Man to the Job

One of the first principles of personnel management is to select the most-qualified person for the job. Looking beyond the requirements of a position, a person must also "fit" the position. The same applies when selecting a person to fill an undercover role. Practically any agent or police officer can do undercover work, providing he is fitted into the proper case and is given the necessary cover. That doesn't mean that every police officer can work every case. What is required is a supervisor who knows the abilities of the individual officer or agent he is about to assign to a case and a genuine knowledge of the suspect and locale of where the case may take place.

One case required the services of an experienced undercover agent for a job in a city in Nevada, a typical western community with a "cowboy mentality." An experienced and very successful undercover agent was sent from New York City. After his initial confrontation with the cowboy-booted suspects, the undercover agent reported very little progress and wondered to the other agents, all local people, "Who are these people, where do they come from, and what do they do?" He had spent his entire life in New York City and the closest he had ever been to a cowboy was in the movie theater. After his second meeting with the suspects, who were trying to sell stolen securities, the undercover agent reported that no progress had been made and they were obviously not going to sell to him. A meeting with the informant determined that the cowboy suspects, who had at first appeared to be tough, hard-nosed thieves, were in fact intimidated and frightened by the "city boy" who they thought had Mafia connections. This undercover agent was replaced with a less intimidating and soft-spoken agent who had had little undercover expe-

A working shift of undercover officers (circa 1970) returning to the office after a night of working the streets.

rience, but who had spent time with horses and cowboys. The meetings went very well, the securities were recovered, and the suspects went to jail.

Most officers would welcome the opportunity to do undercover work, but they are never given the opportunity because someone has tagged them as "average" officers. A person should be given the opportunity to do undercover work by starting on a small case. It would really be quite surprising to see how many so-called "average cops" can be successful in working undercover.

> Harris worked for me for a number of years. He was an extremely intelligent agent who had a typical Ivy-League college appearance and was a successful businessman. I was continually alert for a case for him to gain undercover experience. He was a supervisor and he certainly wanted to work as many undercover cases as possible because he knew before too long, he would have to break in the newer agents and there was no substitute for hands-on experience.
>
> One day, a prominent and well-known advertising agency executive came to my office to give me some counterfeiting information. He probably won't forgive me for not using his real name, but for purposes of this illustration he shall remain nameless. We will refer to him as "P.R. Ads." P.R. indicated that in the normal course of his business he had met an individual who was currently a refugee with political asylum in this country, but who was very influential and well-known in his own South American country. This person was

known as Don Carlo and he had a plan to counterfeit the currency of his native country and flood it with counterfeits (similar to the plan the Nazi's had in World War II with U. S. currency). He believed this plan would ruin the economy of his country, causing a lack of confidence in the current dictator who had been in power for a number years; a coup would result, toppling the regime. His plan found favor and was received with enthusiasm by a large number of Americans who were anxious to be of service and to help him in any way possible. One individual with expertise in photography made beautiful negatives of the currency from which a set of printing plates were made. Don Carlo was currently searching for an experienced printer to print the currency for him. He had received financial backing and support from sentimental ex-patriots who believed in the cause. He had received sufficient financing to employ the best professionals available. The one fact that all these people didn't know, or at least overlooked, was that the Secret Service is charged with suppression of counterfeiting, not only of American currency, but of foreign currency as well. That was what brought Mr. P. R. Ads to my office. He was aware of this, and not only gave us the information, but was willing to introduce an undercover agent to the Don. The agent would pose as the owner of a printing plant who would print the currency from the plates supplied by Don Carlo.

This was the ideal case on which to use Agent Harris in an undercover capacity. He certainly didn't have to look like anything other than a businessman who was willing to do something a little shady to make an extra buck. One of my former counterfeiters allowed me to use his printing business as a front to show to Don Carlo in the event he wanted to inspect the plant.

The introductions went splendidly. There were several meetings in New York and Washington, D.C., where Don Carlo lived. This wasn't the type of case to arouse indignation because it appeared that Don Carlos' motives were purely patriotic. However, during one of the meetings, Don Carlo confided to Harris that once the printing of the counterfeits was finished, he planned to sell many of them and make sure that his future was secure.

Don Carlo delivered the negatives and plates to Harris and Don Carlo was exposed not as the patriotic citizen he pretended to be, but as just another counterfeiter. Don Carlo and the well-intentioned people who had helped him were convicted and duly sentenced. Needless to say, P. R. was quite pleased with himself for the favor he had done for us. The day after the case was disposed of, he approached me regarding a reward we had discussed. P. R. said he knew the worth of the service he had rendered and was expecting a reward. I asked him what it was that he wanted. He replied that he wanted a United States Treasury check payable to him in the amount of $202.12— no more; no less. This request was definitely from the realm of the unusual and had me stymied. I knew he was a good public-relations man and that his forte was generating publicity. With a little prompting, he confided that the Internal Revenue Service, was requesting (demanding) $202.12 which they said he owed them. He thought it would be a great idea and good fun if he could get the Secret Service to issue him a check in that exact amount. He would in turn present the check to the local office of the Internal Revenue Service. He explained that it would only be justice (with a smile).

I realized that if this check were issued, P. R. would hold a press conference, inviting the media — press, radio, and television —the works, and the whole matter would become a three-ring publicity circus. P. R. accepted my refusal with good nature. I did manage to get him $202.12 in cash and presented it to him in my office. Of course he brought along several of his associates for the payment ceremony. This seemed to placate him and took care of the matter very nicely.

Agent Harris continued to work undercover and made several more cases thereafter and was a prime example that there are no typical stereotypes for undercover agents.

Obtaining Cover

One big problem in working an undercover case is obtaining the necessary cover. Very few police organizations have the funds and resources to rent homes or storefronts or to establish businesses for the sole purpose of obtaining the necessary cover for the agent working the case. The FBI's investigation of corruption in Congress (code named ABSCAM) was unique in the size, scope, and expense of the elaborate background setting used to establish credibility. It involved over 100 FBI agents cost nearly $1 million to set up Abdul Enterprises, Ltd., as a business. A yacht, the *Corsair,* was specially rigged and customized for the entertainment and pleasure (and recording) of the bribe-taking legislators, and a luxurious mansion in the Washington, D.C. area was secured as the residence of the "Arab businessmen."

In the absence of such extravagant settings and funding, it is the job of everyone in the agency to locate and obtain locations and props conducive to providing cover for the undercover business without great financial outlay.

This can be accomplished using the imagination, being alert for potential locations, and making friends in various businesses and trades.

Meeting suspects can be the easiest part of the equation. More difficult is the problem of arranging a place to meet and consummate the deal. Hotel rooms, restaurants, and parking lots have been used to a point where it is no longer safe to even suggest them. Most suspects are afraid of entering a private dwelling for fear that police officers (and recording devices) could be planted out of sight.

During the course of working for years in straight investigations or street patrol, an agent or police officer calls on innumerable businesses and makes many contacts. He often establishes a network of friends and settings that could provide potential cover for the undercover people. By investigating government check forgery and counterfeit money cases, I had made many friends in the check-cashing business. These businesses are common in most cities and towns, and are specifically set up to handle large amounts of money for the express purpose of cashing all kinds of checks for a fee. Out of necessity, they are duly protected by bulletproof glass and steel doors separating the busy tellers from the money-exchanging and check-cashing public. The friends I had made in these businesses were more than happy to receive telephone calls for me and they would also occasionally allow me behind the counter to pose as an employee. Whenever I was working an out-of-town case in an undercover capacity, I would always suggest that I could handle larger "lots" of the contraband if they were brought to New York City. I would give the telephone number and address of one of the check-cashing agencies as a place where I could be contacted. I would explain that the check-cashing business was actually a "front" for my other enterprises such as money laundering or handling "under-the-table betting" (a bookie operation). Very often, the people from out of town would come to New York to look at the premises and were generally convinced that this would be a good place to consummate a sale because money was so readily available. This is merely one example of a business and cover story an officer could use. There are plenty of good citizens to be found in every corner of the land, who would allow their premises to be used by law-enforcement personnel to receive telephone calls, messages, and in some cases to consumate a deal. With the proliferation of private mailbox and message centers, even small executive offices with secretaries, it's not that difficult to provide the appearance of a viable business. It is the obligation of everyone in the law enforcement field to always be on the alert to identify and develop locations and relationships necessary for the conduct of surreptitious enterprises. The responsibility will usually fall on the "street" agent or officer who is in touch with the people and businesses in his area on a daily basis.

An undercover agent set up a large counterfeiting deal with a group in the Midwest. After several successful purchases, it was necessary to move the deal to New York City because of the difficulties in working in the suspect's hometown. The suspects were a group who had worked all over the country committing burglaries, robberies, and peddling just about every type of contraband imaginable. They were experienced and "street-wise" and very suspicious of outsiders. They were careful of where and with whom they dealt and wouldn't budge from their established routines and familiar surroundings. It was necessary to come up with a novel idea in order to lure them to New York.

Coincidentally, at about that same time, I had made a friend who owned a large boatyard on Long Island. His business was quite large and always busy. He had many boats in adjoining slips to his business. I approached him and he readily agreed to allow us to use his premises to work the arrangement with the suspects. A cover story was concocted and sent out to the suspects saying that the ultimate purchaser of the counterfeit notes was to be a man who had access to a lot of boats and that he intended to smuggle the counterfeit money, under cover of darkness, out to a ship in the harbor which was bound for Europe. Due to the demands of his legitimate business, the boatyard operator was unable to travel to the Midwest to make the purchase and he didn't trust a courier. Consequently, he would only make the deal under the guise of doing normal business in his harborfront yard.

The leader of the counterfeit group asked for the name and telephone number of the boatyard and he secretly made pretext calls to check it out. He then traveled to New York to look over the premises. Not satisfied with his own reconnaissance and impressions, he had some of his associates also look the place over. They apparently came at various times of the day and week, and of course, every time they came, there was plenty of legitimate business activity. The suspects all agreed that this would be a good place to transact the deal. Needless to say, from our perspective, it was an excellent location. On the appointed day, agents and police officers dressed in work clothes were positioned on various boats and equipment throughout the yard. The contraband was brought into the area and the deal was concluded right outside the boatyard. From there it was easy to effect the arrests — quickly and without incident. One suspect had been armed with a loaded semiautomatic handgun, but he never even had a chance to pull it out. The yard was so staturated with police that the entire group was momentarily confounded and unable to react.

Undercover Telephones and Communications

Receiving telephone calls from suspects is an important part of any undercover case. A suspect legitimately wants the undercover agent's phone number so he can contact him when and if the contraband arrives. Police officers and agents involved in undercover work should use every effort and means at their disposal to find places where they can receive messages. E-mail, voice mail, and faxes have revolutionized inter-personal commnication, but the remaining constant is providing an E-mail address and telephone number for voice mail and faxes. Telephones, E-mail and voice mail must terminate in locations that are not incongruent with the story and cover of the undercover agent. The telephone numbers and addresses have to be placed in locations that cannot be checked and must be available on a 24-hour basis. The person receiving the call must be aware of what calls and messages might be expected on that line so they can be properly handled.

One undercover agent and his partner (working in tandem as a "biker" and his "old lady") managed to gain an introduction into a group dealing in contraband. The "biker" told the group that he was from out of town and because of his transient status didn't have a permanent telephone number. He asked the group for their number so that whenever he needed more merchandise he would call them. The person representing the group absolutely refused to give out a telephone number that could be traced. The "biker" finally proposed giving a pager to the group. The "biker" and his woman argued about whose pager would be left with the group. Finally the female relented and allowed her pager to be left. Thereafter, whenever the undercover agent wanted to make a buy, he simply called his partner's pager (which had been "sterilized"). Within just a few moments, the suspects would call the "biker" and arrangements were made to meet.

Overselling the Agent

There are times, when the informant is trying to convince the suspect to do business with an agent or to establish the agent's credibility, the informant will exaggerate the agent's "connections" or past criminal experience. Introductions and buildups such as these can place the agent in a difficult position. Very often, the suspect will want the agent to participate in an illegal activity with him. Agents should have prepared answers for such situations. In the event the subject comes up, the agent can make excuses and still keep in contact and maintain good relations with the suspect. Unwary agents can become involved in compromising situations if they are not alert.

For several months I had been trying to make a counterfeit money purchase from a colorful midtown character in New York City nicknamed "Shoes." He had earned his nicname because he always wore black-and-white saddle shoes and a small horseshoe-shaped medallion on a gold chain around his neck. Shoes lived in a "fleabag" hotel and made his living dealing in all kinds of illegal material and was well-known in the neighborhood as a pimp.

On one particular day, I saw Shoes standing in front of the hotel so I pulled my car up to the curb across from the front entrance. He strolled over to the car and asked me what I was doing and where I was going. I replied that I wasn't doing anything much or going anywhere in particular. He said, "Hey, wait a minute, I got something for you." I thought it might be the counterfeit money I had sought from him for some time now, so I waited. Instead of the money, he came out a few minutes later with two hookers and told them to get into the car. At the same time he tossed an vinyl-sided suitcase into the back seat. I asked him ,"Where are we were going?" He relied, "To Pittsburgh," to which I queried, "To get the counterfeit money?" He just chuckled, "Heck, no. We're gonna spend a couple of days with the girls." The girls were already in the car and ready to leave. I told Shoes that I hadn't planned on leaving town so I'd have to call my boss before I went. Shoes was under the impression I worked for a street-lottery (numbers) bank.

I went into the hotel lobby, faked a telephone call, and came back pretending to be all excited. I said it was a good thing that I had called because my boss had been arrested. I had to go to the courthouse immediately to begin arranging his bail. I told Shoes that I'd call him as soon as I could get free. The disappointed trio got out of the car and as Shoes turned to retrieve his suitcase from the back seat, he said they would be waiting for my call.

It was then easy to call him back several hours later to cancel the trip because of problems stemming from the arrest of my boss.

In order to illustrate the problems encountered in some undercover cases, it might be beneficial to carry the Shoes case a step further.

The day finally came when Shoes announced that the counterfeit money was ready and we could pick up the notes. He didn't tell me where we were going, but just directed me as we drove. Soon we were entering a main thoroughfare in the Bronx. This began to worry me because I had worked a case in that neighborhood only a few weeks earlier. I had made a case against three principal distributors who were now out on bail awaiting trial. Sure enough, Shoes directed me to the liquor store where the three defendants made their headquarters. He told me to stop the car in front of the store. I didn't stop, but drove on for several blocks and then turned out of the neighborhood. All the while, Shoes was shouting at me. After putting some distance between us and the liquor store, I stopped the car. I angrily turned to Shoes and told him that I knew those guys in that liquor store because I owed them several thousand dollars. I convinced him that I was certain they would kill me if I showed up without the money. Shoes said that he understood. He said he'd go back, get the counterfeit money, and bring it to me and never say anything about my presence in the neighborhood.

A short time later, Shoes returned with the counterfeit money I had ordered and asked me where I was going now. I jokingly said, "Not to Pittsburgh!" He asked me to do him a favor on my way back downtown. He wanted to give some of the counterfeit money to a few of his friends who worked in the bar next to the hotel. He asked me to give one package to the waiter, one to the bartender, and one to the manager. I told him I would as there didn't appear to be any way out of it.

When I left Shoes, I opened each package and put a mark on each bill so I could identify them later if needed. I proceeded to the bar and dutifully delivered the packages to the individuals as I had been instructed. I never mentioned the contents of the packages as they were all apparently expecting them.

Later, a larger purchase was made from Shoes and it was then decided to arrest all the people involved including the waiter, the bartender, and the manager. There were quite a few defendants in the case; as expected, some pled guilty; others opted to go to trial.

I was the principal witness since I had been the undercover agent on the case. I testified about receiving the counterfeit money from Shoes and distributing it to the people in the bar. At the conclusion of the government's case, the judged directed an acquittal of the waiter, the bartender, and the manager. All the other defendants were convicted. The judge called me into his chambers to explain that there was no doubt in his mind as to the guilt of the people he acquitted. He stated, however, that there was nothing in my testimony that indicated that these people knew that they were, in fact, receiving counterfeit money. He felt certain that the jury could convict them and in the absence of any conversation about counterfeit money, he felt they should be given the benefit of the doubt.

Similar situations have come up several times since then. The action and advice of the judge taught me a good lesson. In subsequent cases, I made certain that the people who were getting the notes knew that they were counterfeits. In some cases, we looked at the notes, examined them, and even discussed why we thought they were particularly good or bad examples of the craft.

Preparing for an Undercover Assignment

Physical Preparation

An undercover assignment begins long before the agent is ready to take to the street. Preparation comes in two phases: physical and mental. The physical aspect is the easier to resolve.

Proper Dress by the Agent

Providing an appearance commensurate with the locale, the type of suspect being pursued, and the assumed identity of the agent is usually a matter of anticipating commonly accepted standards. Agents working undercover should be very careful of how they dress. Undercover agents can check with the informant and learn how the suspect and his associates dress. It is highly advisable not to be too conservative or too extreme. A good rule of thumb to follow is to dress to be unnoticeable in a crowd —blending in is the goal. Unless an agent wants to be noticed, he shouldn't dress any differently than anyone around him. It is a generalization to say, but it has often been seen to be true, a person who dresses too conservatively or like he just stepped out of a fashion magazine has been rightly guessed to be a "cop," especially in situations where his dress is not a commonality. The middle ground is everyday dress like work clothes, tee shirts, etc.

A youngish agent (in his mid-20s to mid-30s) who is in excellentphysical condition and is well-groomed , but looks like he just came out of the police academy or the U.S. Marines, should, attempt to alter his appearance to at least to resemble a more typical example of an average American male . Perhaps adding facial hair, letting the hair grow over the ears, even using a hair slickener and wearing thick horn rimmed glasses are minor adjustments that can be made to soften the "military of quasi-military" image usually associated with the police.

Agents preparing for an undercover assignment attempt to create an appearance that will blend into the environment.

Disguises and Props

It is seldom necessary for the agent to wear disguises, invent outrageous cover stories, or make use of elaborate settings. Only in cases on the grand scale of ABSCAM would they be vital components of the operation. In most cases, the agent should be himself and act and do things naturally. The undercover agent can question the informant about what he can expect from the suspect.For example, the informant would be likely to know if the agent needed a special type car, special clothing or anything extra to make the case.

Unfortunately, most federal and city police departments don't have a wardrobe department or a prop room. Here again, the undercover agent must use his imagination to acquire the necessary props. Very often, when prisoners are arrested, some of their personal effects such as cards, memberships in lodges, union books, matchbook covers, etc. are left in the file folder. Periodically, when the prisoner indicates he has no further use for them and doesn't want them they are thrown away. These book and cards can be altered to fit the needs of the undercover agent. Many motor vehicle bureaus will give licenses to various agents and police officers in fictitious names in order to help further an investigation. To simplify remembering names and responding when the fictitious name is spoken, etc., it is best to choose a fictitious name that sounds similar and begins with the same initials as the agent's real name. The agent should practice using and hearing the name as well as writing it. He should even practice writing his initials.

The fictitious license and supporting identification documents, credit cards, photos, and anything else normally carried in a wallet should replace everything that would raise questions or lead to the agent's true identity. To simplify matters in preparing identification, the agent should not carry his normal wallet, but should have a specially prepared undercover wallet for carrying on assignment.

> Information had been received at a local Secret Service office that a man who owned a barbershop in a small Pennsylvania town was distributing counterfeit notes. The Service was unsuccessful in finding an informant who could make the introduction of an agent to the barber. It was decided to send an agent into town to see if he could become acquainted with the barber on his own or force an introduction. The agent was in town for several days and couldn't find anyone who could lead him to the barber. Finally, he decided to try to force an introduction. Since he needed a haircut anyway, he went to the barbershop. As he entered the barbershop, he was immediately recognized as a stranger and conversation halted. The townspeople were suspicious of outsiders and as conversation gradually resumed, it was general "weather" talk and patrons began leaving, one by one. Shortly, the barber was left alone with the agent. The agent mentioned that he was from out of town and was thinking of staying in town for a while. Without actually saying so, he led the barber to believe he was possibly wanted by the police, at least for questioning. The agent said he was seeking a quiet, out-of-the-way place to lay low for a while. The barber didn't seem to be taken with this information and didn't talk much. When the haircut was finished and the barber turned away, the agent tucked his wallet into the back of the barber chair. Before coming to the town he had loaded it with papers indicating he owed money to various people, old paycheck stubs, and a letter from the parole board advising him to report on a certain day. The agent left the barbershop and returned several hours later. This time the barber, who had found the wallet and looked through it, greeted him cordially and invited him into a backroom for a cup of coffee and a little business conversation.
>
> Within a week, the agent was successful in making a substantial purchase of counterfeit money. The barber and his associates were arrested and there was no problem about the protection of an informant in this case.

The props used by the agent were not elaborate; however, they were very effective in convincing the barber that he was the type of person who would be interested in purchasing contraband.

Whatever the prop, the agent must be prepared to answer any and all questions that might arise as the result of the prop. In the previously mentioned case involving the undercover officer and his partner posing as a "biker" and his "old lady," aside from their dress and appearance, their main prop was a Harley–Davidson motorcycle, customized and rigged to fit their image. When they first made contact with the group of suspects, they were extensively questioned about motorcycles in general, but in depth about that particular bike. The agent was later told by one of the group members that if they hadn't been able to answer any question or hesitated too much, the gang was prepared to refuse to do business with them or just "blow them away"

Autos and Rented Cars

In connection with undercover cases, it sometimes becomes necessary to supply the undercover agent with an appropriate automobile. Very often, this car will stay with the agent for a considerable length of time and it is surprising just how quickly the information about the automobile is spread throughout the underworld. Many people connected with gangs and criminal organizations have ways of checking license numbers and telephone numbers so it is important for the undercover car to be registered in a fictitious name, keeping in mind that suspects will attempt to check it out. In one case in California , a notorious motorcycle gang had people watching the local police garage to identify all plainclothes or undercover cars. In another incident, a gang was receiving information about undercover cars and drivers licenses from their girlfriends working for the Department of Motor Vehicles.

In the past few years it has become common for suspects to rent cars or use stolen cars to carry out their work. They are very wary about using their own car, since a license check will immediately identify them and of course the seizure laws subject the car to confiscation by the government. The suspects would rather not jeopardize their own cars; hence, the increase in rented and leased vehicles by underworld figures. Police agencies have also learned the benefits of leasing cars under fictitious names or through front organizations for undercover work. Before using a car for undercover work, the agent should have the vehicle completely cleaned and vacuumed inside. It is surprising how many little things are left in a car that could arouse the suspicion of a suspect. The agent driving the car on a day-to-day basis often overlooks little things such as official forms, parking garage cards, official envelopes, etc. Any of these articles could fall under the seat or into cracks only to be found by a suspicious suspect.

Mental and Psychological Preparation

Anyone involved in public-safety work experiences the whole gamut of the emotions known to man. Stress, anxiety, fear, elation, and depression, are just some of the emotions that are visited upon those who work in high-risk occupations that strain their mental resources and limitations to points sometimes to the breaking point. The person selected to work undercover may experience an entire range of emotions in a 2 to 3-day period. Foremost in an undercover operative's mind is the element of danger and how to deal with it. He is placed in a position where he must mentally spar with criminals without knowing very much about them. Its easy to slip up and he must be ever vigilant. If he were exposed, the criminals wouldn't hesitate to assault or torture and kill him in revenge. Fear and anxiety come with many faces; the undercover agent cannot be certain whether these individuals are out to take his money in a robbery, or whether he will be recognized as a law enforcement officer, or whether he will bungle the case.

Any officer who is assigned to work an undercover case will experience fear. He knows he will be working alone and must make on-the-spot decisions that could place his life or those of his colleagues in danger. He must anticipate every possible consequence of his actions and his response could mean life or death. This type of fear takes its toll, but can be considered healthy because it keeps him alert and aware of everything around him. Usually, once the undercover agent has met the suspect, this fear will temporarily dissipate.

The agent also fears he may say or do something that might jeopardize the case. After spending some time with the suspect(s), the agent forgets this fear. He has an opportunity to listen to the proposition and then make a counter-proposal. The important part of this phase is to listen and let the suspect talk for as long as he wants. In this way, the undercover agent can gain valuable information about the suspect. Is he merely a braggart or does he know what he is talking about? Is he the maker of the counterfeit, or is he just a salesman of the contraband?

Once a deal is made, joy sets in. The agent experiences a sense of elation over the fact that the case is well on its way to its conclusion and he has done his job well. The element of surprise is generally present when the agent makes the arrangements and the suspect involves more people that was initially anticipated. When the case is over, there is a feeling of relief and satisfaction that he has contributed toward the solution to a difficult situation and that it was done correctly and successfully. A job well done.

All of the above are true of an ideal scenario — when everything works out according to schedule and plan. However, as is often the case — things go wrong! There are arguments, fights, and even gunplay. The agent who faces this fear at the beginning of the case and makes plans for these exigencies will undoubtedly come through unharmed. One veteran undercover agent said that when entering into an undercover situation he plans for the worst and expects to get shot. He said this gives him the positive mental attitude that he will survive and overcome his injuries. He further said this helps him allay his fear of danger.

I can readily recall the first time a gun was put to my head. I had always had this fear and if it ever happened I had made plans to talk — and talk and talk! It worked. I came out unscathed. However, my nerves were shot for several days after and to this day I still shake a little when I think of it.

No undercover agent should deny that he hasn't thought about being killed or that he experiences fear during an undercover case. It is onlya natural emotion for this type of work.

Mental preparation is very important when dealing with the emotions of the job. However, there are other aspects to consider that will alleviate some of the worry, stress, and anxiety. This preparation means knowing all there is to know about the contraband and those involved in the selling of it. In the case involving the theft of the Nevada counterfeit gold nuggets, the undercover agent researched every aspect of gold nuggets. The first thing he learned was that gold in the form of nuggets, beyond specks of powder, and an occasional small nugget found in stream beds, were apparently all picked up by 1850. He learned about panning for gold, how it is done, and where to expect to find gold. He read everything he could find about how gold nuggets were formed, where to find them, and prices to be expected for selling them. He picked the minds of everyone with any knowledge about gold. He interviewed people from the Bureau of Mines and visited museums. When he met with the suspect he impressed him with his knowledge which contributed to the suspects eagerness to show him his operation and to sell to him. The same preparation should go into learning about other kinds of contraband. Maybe the security hologram is 1/32nd of an inch too small, maybe there are misspellings, how are CD-ROMs made, what is the price of the contraband?

Mental preparation is recognizing the emotions that will be encountered, learning to deal with them, and continuing the job to a successful conclusion. It is also knowing the contraband product and recognizing it and providing for a means to seize it while arresting the purveyors.

In working undercover, everyone involved in the case should sit down for a good talk session and attempt to think of all the eventualities beforehand. In the session, deliberate obstacles should be brought up in order to see how they could be handled. In one undercover operation, the operative was meeting with a number of gang members in a restaurant parking lot when a group of rival gang members arrived. Several words and gang signs were exchanged and guns were displayed. The undercover agent was in a situation where he very easily could have been taken for a gang member and been involved in a gun battle or "drive-by" shooting. To further complicate the situation, there were several covering officers surveilling the meeting between the agent and the first gang and who could have easily responded with their guns. Fortunately, the supervisor of the police covering team watched the undercover agent for any duress signal and waited to see the development of the situation. The undercover agent recognized that the two gangs were merely posturing and the second gang soon departed with no problems and business continued as planned.

It is obvious that not every eventuality can be thought of beforehand. However, alternate plans should be made. There are very few cases that go according to plan. While each case seems the same on the surface, there are always last-minute changes that don't become problems providing they are discussed beforehand.

An undercover agent should try as hard as possible to make the case, but when it becomes apparent that the situation is impossible for any reason, he should not be afraid to walk away from it, providing he "leaves the door open" for the suspect to contact him. No supervisor should reprimand an agent who walks away from a case. Supervisors who have worked undercover will understand that there are some cases that just can't be made. Perhaps it will be necessary to try several times before a successful case can be made against a difficult suspect.

The counterfeit check case in the Southwest was successful because I realized that the situation had become impossible. But, before walking away from the group, I made certain that they had a way of contacting me. After several days of mulling it over, the suspects realized that they had lost a good customer and then decided to contact me to see if they could salvage the deal.

Instructions to Agents

Supervisors who send agents out to do undercover work should give them a specific target and specific instructions so the agent knows exactly what is expected of him. The instructions shouldn't be too complicated. The undercover agent should be given a certain amount of latitude and should be encouraged to use as much judgement as necessary in keeping with the original instructions. The agent should understand there are certain procedures to follow as dictated for safety and the concern for his well being. An important rule to follow is to not move or change locations without notification or signaling to the covering team. There should be no spontaneous moves. A covering team should, however, be prepared to move and follow the undercover agent in the chance the suspect insists on changing locations and the undercover agent cannot dissuade him.

Probably the most important time during the whole undercover case is the first five seconds when the suspect is introduced to the agent. It is these first few seconds when the suspect makes a personal judgement and decides whether or not he wants to do business with the undercover agent. The first impression is the telling aspect. An agents greeting and demeanor indicate to the suspect whether or not this person is someone worthy of his time and trust. The initial handshake shouldn't be "Mr. Fish" nor should it be "Macho Man Mancinni the Bonecrusher"— in other words, it should be firm, not wimpy; but not so firm as to cause the suspect to wince. The agent should hesitate for a second allowing the suspect an opportunity to initiate the handshake. If he doesn't put his hand out, it is best to let the handshake go past. But if a greeting handshake is made it should be just about the same pressure as the suspects while looking the suspect directly in the eye. Some cultures don't shake hands but the undercover agent should take the lead from the suspect. If a handshake is not given, at least give a nod of the head or other communication such as a small flip of the hand.

In most cases the agent should be friendly and affable but should not overdo it. It is usually best to be conservative and reserved tending to let the suspect do most of the talking. Whenever leaving a meeting with a suspect, it is best to know more about him than he knows about the undercover agent. In some situations, when the agent is cast in a "tough-guy role" he may have to take control of the situation and talk as tough as the suspect, maybe even "setting him on his heel". This technique should be used sparingly and only when necessary to convince the suspect the agent is as "tough" as he is and not willing to take any nonsense. The suspect takes many things into consideration during his first meeting with the undercover agent. He knows he has very little time to decide whether or not this person would be someone he could and should sell contraband to. He takes into estimation the agent's looks, the way he talks, the way he acts, the type of introduction he received and the availability of the contraband. If after reviewing and weighing these considerations, he decides he wants to do business with the new acquaintance, he will enter into a conversation with him. The agent generally cannot sell himself to the suspect if the suspect is suspicious. Some agents occasionally arouse suspicion by saying the wrong thing at the wrong time.

Meetings with the Suspects

Most suspects have one thing in mind and that is to dispose of the contraband that they possess, at the best possible price. The agent must keep in mind that the suspect is a businessman, albeit he may be a trash talking slang spewing profane person. The suspect has a product to sell, therefore the agent should let the suspect sell and not be over anxious to take the first offer nor should he be overly impressed with the quality of the contraband. He should expect the quality of the merchandise to be top quality. The suspect generally doesn't want to socialize with the prospective buyer and is not interested in having the buyer meet too many people in his particular group or organization. Although suspects are anxious to dispose of the contraband, they don't want any prospective purchaser to know too much about their operation. Other than handling the specific sale, they are usually "close-mouthed" and are suspicious of anyone who asks too many questions not relevant to the specific sale.

Frequent meetings are desirable between the suspect and the undercover agent. However, in average cases, these meetings should not be too long and the agent should not be put on display where there is a possibility of someone recognizing him. In other words, it is not necessary for the agent to live with the suspect. He should keep in mind that he is a customer, buying an item and after there is a "meeting of the minds," the sale should be consummated.

The Agent's Attitude and Body Language

The undercover agent should allow his undercover personality and attitude reflect the demeanor of the suspect. Of course the personality of the agent should fit him and be natural and not forced or "acted." An undercover agent should build his own undercover persona, but he should be a great talker. The agent's attitude should be commensurate with that of the suspect. If the suspect takes a suspicious role, so should the agent. If the suspect is "Mr. Rude and Nasty" the agent doesn't have to be "Mr. Manners." Normally the position of the suspect and undercover agent is salesman/customer and the tact is as two average people meeting to discuss a business transaction. As part of the meeting process there are certain ways of saying things that give meaning to the spoken word. Sometimes the difference between success and failure is not the spoken word or verbal attitude we take but, especially when in stressful situations, our mouth may be saying one thing while our body is sending different signals. This is called "body language," a new study explaining the unconscious movement of the body that is either in agreement with or incongruent with what is being spoken. In other words, body language, if not done in agreement with the spoken word will cause the listener to be confused by what he is hearing and will result in distrust or suspicion. The agent should not invade the suspect's "personal space' nor crowd him when in negotiations. Being too close causes a disturbance in the suspect and will prompt him to be distrustful. "Getting in his face" or "up close and personal" is an aggressive move that says that the speaker is taking a tough stance. An approximate distance of at least thirty inches is normally the standard, but the agent can increase this distance without causing stress in the suspect.

The eyes and mouth are the main focal points to consider when interviewing or selling a suspect. A tightness of the facial muscles indicates stress and a possible inability to handle it. Failure to make and hold eye contact can communicate possible deviousness and an attempt to hide something. Pursed, puckered, or covered lips and mouth are often associated with a secretive nature, possibly capable of telling lies. Frowning, looking sideways, or peering over one's glasses can convey an attitude of superiority and arrogance. Rubbing a finger over the nose while talking may tell the listener that what the speaker is saying "really stinks" and may not be truthful. Tapping a foot or finger indicates nervousness and a desire to be elsewhere. Crossing the arms across the body or a tightly folding the hands sets up a barricade and tells the other party that the listener has a closed mind to what is being said. On the other side of the coin, however, open arms and turning up of the hands up indicates an agreement or acceptance for what is being said and an openness to the truth. An undercover agent should be alert to the unspoken "words" of the suspect, but even more so, to what his body language and attitude are telling the suspect.

The undercover agent must approach his assignment with the idea that he is buying and the suspect is selling and he should act accordingly. In the average sale, whether it is contraband or a legitimate item, there are very few people who are willing to put up money in advance, especially if it involves large sums of cash. In most cases, the suspect will always ask the undercover agent to "front" the money. The stock answer for an undercover agent is that he has no assurance that he will, in fact, get a delivery and further it is very possible that someone will try to relieve him of his money by theft. He also explains that the money is not his and that he has no recourse to the law in the event someone decides to trick him or steal his money. Most suspects will understand this because they will rarely or seldom put up money in advance themselves to purchase the contraband that they are selling.

Undercover agents must learn that they don't do everything that the suspects ask them to do. Very often, new agents or police officers working undercover want to be agreeable in order to make the case. Sometimes, this has the reverse effect from the desired goal. Suspects will become suspicious of a buyer who will meet them at any hour of the day or night under any circumstances and pay for the item in advance. Most people purchasing contraband drive hard bargains and are as careful about the sale as they would be in purchasing legitimate items. Many undercover agents have lost cases simply because they agreed with the suspect on many things that were not normal, thereby making the suspect suspicious. When a suspect becomes suspicious he will try various means to "check out" the prospective purchaser. If he doesn't receive the right answers, he will either try to steal his money or drop him completely.

Advance Money

There are occasions when it becomes absolutely necessary for an agent to advance some of the money. These are special cases that cannot be worked any other way. It is usually because the suspect has been the victim of an undercover agent on a previous occasion and he feels that most government agencies will not "front the money" under any circumstances. Each case must be judged on its own merits. Usually, the supervisor makes the decision. He takes into account how much genuine money is available to him and what results he expects from the case. If he has an opportunity to apprehend a major violator, he may find out that it is worthwhile to gamble advance money.

Negotiating With The Suspect

Agents should keep in mind the legal claim of "entrapment" as a defense in the initial conversation with the suspect. They should never indicate to the suspect that they are seeking counterfeit notes or other contraband. It is presumed that this conversation has already occurred between the informant and the suspect, which would preclude the agent from asking for a specific item. Generally, the suspect will ask the agent if he has seen the sample and if he is satisfied with it. The conversation then will generally drift to a price. The agent at this time can indicate that for various reasons he was not wholly satisfied with the sample and can request that he be supplied with additional samples. The samples that we are talking about could be in the form of counterfeit notes, drugs, clothing, CD-ROMs, credit cards, or any other item of contraband.

After the sample is shown, the agent should ask about the price. The price normally fluctuates according to the amount of contraband that is being purchased and the number of times it has already changed hands. The further the distance (the number of middlemen), the greater the price. In the case of counterfeit money, the price of $25 is fair when purchasing $1,000 or less. As the amount increases, the price should decrease. In purchasing counterfeit notes, the price could drop as much as $10 per hundred when purchasing in lots of $25,000 or $50,000. Whatever the contraband item, the purchaser should know the fair market price and the value of what he is purchasing. If the suspect gives a good price, it is not necessary to argue the price. In other words, the agent should "play it on the level." If it is too high, he should say so and negotiate the price until it is right. When the price is right, the agent should indicate that he is satisfied.

In negotiating for the purchase of contraband, the undercover agent should not appear to be the "top man" in his group. One of the principal reasons is that the "top man" should be in a position to make the major decisions. If the "top man" is not there to make a decision about the quality and price of the contraband, the agent cannot make those decisions and it gives him an excuse to back out of the buy at that time or to delay it. It is far better for the agent to indicate that there are other people involved and the he is merely a middleman working on a commission. If during the negotiations, the situation calls for a decision about advance money or place of delivery, the agent can always say he will check with "my people" to see if they are satisfied. This would be a major decision and one that would normally require approval from someone else who is investing the money. The suspect always tries to make things convenient for himself.

As to the method and place of delivery, the agent can agree to almost anything with the provision that he has to check with "my people". If the arrangements are not suitable to the agency conducting the investigation, the agent working undercover can go back to the suspect and say that "my people" are not satisfied. If the suspect is adamant, the agent can agree with him and still keep negotiations open for another time, stating that he will look for different backers because the people he has been working for are impossible. When the door is left open in this manner, the agent can contact the suspect at any time with a new proposition.

Unless there is a specific case that warrants an agent acting as "Mr. Big" or "The Man", the average undercover case calls for the agent to play down his importance. This sometimes has a reverse effect. The suspect may believe that the agent really is an important "heavy-hitter"and that he is purposely trying to conceal his own importance.

> A group of counterfeit note distributors were anxious to dispose of $250,000 in counterfeit $20s. Two of their group had been arrested and money was needed for bail, lawyers, and other legal expenses. They were very anxious to make a deal, yet they were extremely cautious. They certainly didn't need or want another arrest.
>
> An informant had introduced me to one of the group and I immediately started to negotiate for the purchase of the counterfeits that they had. I was quoted a price of eight dollars per hundred which was a fairly good price. I was told to get my money ready and to be on a designated street corner at a certain hour. I would than be picked up by a member of the group and driven to an undisclosed location

where, in some manner, the counterfeit money would be delivered to me. The whole idea was absurd. However, I didn't know if they were testing me. I mentioned that everything sounded all right to me and that I'd give them my answer the following day.

The next day, I met four of the group and at this time I told them that the people who were putting up the money would have no part of the suggested arrangements. The group became annoyed when they learned that I was just a commission man acting for someone else. They tried hard to persuade me to do business their way. I confessed that I could see nothing wrong with their setup. I said I knew I could trust the group and felt that they would keep their word.

I met with them on succeeding nights and carried the story that my people were too suspicious and wouldn't do business. I mentioned that I would try to find another buyer for the notes.

In the weeks that followed, I made it a point to strengthen my relationships with the group and I was pleased to hear that they still had the counterfeits. When it became apparent that they needed money in a hurry for an impending trial, I told them about the Texan I had just met. He had made a good score on some stolen securities in New York City and was anxious to take some counterfeits back home. The group was so pleased about this prospect that they were willing to drop the price to $7 per hundred. I told them the only problem was that the Texan was leaving the following morning so it would be necessary to make a fast deal at the airport. This didn't sit too well with the group so they decided to have a conference. They debated for about an hour and finally reached a decision. Ed, the spokesman for the group, said they had decided to sell the counterfeits to the Texan on the condition that I would make the delivery. For my trouble I was to receive $1 per hundred. It was agreed that I would meet the Texan at the airport. I was to verify that he had the "buy" money. Ed would arrive at the airport and put the counterfeits in a locker. He would turn the key over to me. The Texan would go with me to the locker, pick up the notes, and pay me for them immediately. I would meet Ed and give him the genuine money. When Ed told me of the plans, I could hardly contain myself from laughing. I couldn't have come up with a better plan myself. In their attempt to make a foolproof sale, they had "lockered" themselves.

The next day, all that was needed was an undercover agent with a cowboy hat and a pair of cowboy boots. True to his promise, Ed, arrived on time, deposited a package in the locker box and gave me the key. Two more of the group accompanied him and none of them

> wanted to meet the Texan. The arrests went very smoothly. All of the group eventually made bail, but needed money now more than ever. They switched from counterfeiting to armed robbery. Before the counterfeit case came to trial, one was killed during an attempted holdup. His partner was arrested and received ten to fifteen years. Two others were convicted of burglary and received long prison terms. They eventually pleaded guilty to the counterfeit charges. They were convinced that the Texan was a Texas Ranger on an undercover assignment.

Not being the "top man" paid off in this case. Again, it gave me the opportunity to turn down their original proposal, and still stay in their good graces.

Officers working undercover should be alert at all times, with particular references to license numbers of cars that appear in the area, faces of people that they meet, names, addresses, and telephone numbers. Sometimes covering agents cannot get this information because of the distance they maintain from the action. When it is practical, the undercover agent should make notes as soon as possible. If he is in a public place it would be very easy for him to excuse himself, go to the men's room and jot down a telephone number or license number. When he leaves the company of the suspects, he should immediately go to a computer and make as many notes as he can remember to aid him in making his report. Some agents are required to maintain a small tape recorder in their car and dictate notes as soon as they are alone in the car. They then store the tapes in a secure place for use at a later time. but this must be done with extreme caution and only if there is no chance of discovery. Many are also required to submit reports daily.

Advantage of Obtaining Samples

In attempting to make an undercover case, the undercover officer usually tries to obtain a sample of the contraband that is being sold. This is natural, because most contraband is of varying quality. Drugs sometimes are very high quality, being nearly pure, and other times they have been cut to a point where there is little effect on the user. T- shirts, luggage, credit cards, computers, watches, anything that can be sold on the "black market" come in shades of quality. Anything being bought in bulk should first be sampled. Of course that is as true for legitimate items as it is for contraband.

Counterfeit money runs from very good to very poor. Therefore, it is necessary for the undercover agent to see what he is buying before he can offer a price for the merchandise. If he can acquire enough samples or make a small purchase, his case is made. On the second or third buy he can be a little harder to get along with or to be satisfied. In the event the seller makes any changes, the agent can demand that the sale be handled in the same manner as the first one. At the time of the second buy, the agent can complain about shortages on the first buy and the quality of the merchandise. This would put the seller on the defensive. The agent then could demand enough time to make a closer count. If the buy is large enough, for example in the purchase of counterfeit money a buy of $100,000 was ordered, this would be large enough to warrant delivery by more than one person. Generally, the principal distributors would want to accompany the seller to protect their own interests.

Regardless of the arrangements that have been made in advance, the suspect will continually try to get advance money from the agent. In very rare cases will it be necessary for the agent to "front" his money. The argument that the money is not his and that he has no recourse if the delivery is not made is a valid argument in spite of the fact it is being used all the time. Validation of this argument is evident in the course of everyday transactions in normal business. Even if a person provides a payment with a check (which is never done in the contraband business), once the check is cashed or the money is given over, sometimes the only avenue for redress of a grievance of being cheated or non-delivery of the expected merchandise is the legal system. That manner of solving being cheated is closed to buyers of contraband.

The suspects will try to get a portion of the money in advance. Again, this should not be done, using the same argument. Suspects will sometimes try to have a mutual acquaintance, possibly the informant, hold the money until the deal is completed. This situation should be discussed with the informant before the transaction is effected. If at all possible, the informant should be kept away from the scene at the time of the buy. This should satisfy both the undercover agent and the informant. This can be explained to the suspect as a precaution against possible robbery, or other fears the undercover agent has relative to carrying large quantities of cash. If the informant is not at the scene, this may help him explain why he was not arrested when the deal culminates in an arrest. It is also a good idea for the informant not to be present because at the time of delivery, if the suspect is the least bit suspicious, he may wish to have the informant make the delivery to the agent. If the informant makes the delivery, it then becomes necessary for him to testify at the trial in order to maintain the chain of evidence. If the informant doesn't want to be exposed, all efforts should be made to keep him away from the scene of the buy, especially if an arrest is anticipated.

Signals and Controlling the Place of Delivery

The undercover agent should try to control the place of delivery. This is a very important part of the case. Deliveries in private clubs, in suspect's homes, in cellars, and similar places provide an impossible, even dangerous, situation. In order to make a case successful; it is necessary that the buy be covered so the covering agents know when to make the arrest. Public places, such as bus stops, restaurants, railroad stations, airports, busy stores, parking lots, etc. are very desirable. A hotel room is ideal, providing the agent can pick the hotel and the room and can further arrange for agents to be in adjoining rooms. The suspect will try to make a delivery at a time and place of his choosing that is convenient for him. The agent can use the argument that he is skeptical of a private home or private club because he is afraid of being robbed. If the suspect insists that the agent accompany him to a secluded spot, the agent can tell the suspect that he will go with him but will not take the money. In this way, it will be necessary for the suspect to accompany the agent back to where the agent's money is and, of course, this location can be covered by other agents who can effect the arrest after the signal is given. Signals have always been a source of mild aggravation for me. It was always something that I took for granted. We have been using signals for years and it was something that was usually mentioned in a casual manner before going out on a case. I had one experience that made me give more thought to signals and in the ensuing years I have seen how the misinterpretation of a signal can cause havoc with a case.

> Tom A. Catt was a lovable character. He spent most of his time hanging around the track when the racing season was on. He was not a tout or bookmaker, but he enjoyed the races and found that he could watch the races, bet, and also carry on his "brokerage" business at the track. Tom can best be described as a typical Damon Runyon or Sidney Sheldon character.
>
> I had met Tom in connection with an investigation I was conducting far away from New York City. He immediately recognized I was from New York and kidded me for "talking funny." This from a man who talked from the corner of his mouth and destroyed the King's English with every phrase he uttered . He thought syntax was something having to do with government assessment for payment of illicit sex, drinking, etc. The business I had with Tom wasn't too important. He allegedly had been in a crap game in which counterfeit money had been passed. (Incidentally, it is a common alibi for passers of counterfeit money to play the innocent victim and say they received the money in a crap game or other game of chance such as

poker.) I had contacted everyone I knew who had been connected with the game but never got anywhere with the investigation. If Tom had given me some information, it would have been very helpful because there was very little else to go on. After our official business was concluded, Tom and I had a bite to eat and had a friendly chat. I never saw or heard from him until five years later.

Tom came into the office and was attempting to find out if I still worked there, but couldn't remember my name and was trying to describe me when I walked in. We immediatelly renewed our acquaintance and left the office for a cup of coffee. Tom told me he had always appreciated the fact that I didn't cause him trouble after our first encounter and he felt that he owed me a favor.

He stated that an acquaintance of his was in a position to get counterfeit money. His friend, Dan Amusing, was a very well-known comedian on and off-Broadway and was very heavily in debt to some loansharks. Dan had been offered a "dealership" in handling counterfeit money and was looking for customers. I asked Tom to introduce me to Dan, but Tom refused saying he would be in trouble if it ever came out that I was an undercover agent and Dan was arrested as a result of doing business with me. Tom stated that Dan was an easy "mark" because this was his first venture into crime. We had a long discussion about the possibility of an introduction. I could see that Tom couldn't introduce me so I asked him to keep me apprised of Dan's activities.

At about the same time as Tom's visit, I received a visit from another man who also wanted to do me a favor. In his eary days, Patsy Mack had been a well-known racketeer on the West Coast. Currently he wasn't doing too well financially, he was getting old, and it was becoming increasingly difficult for him to "make a living" in New York. I asked him if he wanted to settle up with me before he left. He said he would do anything within reason, but it would have to be done soon because he intended to return to the West Coast.

I called Tom and asked him if he would introduce Patsey to Dan. Tom said he would have no objection if Patsey as long as he wasn't a federal agent. Patsey was flattered when he heard this, and agreed to meet Dan. Tom eventually introduced Patsey to Dan and before long they became good friends. Just before Patsey was scheduled to leave for the West Coast, we arranged a chance meeting on Broadway. Patsey introduced me to Dan as an old friend who served time with him in a federal penitentiary. I caught Dan's comedy routine in some local nightclubs and managed to have a drink with him on a few occasions. Off stage, Dan was the saddest-looking comedian I have ever seen. For a man who was paid to make people laugh, he looked more like a undertaker with his dark-set eyes, dark hair, skinny build, and his usual outfit of a black suit. One particular day he was really looking down in the mouth because the loansharks were pressuring him for the money he owed to them. He was what is known on Broadway as a degenerate horseplayer. Every dime he earned went to bets on losing horses, and to bookies and loansharks. He confided to me that he hadn't been out of debt in the past 20 years in spite of the fact he was working regularly and making good money. He was particularly distressed this evening and asked me to accompany him to a local bar. When we got there, he showed me $10 and a $20 counterfeit bills and asked me if I could use any. He said he had a connection and could get the counterfeits in any amounts. He quoted a fairly good price and bragged that he had handled hundreds of thousands of these particular notes. I knew that the note had fairly good distribution , but they were nowhere near what Dan bragged. I told him that I was interested. He then put on a very somber face (which is saying something because his usual Sad Sack-look was just beyond death warmed over) and warned me that I would be killed if anything went wrong or if I "squealed to the cops." I could barely keep from laughing at Dan's amusing performance at being a tough guy. He took my order for $100,000 in counterfeits and arranged for me to meet his friend, Whitey, who was to make the delivery.

Whitey tried to acquire the "buy money" in advance and after much haggling he agreed to deliver the notes the following day at a local hotel. We managed to get adjoining rooms for the covering agents at the hotel and we set everything up for the arrest after the delivery. Before leaving the office, the senior agent asked me what signal I would use to show that I had actually received the money as a cue to cause the agents to enter the room and effect the arrests. I said I would look at the package and say, "This goddammed crap is no good!"

Whitey arrived right on time at my room carrying a package. I opened it and found that it contained a sizeable amount of counterfeit money. In a voice louder than I had intended, I said, "This junk is no good!" I waited. Nothing happened. I said again, "This stuff is lousy!" Again nothing happened. Suddenly I realized that I had completely forgotten the signal. I tried everything, in a voice louder than normal. I tried counting the notes out loud, complaining about the quality of "these here counterfeit notes" and trying to reduce the price. All this was causing Whitey great concern. He wanted his money and wanted to get out. He thought I had "slipped a cog" because I was walking about the room talking in a loud voice. In the hallway, Whitey had two people waiting next to the elevator for the good money. I tried stalling for what seemed like an eternity, then in desperation, I opened the door to the adjoining room and told the agents to come on in and make the arrest. I totally blew my cover and had it been any other case, I probably would have gotten the informant hurt or killed. In this case, the informant was from California and didn't care whether anyone knew him or not. The men in the hallway were arrested and the following morning Dan was arrested. His arrest was the most pitiful thing we had seen in a long time. He was well respected in the entertainment field and most of his friends and associates thought he was financially well off. Even though he managed to arrange bail, it was a long time before he could find work again. Although he didn't appreciate it at the time, the arrest was the best thing that could have happened to him, especially considering the options the loansharks were promising him.

Several years after, Dan was working "the circuit" again and I met him after a performance. We talked about the case and he told me the loansharks had cancelled out his debts as a result of his arrest. This, he explained, is apparently part of the bankruptcy code of the underworld: "Get arrested, go to jail — have your debts cancelled!" Dan is now back in "show business" making regular appearances in clubs on and off Broadway. Though I am certain he is still also a regular with the loansharks.

How about Patsy Mack? Well, it later developed that he and Dan had become closer buddies then anyone had thought during their brief acquaintance. Before he left for the West Coast, Dan sold him a small package of counterfeit notes. Patsy managed to pass three notes before his arrest.

The case turned out very well, even as it seemed the covering arrest team would never get the signal, and from that time on I paid strict attention to the importance of signals and of giving the correct cue. I learned through sad, nearly hysterical, though possibly dangerous, circumstances that one of the most important acts in the undercover case is proper planning and use of signals. The signal triggers a series of events that hopefully ends with the seizure of the contraband and the arrests of the suspects. There are also signals to denote duress or impending danger. It is the responsibility of all people involved in the operation, the undercover agent and covering team, to be on the same page to understand, remember, and react to the correct signals.

The signal is very important in any case. Any signal can be usedas long as it is simple, and can be seen from a distance and that it cannot be misinterpreted. The idea of lighting a cigar or smoking a cigarette sounds good but it can be dangerous. The undercover agent may inadvertently light a cigarette, thereby launching the arrest team prematurely. Again, any signal should suffice as long as it can be easily understood.

If the agent states that the money is in the trunk of his car, the opening of the trunk is a signal that cannot be misinterpreted. Certainly it can be seen from a distance if the covering agents are careful to place themselves in a position where nothing will interfere with their line of vision. When an area is selected for the delivery, it is a good idea for several agents to visit that area long in advance of the proposed buy. They will look for many things. One important thing is the necessary cover and concealment so that the agents covering the deal will not be exposed. Secondly, it is important to look over the area; perhaps there will be a friendly institution or business in the vicinity that could be used as an observation post. Sometimes in surveying the area, agents will recall that they have a friend or relative in the neighborhood whose premises could be used. In a counterfeiting case, it is a good idea to canvass the business section of the neighborhood with thoughts of trying to locate a print shop or publishing business that could be responsible for the production of the notes that are being sold. This is especially true if the suspect selects the neighborhood.

Crime in the Printing Business

At this point, it might be a good idea to discuss the type of activity that occurs within a print shop. Law enforcement officers can go their entire careers without ever having been inside a printing establishment nor have they given much thought to the crimes that can committed there. In what has become a common business, there are 24-hour reproduction centers on nearly every corner with copy machines capable of reproducing the finest-quality color documents and photographs. With the advent of computer typesetting, high-speed laser printers, and color copiers, the term "print shop" has become an outdated term. The art and equipment of printing has changed, but in the final analysis, the end product is the same.

In order to keep an illegal lottery operation (bookmaking) going in a city, it is necessary to have a printer make the tickets. This applies to any type of bookmaking or lottery from sports betting to the stock market daily averages. Very often the printing of unauthorized or unofficial tickets is what leads the printer into a real life of crime. He learns that printing tickets for the local street lottery is far more profitable than printing wedding invitations and business cards. Some printers who are having financial difficulties or owe a "favor" are approached to print a few items that may not be exactly legal, for a group or syndicate of underworld citizens. After the smaller jobs are completed, the printers are propositioned to print pornography in the form of pictures and text. This too can be very profitable for the printer who is then subsequently asked to make counterfeit checks, counterfeit stock certificates, counterfeit bonds, driver's licenses, birth certificates, marriage certificates, credit cards, bills of sale, and counterfeit money. The range of items that can be printed to look like the authentic documents is infinite. The printing of vehicle ownership cards and driver's licenses are small items, but they are very valuable to car thieves and people who need identification documents

A printer may also enter the business accidentally. He may be alone in the shop late one night and decides to experiment with making a counterfeit $20, $50, or $100 note just to see how good he can make it. Impressed with his results he makes more. In a short time he has a cache of money that he decides to sell for a profit. With the sophistication of the high-tech printing and reproduction equipment, it is becoming a simple matter to print out thousands of dollars worth of fictitious documents or currency in just a short while and there is a minimal amount of clean up and no evidence is left behind.

A computerized camera is capable of extremely high-resolution output. It can reproduce details invisible to the naked eye. With this camera, a counterfeiter could make copies of the original documents that would be virtually identical to the original. (Courtesy of FROMAX and Paul Sohn, Marina Del Rey, CA.)

Interior view of a typical modern print shop. The employee in the back is working with a computer typesetter. (Courtesy of West LA Printing, Los Angeles, CA.)

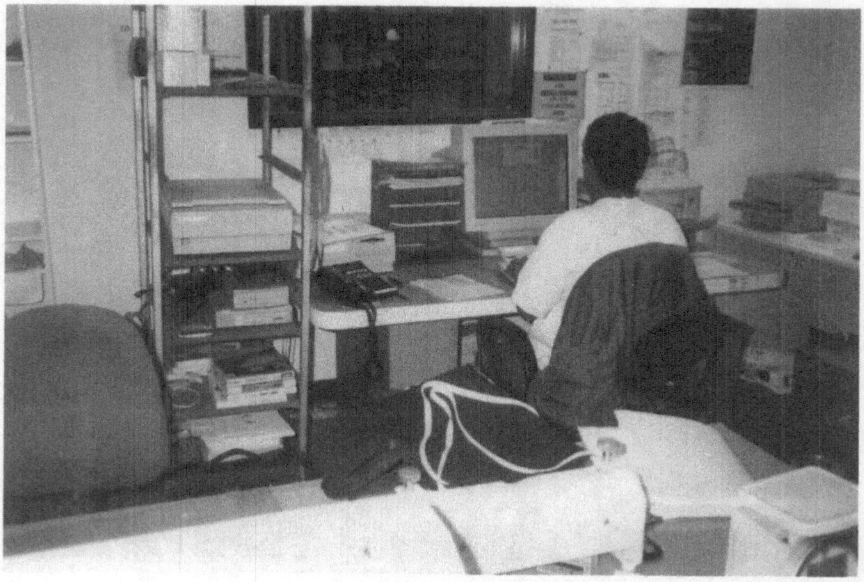

The typesetter is using a computer to prepare the copy. The document to be counterfeited is placed in a scanner, downloaded into the computer, and printed using the latest in laser technology. (Courtesy of West LA Printing, Los Angeles, CA.)

A high-definition laser color printer. Turn it on, place the document to be copied onto the glass, select number of copies, and instant counterfeit — no mess, no cleanup, no evidence to destroy! (Courtesy of West LA Printing, Los Angeles, CA.)

A Megalith platemaker. The image of the document to be printed is transferred from the high-resolution photo-negative onto the printing plate without any loss of detail.(Courtesy of West LA Printing, Los Angeles, CA.)

A typical offset printing press. Although it is somewhat messy with inks and solutions, it produces excellent-quality printing. (Courtesy of West LA Printing, Los Angeles, CA.)

Pressman operating the offset printing press. (Courtesy of West LA Printing, Los Angeles, CA.)

When a counterfeiting plant is located and the printer arrested, a complete search of the premises can be of great help to other agencies. It is not uncommon for an undercover agent expecting to purchase counterfeit currency to also be propositioned about buying driver's licenses, vehicle registration cards, personal identification papers (immigration "green cards") etc. Besides looking for print shops, the city should also be looked over for possible book-making facilities, warehouses, or liquor and other stores that don't seem to be storing much merchandise. They may be possible locations for hiding the contraband before a delivery is made. Identifying these places and keeping them under surveillance can be great help at the time of the proposed buy.

Working Undercover with More than One Agent

For many years, various agencies have worked under the mistaken belief that one undercover case deserved one undercover agent. Over the last 10 or 15 years, I have decided that if two or more people can purchase contraband from friends and acquaintances, there is no reason why two or three undercover agents cannot do the same thing without arousing undue suspicion. Wherever possible, at least two undercover agents should be used on the case. Very often when one man is used, situations can arise where he is not in a position to report it to his supervisors or to the covering agents. In a case where an undercover agent has s partner with him, he could be introduced as a partner, a driver, a delivery person or anything that will fit the particular situation. In the case involving the "biker," his partner was a female undercover agent dressed in the role of the biker's "old lady." During the course of a subsequent meeting, a third "biker" was placed in the restaurant where the transaction was to be made before the suspect and his entourage arrived with the contraband. When the suspect noticed the scruffy looking "biker" sitting in a nearby booth, the undercover agent called the third agent and introduced him as a partner.

A second or third undercover agent can be valuable as cover, support, or as another prospective buyer. In some instances, where the potential danger level is very high, the undercover agents can stand apart from each other in such a position that makes it difficult for the suspects to cover them both at the same time, yet affording the undercover agents to be in an advantageous position to take defensive action if necessary. In the event the undercover agent needs to send a message to his headquarters, he can send one of his "partners" on an errand or other duty. Depending upon the contraband being sold, the second or third agent can pose as an expert in that particular type of merchandise.

A group of counterfeiters had decided, for some odd particular reason, they would print several million U.S. postage stamps. They didn't make "collectible" stamps, but rather the plain ordinary postage stamps. They could have just as easily decided to counterfeit food stamps and would have been more successful in selling them. Like many groups before them, they were able to successfully counterfeit the stamps, but they needed to market them. They found it very difficult to find an outlet for the product. Most businesses and people that use large amounts of stamps use postage meters and pay bulk rates and most people who buy stamps in bulk at a discount generally don't use more than four or five sheets. The suspects had made the counterfeits but they hadn't done their market research to determine if there was a market for the stamps nor had they done their homework regarding a distribution system.

> This particular group gave an informant a sheet of stamps to be shown as samples in the event the informant was able to interest a prospective buyer in taking over the whole lot. The informant took the sheet of stamps to the Secret Service office and it was decided to use an undercover agent to contact the group. Arrangements were made whereby the informant could introduce the suspect to the prospective buyer in a hotel in Ohio. This was the type of case where the informant could not be exposed and it was decided that the agent doing the undercover work would call in an "expert" before he actually purchased the stamps.
>
> The meeting took place in the hotel as scheduled. The suspects were registered in the same hotel but had different rooms. The undercover agent was introduced to the suspect and the suspect asked the agent if he had seen the samples. The agent replied that he had but before making the purchase, he wanted to call in an expert to attest to the quality of the work. The suspect became annoyed at this small turn of events but he left to check with "his people" and returned to say it was agreed to let the expert look at the stamps.
>
> I posed as the expert and later that night met the suspect. He gave me the keys to his car, told me that the stamps were in the trunk and stated he would give me an hour to take the car wherever I wished to make an examination of the stamps.
>
> I took the car to the local Secret Service office and discovered that there were several million counterfeit stamps in the car. I returned to the hotel and told the undercover agent in the presence of the suspect that the stamps were actually of very poor quality and probably wouldn't even fool the first mail carrier. My advice to him was to not purchase them. The suspect became angry at this state-

ment and tried to convince the undercover agent that he should purchase the stamps.

He stated that he supplied a sample well in advance of the sale and that the agent was obligated to make the purchase because his group had gone out of their way to bring the stamps a great distance for the sale. It was very easy for the undercover agent to explain that he went through the expense of getting an expert and that he would abide by the expert's decision and advice. This argument went on for several hours.

The suspect left the room several times to check with "his people" whose room was nearby. When he returned each time, all his suggested offers were rejected on the grounds the stamps were no good. After each argument, the suspect reduced the price until finally it was down to one-fifth of the original price. Our original plan was to not buy the stamps but to force the suspects to leave with the stamps and then place them under arrest while they were en route home.

The undercover agent maintained the position that the stamps were of such poor quality that buying them won't only cost him a lot of money but might also be the cause of him being arrested as the expert said the stamps won't fool anyone. During these negotiations, a telephone call was received from the informant in which he stated that the group was getting desperate and they had decided to come to the agent's room with guns and take his money. After receiving the telephone call, the agent and I excused ourselves, left the hotel room, and never returned. The suspect soon got tired of waiting for us and joined his friends. All four of them left the hotel several hours later, got into their car and as soon as they attempted to drive away, they were arrested and the stamps, which were still in the trunk, were seized as evidence.

This is a good example of how a case can be worked with more than one agent working undercover. Certainly, in this case one man complimented the other and both their actions helped make a successful case. The defendants believed that the expert was the person who "leaked" the information to the authorities.

Testimony at Trial

Undercover agents have a tremendous responsibility in police work. Generally it is their testimony that convicts the violator. All police officers must tell the truth when called upon to testify in court. Truth is also stressed with an

Mr. Motto (second from left) posing with postal inspector and other agents following a seizure of several million dollars worth of postage stamps.

undercover agent. It is generally his testimony about dealing with the day-to-day meetings and conversations he has with suspects that will convince a jury to convict the defendant. Any deviation from the truth at any time during the case or trial is unconscionable on the part of the agent. Agents are sometimes tempted to say something that is not true in order to possibly hide the identity of the informant. This may be a "white lie" in his estimation but it is perjury under the law and certainly should be avoided. Any factor that is not the truth and is determined to be contrary to fact will ruin the agent's credibility with the court and jury and his entire testimony will be discredited. Informants sometimes think that their identity can be kept secret by the undercover agent inventing lies while testifying in court. It should be explained to them that no one, especially a police officer, has a license to lie in court. If it is that important to hide the identity of the informant, it is far better to lose the case than to reveal the informant's identity or to lie. As an undercover agent testifying in court, you will note that the jury will intently listen to every word given in testimony. They realize this witness is risking his life every time he works undercover. They are inclined to believe everything he says. The agent must realize that he has a tremendous burden and responsibility not to deviate one iota from the truth.

Cross Examination at Trial

In a court case involving an undercover agent, it is very difficult for the defense attorney to find something to "hang his hat on" when he is cross-examining the undercover operative, especially if the agent has steadfastly told the truth. The attorney must, therefore, rely on such things as what time it was, how far away was the man from you, how was he dressed, and other seemingly insignificant items. He has to do this because he generally cannot weaken the main portion of the agent's testimony. After he asks the small details of the undercover agent, he will question the covering agents along the same line to try to show discrepancies in times, distance, etc.

In a major counterfeiting case, I was the undercover agent and faced two days of extensive cross examination. At the end of the testimony phase, the defense counsel made a very unusual summation. He said, "You heard Agent Motto testify. He let you know that most of his cases ended in convictions. He told you how he posed as a convict, a soldier, a manufacturer, and the Lord knows what else. Here is a man with many years of service, he knows the in's and out's. I tried for two days to trap him up, but he is too clever. Clever is the word, I don't know how much of what he told you is the truth, all I know is that I wouldn't want the government to put Motto on my trail at any time. Believe me, he makes cases even when there is none. The method that the government uses smacks of entrapment. Please keep this in mind when you deliberate."

To me this was the silliest approach that I had ever heard. I was sure the jury won't fall for it. The U.S. Attorney made an excellent summation and characterized all undercover agents as heroes and said "Thank goodness we have them."

The jury was out longer than I had expected. After two days they returned to the courtroom with a verdict finding all defendants guilty. I spoke to one of the jurors after the trial and he said that three of the jurors were impressed with the defense counsel's summation. For a while it looked like there might be a hung jury. Better heads prevailed and all defendants were found guilty. You never can take a jury for granted.

Summary

In working undercover, there are many fallacies concerning the undercover agent. Contrary to popular belief, he doesn't have to be a good actor. His character must be himself with the same problems, concerns, etc. as anyone trying to "make a buck the easy way." He must, however, be quick of mind, often thinking way ahead of the conversation and planning his response before it is required. He must be able to anticipate any questions regarding his role, the product he is seeking to purchase, and ways to inveigle the suspect to deviate from his normal routine for delivery of the contraband. The undercover agent who is properly mentally and physically prepared will be able to, under most circumstances, successfully and safely conclude the case. It is good practice and procedure to assign two or more undercover agents to work on a case. The second or other agents support the main undercover agent as a "buddy," a driver, an expert or other imaginative position. If the case comes to trial the agent is expected and has the responsibility to be truthful regardless of the outcome and even if it means losing a case he shouldn't "invent" to protect the identity of the informant.

The Arrest or Raid

5

Once the undercover agent has given the prearranged signal that he has received delivery of the contraband, the undercover phase of a case is concluded. This signal triggers the arrest (if it has been decided that an arrest is to be made). We have previously discussed how, in order to avoid confusion and misinterpretation, the signal, should be simple: easily understood, easily seen, and easity heard by the covering agents who are standing by, ready to move in to effect the arrest.

The timing and execution of the arrest are crucial. The suspect has been caught in the act of committing a felony. This is his moment of "fight or flight." He will respond either by attempting to escape — by running or shooting his way out of his predicament — or he may realize the futility of the situation and surrender. The covering/arresting agents should be ready for all contingencies and try to anticipate the suspect's next move. Each case will present its own particular problems. However, there are times when we can lay the groundwork on a particular case and try to make it fit a pattern. At best, this will give us a general idea of how we wish to make the arrest. There will be many variations that can be used to suit each specific situation, but there is no substitute for meticulous planning.

Today, we are dealing with larger amounts of contraband than ever before and the amount is increasing all the time. Sometimes the amount of contraband seized is quite staggering. In the not-too-distant past, a $1 million counterfeit seizure was considered to be extraordinary; the seizure of a kilo of cocaine was thought to be a sizable haul and a newsworthy event. In 1993, $2.7 million of counterfeit money was passed in Los Angeles County, California; in 1997, that figure had jumped to $4.2 million. In neighboring Orange County, the amount of counterfeit money passed rose from $288,000 to $765,000. This example from official Secret Service statistics accounts for only a tiny fraction of the counterfeit money foisted upon the unsuspecting public. In 1997, counterfeit money in excess of $31 million managed to find its way into nationwide circulation.* A statistical analysis isn't necessary to project the amount of counterfeit money that was produced that year and to imagine what the amount victimizing the public might have been. Just a few years ago, a truckload of 3 tons of cocaine was discovered in a southern California warehouse through the efforts of an undercover investigation. It has become commonplace for an investigation to end at warehouses full of counterfeit or stolen merchandise. This makes it even more necessary for the distributor of the contraband to invest more of his money in order for him to make larger sales. If his investment is large, he will naturally want to protect it from falling into the wrong hands; that is, rival gangs and the police. We are witnessing an unprecedented arming of the suspects with semiautomatic and automatic assault rifles and 15-round magazine handguns. They are also prepared to use whatever force or violence is necessary to ensure the shipment, delivery, and storage is not intervened upon by those with other intentions. We have to anticipate their every move and try to be in a position to effect the arrest without jeopardizing our own people or innocent bystanders.

One wrong move by either side can, and most probably will, set off a chain of events that can have tragic consequences. Premature exposure of the officers or unnecessary shooting by the officers, or allowing a suspect to draw his weapon in the course of the raid and arrest can all contribute to the confusion. There is shouting, (possibly shooting), people running all over the place, and generally speaking, a whole lot happening at the same time. Before the raid and arrests occur, it is advisable to discuss and plan for every contingency and all personnel involved in the raid to be thoroughly briefed. Everyone should know what their role is, who the offenders are, any undercover officers or innocent people present, and the physical layout of the premises, including all avenues of possible escape. Intelligence and imagination play an important part in the planning of a raid and the arrests that will be made: intelligence about the operation and location and imagination to anticipate all possible counter moves and security, including counter-surveillance, by the subjects of the operation.

In cases involving large amounts of money, big-time violators, or people and situations having a potential for violence, we have found that a surveillance vehicle is extremely helpful. This vehicle, can be in the form of a nondescript truck, a taxicab, a bus or other commercial vehicle common to the area at the time of day or night. Such a vehicle can allow surveilling officers to get close to the scene without arousing undue suspicion, and at the same time affording maximum cover and protection for the officers. Surveillance vehicles can be equipped for nearly any exigency including videotaping and photographing the activity. Support personnel can be secreted

* *Los Angeles Times*, Nov. 5, 1998.

inside, ready to respond to the undercover agent's signal or transmissions. Of course, with the use of a surveillance vehicle, there comes a certain amount of responsibility and some caveats. This vehicle should not be unmasked except in the event of an emergency. Routine arrests should not be made from the surveillance vehicle. The reason being that the underworld intelligence will soon realize that the police are using specially equipped unmarked vehicles. The description of these vehicles would soon circulate throughout the lawbreakers' network and their revelation would render them ineffective for further surveillance purposes. However, in an emergency, the identity of the vehicle becomes secondary to aiding an officer or saving a life.

Another vehicle, a standard police car, replete with lights and siren should be in the vicinity to respond as needed, but until that time, should remain out of sight. It is important that covering officers, the raiding team, and surveillance personnel remain alert to the possibility, and likely probability, that the violators will attempt some type of countermeasures. They will post lookouts and counter-surveillance teams equipped and with communications as advanced as those of the police, to scout the area for police or rivals. Armed guards at the scene are also likely to be encountered. As stated above, the more that is at risk, the greater the likelihood of armed and alert counter-forces. Many (or most) of the groups today have had some type of training and are aware of most police techniques. They have either had paramilitary training, a street or prison education, or they at least watch television with much of the media, through news programs or entertainment dramas, disclosing police procedures in "buy" or undercover operations. Consequently, the officers in a "standby" position must remain cognizant at all times of the sensitivity of their positioning.

It is no secret that in working undercover, officers are now using cars that not only don't look like police vehicles, but they also could withstand the most minute inspection by the suspects. Therefore, when the arrest/raid begins, the standard police car should be in a position to move in close so they can notify local police officers that an arrest is in progress. Generally in an arrest situation there are two groups of officers: an inner and outer perimeter. In the inner perimeter are the officers and agents who will be directly concerned with taking the suspects into custody. They will be dressed in "raid" jackets and caps with the words "Police" or "Agent" or a similar designation emblazoned across the front and back. The outer perimeter will act as a reserve. Their duties will include notifying any other police officers who might respond to the scene that an arrest is taking place. They will also be alert for less-obvious covering suspects and people involved in the crime that may be attempting to escape or flee the scene. These officers should be dressed in business clothes or "raid" jackets and should be in a position to immediately identify themselves as officers when the arrest is in progress. All officers involved in the arrest, both inner and outer perimeter, should place their shields on their persons as soon as practical, so there is no doubt as to who the officers are. Wherever possible, a member of the local police agency should be on the scene at the time of a contemplated arrest. Out of necessity, he should be a member of the outer perimeter team because of the possibility of recognition if he is too close to the action. The local representative should be teamed with a member of the agency controlling the case. The officers in the outer perimeter, will be in a position to identify fellow officers who may come upon the scene at the time of the arrest or shootout. Sometimes it may be necessary to have a Special Weapons and Tactics (SWAT) team positioned for immediate response should the conditions dictate. Adequate communication between participants is imperative!

The above are some of the considerations that must be addressed in preraid planning and briefings. Before we can discuss how a physical arrest is to be made, we have to explore how the undercover case is being handled and how it is expected to be resolved.

For the purpose of an example, let's say that a buy has been set up for a hotel room. The same rules apply regardless of where the delivery is made. If at all possible, the undercover agent shouldn't agree to make the exchange in the suspect's home, in a warehouse, or any other place where arresting officers cannot be close enough to be able to surprise the suspects.

In our example, the undercover agent has arranged with the suspect that it will be a hand-to-hand delivery in the hotel room. At the appointed time, the suspect is observed entering the hotel lobby. Covering agents in the outer perimeter should immediately forward this information to the agents in the inner perimeter. The inner perimeter in this case would probably be the agents who are in an adjoining room to where the buy is to take place. They should be notified when the suspect or suspects arrive, the method of arrival, how many people are involved, a complete description of the suspects, and if it is obvious, that they are carrying the contraband. It is rarely obvious that they are carrying contraband; however, they may be carrying a suitcase, a briefcase, a cardboard box, or a large wrapped package. This doesn't mean that the package actually contains contraband; it may be a lure to trigger a premature arrest. This is a device used many times in the past and is still an effective tool of the contraband suspect's trade. Under no circumstances should an agent feel that what the suspect is actually carrying is contraband and effect his arrest. The case must proceed as planned and be allowed to run its course. A suitcase full of old telephone books is a poor substitute for the anticipated contraband at the termination of the case!

Once the suspect proceeds to the lobby or the room of the undercover agents, a listening device will generally alert the agents as to whether a bonafide delivery is taking place or not. If the delivery has been made, the undercover agent must be in a position to make the payment. He generally won't admit that he has the buy money in the room (he is concerned about a holdup). He will either send another agent to pick up the money while the suspect waits in the room with the contraband, or he will personally go to a safe at the desk where he has left a package. The suspect will either accompany him or he will go alone. The suspect may have a partner accompany the agent while the original suspect stays with the contraband.

If the suspects separate during the transaction, the arrest can be effected as follows. After the signal has been given that a delivery has been made, the inner perimeter agents can either enter the undercover room by an adjoining door or with a key that has been obtained in advance. The suspects in the room can be placed under arrest and the outer perimeter agents advised that the arrest has occurred. If the suspects have split up and one is accompanying the undercover agent, the arrest can quietly take place at the desk by the outer perimeter agents. An agent and a local police representative should be nearby to intercede and advise any local police that an arrest is taking place and also to help the arresting officers, if necessary. In the event there is trouble, a marked police car or unmarked car with lights should turn the lights on to signal local police that a law enforcement activity is under way. The surveillance vehicle in the vicinity has been observing the area for some time. If the men inside see anything that needs attention they can take care of it. During all these phases, radio or other types of communication must be maintained with the command post that is usually located in the same hotel in a nearby room.

There are times in some cities where the agents are friendly with the owners or employees of hotels and motels. Sometimes these people can be taken into confidence in order to obtain the necessary rooms and cover. As long as the hotel or motel doesn't get any unfavorable publicity, they will often cooperate with authorities. Each case and situation must be judged on its own merits. However, under no circumstances should any unnecessary risks be taken. At the time of the arrest, plainclothes agents should put on their shields in full view to prevent being mistaken for one of the violators.

The suspect will most often not agree to sell the contraband in a hotel or motel room. He may have had a previous experience with a buy that went bad or knows of someone who did. This person will want to proceed as cautiously as possible. Generally, he will want to choose a location that totally assures his protection, yet it may leave the agent and his money in a vulnerable position. The agent can decline to meet under those circumstances saying he is concerned about the possibility of a "rip-off." He should make a counterproposal for a neutral site. If the agent is posing as someone from out of town, or if the money is allegedly being brought from out of town by a trusted "money man," it can be suggested that the airport be the place of delivery. The agent can argue that just as soon as he gets his product, he wants to leave immediately to get the contraband back to his people. This will have the added benefit of reducing the possibility of the suspects being armed, especially if the transfer of the money can be arranged inside the security checkpoints. If the amount of contraband is too great to fit inside a piece of luggage that will pass through screening without arousing suspicion, the agent can say he has arranged for a "hired" means of transporting the material. Another argument can be that it isn't the suspect's business how the agent will transport the product back to his people.

The agent can give the suspect the time he will be at the airport without mentioning the exact time or flight numbers. If these arrangements are agreeable to the suspect, the agent can also indicate that he will leave his money in a locker box at the airport so he can pay for the contraband as soon as he has inspected it and arranged for its transfer. In this case, the inner-perimeter agents can cover the vicinity of the locker where the agent has placed his money. They know that the agent won't take the suspect to the box nor will he open it unless he has seen the notes or has actually taken possession of the contraband. When the buy money is being retrieved from the locker, this can be the signal to make the arrest. The inner perimeter of covering agents will take the suspect into custody; the outer perimeter will be on the look out for any accomplices and arrest any that have remained in the background. At the same time, other agents, perhaps from the police car or surveillance van, can seize any vehicle the suspect may have used. This should all be done as quickly and inconspicuously as possible. It is best that the fewer people who know about the arrest, the better.

The evidence at the scene should be immediately secured. One agent should be in charge of the evidence and take custody of the contraband and keep control of it so the "chain of evidence" isn't broken and there won't be any trouble in entering it as evidence at the time of trial. In other words: one agent obtains the evidence, initials or marks it, and puts it in a safe place and secures it for storage until he needs to take it to court. This will prevent the necessity of having several agents being called to court for the purpose of identifying the evidence and establishing the necessary chain.

The same procedure can be used for a subway or railroad station, bus terminal, or any other public facility. There will be little variation in these types of cases except that the subject may want to make the transfer in a car in the parking lot. This shouldn't create a problem because the agent will have to retrieve his money from a locker or his car. He should have seen the contraband and the agents from the outer perimeter should be in a position to cover the transaction while the agents in the inner perimeter make the necessary adjustments.

There are times when the suspect insists upon making a deal at a restaurant on a busy street, expressway, or highway. This will necessitate the use of cars by both the suspect and the undercover agent. The suspect will generally arrive at the restaurant early to look it over. He will also make a couple of passes through the parking lot to see if there are any people just sitting in cars. He will then meet the agent in the restaurant or bar and have a conversation with him. He may have the contraband with him or he may be expecting a delivery. He might leave someone else in the parking lot as a lookout or backup. He probably will be equipped with a cellular telephone to call another person to bring in the contraband if he doesn't have it on his person. Of course it is also possible that the suspect can also receive incoming calls from his counter-surveillance team if any police or unusual activity is determined.

The agent may have the buy money with him or it could be locked in his car. If the intended plan is to "cut-out" the agent, at least temporarily so he can continue to bring in other conspirators or wrap-up any loose ends such as immediately meeting the source or other middlemen, the exchange of money and contraband can go as planned inside the restaurant. As soon as the suspect exits, the covering officers arrest him while the undercover agent "escapes" out another entrance. The arresting officers continue the charade about the "escaping accomplice" as long as possible.

If the agent's money is in his car, he tells the suspect that he is ready to complete the deal but will have to go to his car to get the money. The suspect may also have his contraband in his car or with an "outside" accomplice. The outer perimeter is, of course, either in the parking lot or close by where it can be kept under surveillance. Here again, it must be remembered that nothing can happen until the agent goes to get his money or the signal is given to make the arrest. The outer perimeter will cover the agent while he goes to get his money. If the suspect is with him, both will be placed under arrest in the parking lot. The agents in the restaurant who were in the inner perimeter will leave the restaurant and lend assistance to the arresting officers, and carry on the normal functions of the outer perimeter.

Very often the suspect will insist on making a deal at a large shopping center. Here the agent can control the activity by again using a car and keeping the buy money in the car. Whatever contact he has with the suspect can be loosely followed by agents of the inner perimeter while agents of the outer perimeter cover the car and parking lot. In an area such as this, a surveillance vehicle will easily fit into the area as there so many different types of cars, trucks, and vans coming and going. After the agent has seen the notes, or accepted delivery of the contraband from the suspect, he will go to his car and get his money from the trunk or wherever it has been placed. This signal will notify all agents that the undercover agent is ready for an arrest. Again, agents from the inner perimeter can effect the arrest of the suspects while the undercover agent can be taken into custody by the outer perimeter. Other agents will act as reserve and be in a position to notify local police, etc. of what is going on.

There are times when the suspect absolutely insists on doing business either in his home or an apartment that he maintains away from his home, where he is confident the conduct of business can be concluded safely. With the popularity of closed-circuit television cameras and monitors, alarm systems, decorative security lighting, enclosed compounds, etc., it is nearly impossible for covering and arresting agents to penetrate without being detected. If this is a significant transaction, the undercover agent can go to the home or apartment, but insist that he will not take his money there because he doesn't know what to expect when he gets there. When he sees the contraband, and knows it is on the premises or gets the delivery, he can ask the suspect to accompany him to his car. When he goes to the car he gives the signal, and the arrest can be effected on the street.

One new undercover agent couldn't get out of meeting with the suspect in his home. Concerned that a body transmitter would be detected by the suspect's electronic detection devices, the agent went into the meeting without any communication with his covering agents. His supervisor told him that should a problem arise necessitating interference or rescue, the agent should throw a chair through the window. Upon entering the house, the young agent kept that instruction in mind. Much to his concern, he wa confronted with a living room that contained only a large sectional sofa and overstuffed chairs that even the "Hulk" couldn't pick up, let alone throw out a window.

Another method of delivery can be car-to-car. The suspect arranges to meet the undercover agent in a neighborhood and tells him to park his car at a certain location. He will then cruise the area before delivery to make sure that there aren't any suspicious cars or personnel in the vicinity. It is very important in cases such as these to use a surveillance vehicle to get the maximum amount of cover for the agents who are to make the arrest.

In all of the above scenarios, once the signal is given, no time should be lost in effecting the arrest. A few seconds could make the difference between success and failure. It is vitally important that control of the suspect and accomplices be accomplished before they have an opportunity to take evasive or violent action. If the suspect is armed, even the loss of a few seconds can trigger a sequence of events that could be disastrous.

If the case is significant enough, it may warrant giving sufficient notice to the assistant United States Attorney or deputy District Attorney handling the judicial proceedings so they can be immediately available after the arrest to take care of the legal issues that might arise. Having an Assistant U. S. Attorney or deputy D.A. on the scene is very helpful and he can generally take part in interviewing the suspects. He can make certain that the suspects are provided with information regarding their rights and immediate options.

If the means of delivering the contraband to the transaction point cannot be readily determined by the covering agents, the informant and undercover agent should be debriefed privately regarding their observations at the time the delivery was made. Very often the undercover agent will be able to tell how the delivery was made, who made it, and whether or not the delivery person is still in the vicinity.

In most instances, the case is important enough to have photographs and videos made of the seized plant. Arrangements should be made ahead of time for the photographs and videotape so time isn't lost waiting for someone to arrive with the proper equipment. The photos and videos should be taken of the plant before and after it has been searched to show the condition of the plant before and after the agent's arrival and departure. The contraband and evidence seized at the plant should be inventoried, marked, and secured as soon as possible.

As soon as is practical after the arrest, search, and seizure, the undercover agent should be allowed an opportunity to make the notes necessary for his final report. He should be provided with a room, computer, tape recorder, etc., so he can make these notes while the events are still fresh in his mind.

Each participating officer and agent at the scene should be given a specific responsibility after the arrest such as transporting the arrested people to the office for questioning or to jail, taking inventory of the evidence and seized contraband, and maintaining custody of it. If these assignments aren't planned in advance, time will be lost at the scene of the arrest. It also opens the possibility that something will be overlooked or forgotten or assumed that someone else will take care of it. All assignments should be carried out as quickly as possible and all agents should depart the scene as quickly as possible. The supervisor should make sure each officer at the scene prepares a report detailing exactly what he did and what he saw at the time the deal was being consummated. If too much time is allowed to elapse, officers will be unnecessarily delayed in compiling their reports to headquarters. It is the supervisor's job to see that all reports are accurate and received on time.

Publicity

A successful case usually ends with an arrest and a sizeable seizure of contraband. This type of case is newsworthy and is of great interest to the press.

The folowing pages show examples of photographs used for publicity purposes displaying sizable seizures of counterfeit money. Whether to allow publicity, is a decision that faces each agency after a successful case. Most agencies have a public affairs departments that have a cooperative attitude toward the press providing as much information as possible to the media. It's a good policy that all inquiries regarding an investigation be funneled through one spokesperson who usually has a good working relationship with members of the news media. This prevents contradictory statements, misquoted material, or release of sensitive information that normally is attendant in undercover operations.

Publicity is a double-edged sword that cuts two ways. Most agencies wage a never-ending budget battle and in order to obtain a workable budget commensurate with the types of programs, policies, and operations it maintains, the agency must generate favorable publicity for the work it is doing

The various governmental bureaucratic lawmakers generally hold hearings and council debates in order to determine the size of the budget they will authorize and fund for enforcement work. Favorable publicity generates public support for any special operations that have been shown to have positive results. Public opinion translates to political influence. The police administration must be armed with statistics that will help them gain favorable press, public, and political attention, and to obtain the funds necessary to wage a successful war against crime. Thus, whenever an undercover case is successful, the media should be considered as a publicity tool. Legislators remember the publicity that the department receives and they are undoubtedly influenced by what they read in the papers and see on television.

The other side of the proverbial sword cuts another way also. The police must decide whether to meet the press and issue a news release at the conclusion of a successful case. The decision shouldn't be whether to meet the press or not, but rather, how much information to provide. To give the press the facts as they happened will tend to expose the informant and operating procedures. To mention that it was an undercover case would indicate that there was an undercover agent involved and this will alert the defendants that they were "set up" and again the informant will be in jeopardy. To try to distort the facts or mislead the press is undesirable and dangerous. Most reporters are familiar with the workings of an undercover case and if they feel that they are being deceived they will dig deeper into the facts and go an extra mile to determine the exact truth.

Time and timing are important factors in many cases and they are something that most police departments desparately need when they are involved in a lengthy and complex investigation, especially if it involves undercover work. An important phase of the investigation may be concluded, but there are many other phases that need further investigation. If all the facts are published in the press the case can be ruined. That is another of the consequences of the "double-edged sword" of publicity. Reporters realize that undercover work and "daring do" provide interesting reading and viewing. Interesting topics attract readers and viewers, sell more newspapers, and gain a larger "ratings" and market share.

However, the premature publishing of the facts in a case can do irreparable damage to the investigation. The only other alternative is to completely ignore the press and thereby incur their displeasure; a sure way to garner adverse publicity, there is a workable middle ground. There are some jurisdictional areas where the police and press have a good working relationship and the press will cooperate by not printing anything that will jeopardize the informant or the judicial outcome of the case. There are also some investigations where all the facts can be given to the press when the investigation ends. In these cases, there ususally aren't any informants involved and no undercover agents at risk. The police can feel free to answer most questions asked by the press.

In some jurisdictions, the cooperation between the police and press is so good that on an occasion the police will invite the press along on an arrest or raid. This is good for the relationship and it generates publicity. But the negatives far outweigh all the "flag waving." Anything can, and so often does, go wrong in a case, especially one involving informants and undercover agents. To have the press on the scene only compounds the risk factors including liability for any injuries to the media personnel. Not many alternatives have been offered to handle the press and a decision is difficult to arrive at. The overriding factors however, must always be concern for the safety of the undercover agent, protection of the identity of the informant and agent, and premature publicity of the case which might jeopardize the judicial outcome.

Summary

An undercover agent meets the suspect and exchanges money for the contraband. A signal is given and covering agents move in to effect the arrest. A very simple scenario. It is simple if every contingency has been preplanned, all participating agents are thoroughly briefed and properly equipped and prepared for their assignment, all signals are understood, and each person performs his role as planned. However, the scenario can quickly deteriorate to the point where he suspect resorts to violence in an attempt to effect an escape if there is a breakdown in communication between the covering agents and the undercover agent. There may be premature action taken by the agents or the suspect or his counter-surveillance personnel detect the presence of the hidden agents who are waiting to make the arrest. All means must be taken to prevent adverse action by the suspect. That will mean controlling the place of contraband/money transfer, placing agents as close to the scene as possible through deception and/or the use of a vehicle common in the area as a surveillance vehicle and transportation for the agents, and quick response to the arrest signal of the undercover agent.

There will be many variations that can be used to suit the particular situation, but there is no substitute for meticulous planning and safe execution.

The amount and degree of media publicity afforded to an investigation should be commensurate with the departmental policy. One spokesperson should be the single voice disseminating information to the news media thereby preventing premature disclosure of sensitive information, dispelling rumors, and in protecting the identities of the informants and undercover agents. There are not many choices offered in dealing with the press. The best alternative is the truth, but the timing of the of release any information must be carefully chosen.

The photos on the following pages are samples of publicity photographs that are suitable for release to the news media. Care should be taken not to include the undercover agent or the informant. Photographs of this type will usually satisfy the media requirements while providing excellent publicity for the agency.

Attitudes

6

It doesn't take a *Wheel of Fortune* viewer or a crossword puzzle fanatic to be able to come up with a six-letter word that doesn't belong in any law enforcement department. That word is *apathy.* There are other words that describe the same attitude: lack of interested involvement, disregard, indifference, lassitude, unconcern, and unresponsiveness. As apathy takes many forms in letters, it also takes many forms in investigative work: the unwillingness to take an honest gamble, the fear of "rocking the boat," the desire to only work on the big case and avoid the small one, the unwillingness to take on the slightest responsibility, and certainly not to get involved doing something as proactive and responsive as undercover work. One cannot expect to be an effective undercover agent with less than a positive attitude.

Apathy is a negative attitude that knows no age limitations. The rookie as well as the veteran officer can be equally guilty of being apathetic. Sometimes it is a learned attitude. Several years ago when a young man, who later became a federal agent, was beginning his law enforcement career as a police officer for a medium-sized city, he was assigned to a police patrol car with a much older veteran officer. The assigned hours of their shift normally were 7:00 P.M. to 3:00 A.M. or 9:00 P.M. to 5:00 A.M. For the most part, the veteran officer made contacts with the people in his patrol area only if directed by the radio dispatcher. As soon as the early evening activities began to settle into a quiet routine, the older officer would direct the younger officer to "go to the hole." That was a term meaning, "find a quiet, unobserved spot to park the patrol car and sleep for a couple of hours." The young officer soon learned that his "training" partner was only one of many officers following that routine. He also determined that many younger officers, who had joined the police department at the same time as he, had accepted that routine attitude as the normal pattern. When he was assigned to a plainclothes decoy detail in the "lower end" he was told by the veteran officers not to make more than two arrests per day, however one was preferred because any more than that would put pressure on them when they pulled that assignment. The unofficial instruction was to "make your arrest early in the shift; then go to the movies."

Hopefully, the "going-to-the-hole" attitude has passed into another era. But the overall disinterested attitude may still be pervasive in many localities. There are many old-timers who have "put in their time" and don't want to become involved in anything more than the most routine of matters. There are also some young officers who are so intent and preoccupied with studying for a promotion or for degrees in higher education that they don't seem to have the time for the duties for which they are being paid. To be assigned to respond to a complaint or to be flagged down by a citizen on the street seems to come as an intrusion upon their "personal" time. There are some investigators who constantly shift around and try to pick out the "big case" that might bring instant recognition or some other form of reward. The small case that has been kicked aside though could possibly be just as rewarding, or perhaps more so to the officer and people involved. Perhaps not in the form of monetary gain or departmental recognition, and it may not be a "career" case, but just in knowing that the job was done right and an honest effort, which paid off, was made to properly resolve it. The "big one" may never come along but any number of the small ones, if worked properly, can lead to the big one or at least to a measure of personal and professional satisfaction. When police work becomes dull and routine and the desire to solve the case is no longer there, or the challenges no longer bring a degree of response, then it is time for the officer or investigator to seek employment elsewhere or to be in another line of endeavor.

Apathy is a symptom of "burn-out" and can be cured only with a change. Police work is not always the best paying job, but most of us who have been involved with it get a sense of fulfillment in trying to prevent crime, arrest violators, and making the world just a little bit more safer. A good example of putting maximum effort into a small case that paid off and was rich in satisfaction is the case of "The Spider."

> He was called Spider, because of a malformation of his teeth and jaw and the fact that he was so gangly — all arms and legs — contributed to the moniker as well. Spider had a penchant for getting involved in matters that didn't concern him or that caused him trouble. He'd had more than his share of "brushes with the law" but never had served any real jail time, just a few short sentences here and there, nothing of consequence. However, his escapades and several arrests had earned him a reputation in his neighborhood and in police circles as a "troubled youth." He had long forgotten, if indeed he had

ever known, what it was like to have a decent family life. He was orphaned at an early age and had run away, "escaped" was his term for it, from every foster home into which he had been placed. He preferred to make his own way on the streets of New York.

One day, Spider, was identified as the passer of a counterfeit $20 bill that was making its first appearance. He was picked up by the police and then turned over to the Secret Service for further questioning and prosecution. Spider maintained that he had found several bills on the street, and that he didn't know they were counterfeit. He would normally be considered as just another passer with a trite and tried story common to counterfeit passers and would be questioned and either released or arraigned. What made Spider so special in this case was the fact that he was the only person who had "redeemed" any of these particular notes. The notes were new, they were of excellent quality, and no others had appeared in circulation. We believed that Spider was either in a position to steal the notes or he had access to where they were being printed. We felt sure that he had enough information to help us locate the plant and printer before the notes were extensively distributed. While we were still questioning The Spider, information came to us that another police department wanted to talk to him in connection with the murder of a taxi driver. The police wanted to have some time to further their investigation and to do some background work on him and then wanted him made available at a later date for questioning about this particular homicide.

After spending several hours with Spider, I felt that he was putting up a brave façade but deep down he was just a scared kid and if we could press the right buttons, he might decide to cooperate. At times during the interview it appeared that he might be softening just a little. But just as soon as he was asked pertinent follow-up questions, he would quickly regain his "tough-guy" front. Getting him to admit that he had passed the counterfeit notes wasn't the problem, as he had already admitted to that. We had to find a way to shake his story that he found the notes on the street. We learned that 18-year-old Spider had a special interest in a physically handicapped girl who lived in his neighborhood. The idea that he might be separated from her for a long period of time, and nobody would look after her seemed to cause him some concern and worry.

I was able to obtain permission from the United States Attorney's office to get a quick arraignment on Spider just before the court closed for the day. We wanted to be sure he was arraigned and released on his own recognizance without any publicity. We didn't think Spider's case was newsworthy enough to draw the attention of the press as he was only being arraigned for a one-note pass. After the arraignment, I decided to take a chance and asked Spider to talk to us after he was released. He agreed to come back to the office after the court proceedings to discuss the case. Of course he could assert his Constitutional Fifth Amendment rights and refuse to have anything to do with us. He was also absolutely free to go back to his source and let the source know he had been arrested and the Secret Service was investigating the appearance of the new counterfeit note.

When we arrived back at the office, Spider was once again reminded that he could terminate the interview at any time and that he was free to leave at any time. His attitude began to change because for the first time in his life he felt that he was talking to someone he could trust. We spent quite some time engaged in small talk. We had food brought in and over the meal returned to the topic of the counterfeit money. After he had finished eating, he abruptly stated that he didn't want to go any further in the questioning. He got up and started to leave the office. No one stopped him and we wished him well. He got as far as the door and turned and came back. He decided that he would cooperate after all. This appeared to be a test to see if he was actually free to go when he pleased.

As he sat down again he announced that he was ready to tell the whole story. Yet, he again asked if he were still free to go home. We assured him that he could go home that night regardless of what he said. He took a deep breath and began his story. Several months earlier, he got a job in a neighborhood print shop. He said that he did odd jobs around the shop and ran errands for the owner, George Franklin. Franklin wasn't an ordinary printer. He was a third-generation printer and engraver. He knew lithography, photography, and all the allied arts. A few weeks after Spider had started his job, he noticed that Franklin was experimenting with making counterfeit notes. on one occasion, Spider had entered the print shop after hours and saw evidence of counterfeiting. Spider confronted Franklin about what he had seen. Franklin took him into his confidence and promised to make Spider a partner in the counterfeiting activities. Franklin continued with his experimenting, but being the perfectionist he was, he never seemed satisfied with the result of his work. Althugh the counterfeit notes passed by Spider were of excellent quality, Spider said Franklin wasn't satisfied and felt he could do better still. Spider told us that Franklin always destroyed the negatives, the plates, and the notes once he completed his experiments. He went on to say that on several occasions he had helped to destroy thousands of dollars in counterfeit money that weren't good enough to pass Franklin's high standards. Spider managed to steal several of the discarded experimental notes before they were destroyed, hence his present predicament. Spider stated that he didn't have any problem passing the notes and denied that he had any more left.

He assured us that Franklin's shop was absolutely clean and devoid of any evidence of counterfeiting activity, so it would not only be counterproductive to get a search warrant, but a waste of time as well. There wasn't amy way of knowing when Franklin would resume his activities. Spider knew Franklin was under financial pressure because he had been getting visits from several characters who wanted him to make counterfeit money and checks, to pay off some of his debts. We didn't want to expose Spider by using him as a witness against Franklin. It would be a weak case at best and our only chance was to gamble with Spider and trust him to keep us informed as to Franklin's counterfeiting activities.

Spider seemed to enjoy the prospect of working undercover for the government. He promised to return to his job in the print shop and report to us several times a week. Surprisingly, he kept his word and was prompt and accurate in his reporting. He gave us the names and license numbers of the unsavory characters that visited Franklin and he reported on his movements and the conversations he had with him. Franklin had plenty of legitimate business to occupy his time and he postponed his counterfeiting activities until he had more time to spend on it.

While we were waiting for Franklin to resume his experiments, we found time during the lull to let the police interview Spider about the homicide of the taxi driver. Spider cooperated with the police, answered all their questions, and was subsequently cleared of any complicity in the crime. For the first time in his young life, Spider was seeing daylight and he liked the idea of not having to run from every policeman he saw. He continued making his reports on a regular basis. On his visits to our office he joined in small talk with several of the agents, he had breakfast with us two or three times a week, and even borrowed money on a payday-to-payday arrangement. He was as prompt with paying his loans as he was with his reporting. Spider began to go to the dentist to take care of his teeth. He bought himself some new clothes, got a part-time job to supplement his income from working for Franklin, and started dating Edna, his disabled girlfriend. So it went for 8 months. We began to wonder if Franklin had been tipped off or if Spider had double-crossed us. I took a lot of good-natured ribbing from some of the personnel in the office. A lot of them felt that Spider was bad to the bone and we had made a mistake in trusting him. I still felt he was being honest with us. No new notes were appearing so it was obvious that Franklin wan't back into the counterfeit business yet. Surveillance on the print shop didn't indicate that Franklin was engaged in any illegal activities.

Finally, one day Spider reported that Franklin was talking about making $100 bills. Franklin had told Spider that he had developed a new process for making counterfeit notes and he was sure that he could make a very deceptive bill. He had begun buying supplies and working a little at the end of each day. Spider was allowed to stay around while Franklin worked on the plates. After several weeks, Franklin announced to Spider that the plates were finished and he was thoroughly satisfied with the way they had turned out. He told Spider that he had some large orders for these counterfeit bills and that very shortly he would start printing.

Spider was now reporting daily and one day he told us that Franklin was going to start printing on the following evening. We wanted to obtain a search warrant for the print shop premises but didn't want to use Spider as a witness. The print shop was on street level and was easy to cover, but the windows were painted black and we couldn't see into the plant. The night before the printing started, Spider made sure that enough of the paint was scrapped from the window to give us a view of Franklin's activities. Franklin didn't deviate from his schedule and began printing in the late afternoon. He planned to stay in the shop all weekend, if necessary, until the job was finished. That night we observed Franklin at the press, printing the notes. Based on what we had seen, we were able to obtain a search warrant for the print shop.

The following day, we went into the shop while Franklin was printing the counterfeit $100 bills. Spider didn't show up for work that day and wasn't present when the arrest was made. George Franklin was a very intelligent individual and was tops in the printing trade and could have a good living by working legitimately. He apparently got carried away with his own talents and wanted to compete with the Bureau of Engraving and Printing. Several hundred thousand dollars in finished notes were seized from the plant as well as Franklin's press, camera, and other equipment used in manufacturing the notes. It had first appeared that Franklin was going to fight the case, but after speaking with his attorney, he decided to cooperate and assist the government in identifying and testifying against the others who were with him in his previous counterfeiting activities. The others were subsequently identified, arrested, and convicted.

For his cooperation, along with his previously clean record and good citizenship, Franklin received a suspended sentence and was placed on probation. He later became a good friend of the Secret Service as he stayed in the trade and was responsible for helping us with several major cases. Franklin married, bought a home in another part of the country, he and his wife have a growing family and a very successful business. The last time I talked with him, he told me he was going to write a book. It is hoped it will be a textbook about printing.

But what about Spider? Things couldn't have worked out better for him. He also received a suspended sentence. He married his girlfriend, Edna, and moved away from the city. They are happily married, living in a small town, and raising a family. Spider opened a plumbing business and hasn't been in any trouble since that time, long ago when he was arrested for passing the counterfeit note.

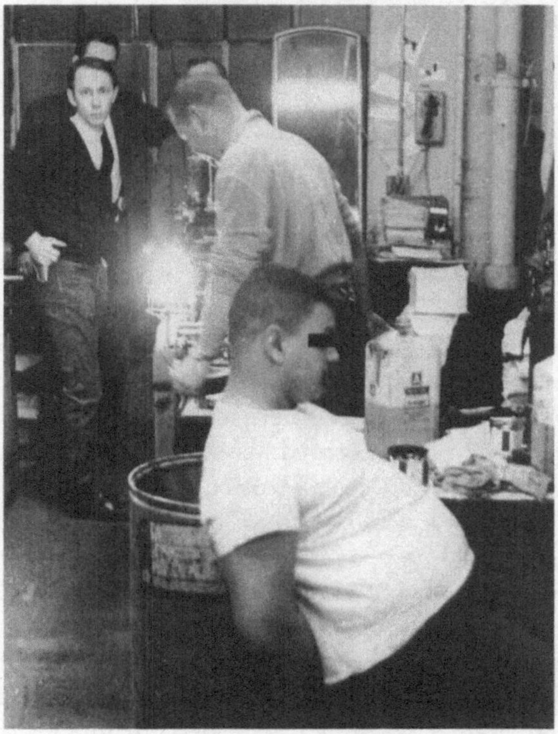

Counterfeiter caught in the process of printing counterfeit money.

Interior of print shop where counterfeit money was made.

This case couldn't have been scripted any better. It was a gamble that paid off and I hate to think of how many other cases that didn't work out as well and died because we didn't take the time and patience for positive action. In the final analysis of this case, there really wasn't much of a choice. Fortunately, our trust wasn't misplaced and no unforeseen event had "tipped the scales" against us. We could have simply placed Spider in jail or held off with the arraignment until the next day and asked for a high bail. Franklin would eventually have heard of Spider's arrest and decided that he couldn't be trusted to be in on his plan to counterfeit and he undoubtedly would have been more careful with his discarded material and perhaps dropped Spider as too great a risk. Or, if we had trusted Spider and he didn't want to cooperate, he would have told George of his arrest and encounter with the Secret Service we would have lost. Either way, we would have been no closer to the plant. So this case, and many similar ones, left few alternatives. The right choice was made and it paid off.

It would be foolish to think that all of the cases where we trust someone would end as well as this one did. All we can do is play with the possibilities and take the one case that we think has the best chance of success. There may be some possibilities in even the most benign of cases, but a positive attitude is needed and the desire to extend one's self beyond the point of just "getting

Examining an uncut sheet of counterfeit money retrieved from the trash barrel in the print shop.

by." The main thing to remember is "do something." Even a placebo might work if there is confidence that it will be effective. You can never be sure a plan will work unless it is tried. It definitely won't work if it's "left in the box." It was refreshing to note that in this case all the personnel involved were enthusiastic about its possibilities. Long hours were involved and there were many times of doubt and glitches with their attendant headaches, but not once did apathy rear its ugly head.

I have to admit that Franklin's work was the best I have ever seen. The effort that went into this case paid off handsomely. If Franklin's counterfeiting activities hadn't been curtailed when they were, he could have continued his activities for a long time and the public would have been victimized by untold thousands of dollars in these counterfeit notes.

Summary

Attitude: that definable something that can tip the scale into a negative or a positive. It is the effort recognized in people and causes that is translated into a professional and/or personal winning situation. A law enforcement officer can easily "get by" working daily in a capacity of providing only the most routine of services. To those people, their job is nothing more than an opportunity to make a living while waiting for their pension or it can be a "time filler" between other off-duty endeavors such as running a business or working semi-police jobs like private security. Their attitude is one of protecting their retirement and serving their own personal needs. They are, in other words, apathetic toward the needs of the people, their agency, and in the end, their responsibility. Modern law enforcement agencies have no place for these people and hopefully apathy is not a contagious attitude.

One young police officer and his equally idealistic partner adopted a motto that precisely summed up their attitude: "We are here to help." They knew that no one turned to the police unless they were in need of help. That was a positive attitude that brought them many professional rewards such as the number of cases they favorably resolved. But more importantly, they also experienced satisfaction on a personal level —they knew that at the end of their shift, they had helped someone who needed their help and they knew that the job was done right.

There is no room in undercover work for a lackadaisical or apathetic attitude. The job requires a person with the determination to want to make a difference, who will go the extra distance to do the things that if left undone would result in a less than satisfactory job. It is people such as there who are successful in their chosen roles or profession. For them, "good enough is *not* good enough. " This attitude makes them winners.

Questions and Answers 7

Younger agents-in-training always have questions about undercover work. Although most of the questions usually reflect their own personal concerns, there is a commonality that can be predicted, even from veteran undercover agents. It is with this in mind that this chapter is devoted to anticipating and answering many of the most frequently asked questions (at least to the degree possible from experience that has been shown to work or that has been encountered by other undercover agents). Undercover work isn't like working at a regular job. The undercover agent is placed in a position where he assumes a role. The degree of success he achieves is dependent upon many factors. Chief among them is the agent's self-confidence. If any of his doubts can be eliminated or his questions can be resolved in a training situation, he will carry a greater proportion of confidence into his role.

Q: Should a police officer or agent be armed while working undercover?

A: As we keep iterating, undercover work is not an exact science. Each case is different and must be judged on its own merits. The answer to the question of whether an agent should be armed while performing undercover work will vary depending on the circumstances. In many settings a weapon is a standard tool of the trade. In drug transactions, for example, it is not at all uncommon, in fact it is actually expected, for both the buyer and seller to be armed. In gray or black market transactions it may not be as common for the participants to be armed. If the circumstances do not indicate a possibility for violence, then a weapon may not be necessary. If dealing with "respectable businessmen" such as corrupt public officials, "black marketeers" selling counterfeit merchandise, then a gun might be more of a hindrance than an necessity. It must be remembered that a weapon should be used only as a defensive measure. In most situations a gun would only raise unnecessary questions or suspicions that would be difficult to explain and it could have unintended consequences such as the suspects feeling they must be armed, or it could even be used against the undercover operator.

However, whether to carry a sidearm is a personal decision. If an agent feels more confident and knows he can readily explain its presence if it is detected, or if the other side might expect the agent be armed because of his role, then a weapon would be appropriate. The anticipated need should be the overriding criteria. Some undercover agents have worked their entire careers without carrying a weapon. If the decision is made, either by the undercover agent or his supervisor, to carry a weapon, based on the likelihood for potential violence, the degree to which an agent can be covered by other agents, or other mitigating circumstances, the undercover agent doesn't necessarily have to carry the usual standard issue sidearm. A small gun, which can be easily concealed, may be more advisable.

Q: Should undercover agents use pagers and cellular telephones?

A: Pagers and cell phones have become so common that only in very unusual circumstances would their use raise any suspicions. These days, nearly everyone involved in business carries these symbols of "being in touch." If an undercover agent is using these tools, the same precautions as the use of a regular undercover telephone should be observed. The pager and telephone should be neutralized so that an innocent page or telephone call will not provide the suspects with the potential of learning the undercover agents true identity. The telephone numbers should be listed to a "straw name" and all incoming calls should be in keeping with the agent's role. As with all tools of the undercover business, there are advantages and disadvantages in carrying pagers, cell phones, or whatever the latest "gizmo" is. Their use should be limited and they should be used only under the appropriate circumstances.

Q: Should an agent be covered at all times while working in an undercover capacity?

A: This can be answered in the same way as the previous question. That is, the circumstances of the situation will dictate the need. An agent working in a "buy" situation should be covered at all times, especially if an arrest is imminent. There are times, however, when undercover agents cannot possibly be covered or it would be impractical to do so. An agent working undercover in a business, labor, or manufacturing setting to detect company theft, corruption, etc., for example, is expected to be on his own and is left to his own devices. There are times, as described earlier in this book, when undercover agents must accompany suspects on short trips either to pick up the contraband or to meet other violators and it is just not possible to have accompanying cover. Arrangements and preplanning should be made in advance for the undercover agent to contact his supervisor or "contact person" as soon as it is practical so that he can advise of his location and the surveillance can be taken up on that end. If an agent is working on long-term, intelligence-seeking assignments, there are times when he will be out of contact for long periods of time. That is to be expected. Here again, arrangements are made in advance for the method to be used to contact his supervisors, a partner, or the designated contact person. To reduce this question to its lowest common denominator: the rule of thumb is that wherever practical, an agent working undercover should be kept under surveillance by his fellow agents to render assistance in the event he needs it. The case should be controlled in such a manner that there will be no problems in covering the agent.

An illustration including both situations of whether an agent should be armed or whether he should be covered at all times while working undercover follows.

> I had just completed an assignment in Philadelphia and was preparing to depart the local Secret Service office to return to New York, when a telephone call came into the office. It was an informant, saying he had been propositioned to purchase counterfeit notes and was in a position to obtain a sample. As the informant was tending bar in a town that I would have to pass through on my way back to New York, and since I knew I would be assigned to do the undercover work in the case, I volunteered to stop by on my way home to see whether a case could be developed.
>
> It was night when I arrived at the informant's business establishment and the bar was doing a brisk, but not unusual. amount of business. I located the informant. who was the bartender on duty and introduced myself. He told me that a patron of the bar had shown him a sample of a counterfeit note and wanted to sell the notes in large quantities. As we were talking, the suspect entered the bar and the bartender introduced me to him as a friend from New York. The suspect and I engaged in small talk for the next hour or so. Eventually the conversation settled on the subject of various types of contraband and he showed me a sample of counterfeit money that his group was selling. He asked me if I would be interested in making a purchase. I told him I wasn't in a position to make a large purchase at that time, but I could invest a few hundred dollars in some notes, take them with me to New York, and return later with a larger order. He asked me to stay for a while longer to meet some of his friends. The hour was getting to be fairly late and there was no way that I could make contact with the office. Yet, I agreed to wait.
>
> At about closing time, the suspect and I went out to the parking lot where two men were waiting in a car. I was invited into the car

and a conversation ensued about counterfeit money. The driver of the car became suspicious of me and started asking a lot of questions. The situation nearly deteriorated to the point of argumentation. I was apparently not giving him the answers he wanted to hear and he was becoming annoyed with me. Both he and his friend were armed (and of course I wasn't — I never carried a weapon in undercover work). The suspect I had just spent the past several hours with in the bar told his friends that if he thought I was "wrong" he wouldn't have any hesitation about killing me and dumping my body into the nearby river. Both of his friends agreed with him and the situation became critical. The driver continued asking questions about who I knew, who I worked for, what my connections were, what my intentions were for the counterfeit money, how was I going to sell it, and similar "third-degree"questions. He demanded answers, but didn't even always wait for my reply before firing-off another question. In reply to one of his questions, I told him I was in the garment business in New York. He replied that he had good connections in the business and asked me the name of my employer. At random, I picked the name of a dress manufacturer in New York, confident (and hopeful) that he wasn't in a position to contact this person at that time. He went through some motions of making telephone calls and trying to check out my story. Then, for some reason, they suddenly decided to let me go and released me from the car at about 4 o'clock in the morning. Needless to say, I didn't buy any counterfeit money from them!

Some time later, after a case was made against all of these individuals, it was learned from one of them that on that particular night they had been deadly serious about killing the man who they had in the car, as they suspected he might be an informant or an undercover agent.

Working this case "cold" and without cover was very foolish and unnecessarily risky on my part. It was one of the rare times when the office had no idea of where I was or what I was doing other than the fact I mentioned I was going to meet with an informant. It would have been far better had I been kept under surveillance, not only for safety's sake, but because the government would have been provided with the several more witnesses needed to corroborate the testimony I gave in court after the defendants were arrested. It was very hard for a jury to believe that a man would be working undercover in such a situation with no other agents in sight. The question of whether it would have been better to be armed at that time is debatable. Perhaps if I had been armed and drew the weapon during the argument in the car, it might have caused a shootout as at least two of the other people were armed and most probably someone would have been killed.

Q: Should an agent tell his family that he is working undercover?

A: Yes. The families of most undercover agents have accepted the fact that their husband (or wife) or relative works undercover, and that there is a certain amount of danger connected with their work. Most undercover agents advise their families early on that they are working undercover, that they will receive telephone calls at all hours of the day and night, that they will go out at very odd hours, and they will be seen in the company of some strange people. The agent's spouse and family must accept this way of life or the domestic tranquility of home will be upset. Once the family is aware of the undercover agent's role, it is not necessary to give them a daily update or report on the case. Very often, the life of the undercover agent depends upon the facts of the case remaining confidential until a certain stage in the case is reached. Revealing too much information, even to one's family, might be dangerous and not only adversly affect the case, but put the agent in a perilous position.

One undercover agent, who spent a great part of his career working high-risk national security cases, told his family "If you see me on the street or in a public place, don't approach me. Instead, position yourself so I will see you. If I know it's safe to talk with you, I'll make contact." Other agents, such as the "biker" mentioned earlier, have made working undercover a family affair. In that example, he married his partner, and they continued to work undercover cases together. He has since moved into other areas of investigative endeavors, while his wife continues to work undercover. Other agents have responded by saying that their assignment is none of the family's business. That is a very short-sighted and selfish attitude. They may feel they are shielding the family from the stress and anxiety that comes with worrying about a loved one being in a potentially dangerous situation, but it calls into question suspicion and doubt about the undercover agent's sometimes strange activities and unusual comings and goings.

> All agents and officers working in sensitive positions (such as undercover work) should make their families aware of their potentially vulnerable employment and as a consequence the all should follow certain safety precautions such as being aware of strange cars, people, and circumstances. In one case an investigator, although he wasn't working undercover at the time, told his family he was working to arrest some very high-profile "biker" criminals. The group was noted for their capacity for violence and their total disregard for rules of society. He had instructed his family to be cautious and alert for

> strangers or anyone who appeared questionable. One morning the investigator's young son left home to walk to his nearby junior high school. Along the way he noted a strange car with two scruffy men parked on the street about a block from his house. The boy stopped at a nearby telephone booth and called his father who was still at home. The father then called the sheriff's department to check out the occupants of the suspicious car. The car contained several guns and the men were members of a local chapter of notorious social misfits that the father was investigating. It was determined that the men were planning to assassinate the investigator that morning as he left for work. This alert young boy saved his father's life.

The undercover agent's family should be advised, aware, and alert, but they should not be concerned to the point of unecessary paranoia. That is where the line of advising the family of the agent's occupation must be guided by common sense. The family should be knowledgeable that the agent is working in a position that shouldn't be freely discussed outside the family or beyond the point that he is working in a critical occupation.

Q: What is it like to work undercover?

A: Have you ever jumped from an airplane at 10,000 feet? You have packed your own parachute and that it was examined by the jumpmaster, and everything should be all right. But during those seconds of free-fallling as the wind whips past your face at over 100 miles per hour and your body is spinning as you see the Earth rushing up to meet you, there is time to worry about all the things that can go wrong. But it is really too late to eventhink about it because there is no turning back! When the parachute pops open and you look up to see that big canopy slowing your speed of decent, you breathe a little easier, but you don't relax. As your feet touch earth and you have executed a perfect landing, the exhilaration is beyond belief and you can't wait to try it again.

That is the ride you get working undercover work. You have prepared for the assignment, made plans for every conceivable contingency (but be aware of Murphy's Law — if anything can go wrong...). You fret that the unforeseen and unplanned could occur at any moment threatening the success of the case or placing you in imminent danger. When the arrest of the suspects is made and the case enters the final phase, the feelings of wrapping up a successful case and knowing that this time you did everything right, makes you want to do it again and the ebullience rivals winning the Lottery.

Q: What should an agent do if he is riding in a car with a suspect and the suspect detects a surveillance.

A: Very often the suspect will mention to the agent that he thinks he's being followed. He will then test to see if the car behind him really is following him by trying to shake his tail — stopping, double-parking, turning onto a one-way street, speeding, jumping a red light, or anything else that may come to mind at the time. Some people being followed have been known to wait until they come to a dip in the road where a car seemingly disappears from sight for a minute. During that brief period of time the driver makes a sudden U-turn in the street and proceeds in the direction from which he was coming. Any following cars have to either continue ahead or also make a quick turnaround. Either way the suspect either detects the following car or loses it.

If it is obvious to the agent, as well as the suspect, that they are being followed, he should agree with the suspect that there is a surveillance. He should then request the suspect to drop him off as quickly as possible because he feels he is not in a position to be questioned by the police. He can say it is because he is carrying contraband or because he is on parole or some such excuse. He can even say something to the effect that the District Attorney's office is looking to serve him with papers for delinquent child support. Under no conditions should he insist that they are not being followed. This would only tend to make the suspect suspicious of the agent.

Q: Is it a good idea to try to meet a suspect without the use of an informant?

A: Yes, if it can be done its a great idea. I find it is almost impossible to meet the suspect without an informant unless the undercover agent spends a great deal of time in the area where the suspects are known to operate. In most of our cases we don't have the luxury of time and manpower to invest in a case that may bring nebulous results. In the event it can be done, a lot of time, effort, and stress are saved in trying to protect and safeguard the informant.

> In a case worth mentioning, I was to meet a suspect in the lobby of a motel at a certain hour. The case was in the mid-west and someone else was handling the informant. When I arrived in the city, somehow the time element had become all fouled up. The suspect was to arrive at the motel looking for me at 2:00 P.M. Rushing quickly, I could just barely arrive by 1:00 P.M, not allowing much time for settling in or to be briefed. The informant was also to arrive at 2:00 P.M. The only information I had was a very basic description of the informant,

whom I had never met, and the informant had told the suspect that my name was Felix Marlowe.

When I arrived at the motel and was checking in under the name of Felix Marlowe, I found that "Felix Marlowe" was being paged. I also learned that the suspect was in the bar waiting for the informant and me. I proceeded to the bar and asked the bartender for the man paging Felix Marlowe. He pointed out a man named Alex who was sitting at a corner table where he could observe all the people who entered the bar. I walked over and introduced myself to him. We had a short, very casual, and carefully worded, conversation. After about 10 minutes, the informant finally arrived. As I had never met him and only had a general description, I took a chance that the person was indeed the informant. I met him halfway across the room and was able to whisper to him, out of earshot of the suspect, and tell him who I was. The informant was quite upset at the way things were progressing, but he settled down after we all shared a few drinks. However, the prospect of making a case didn't appear to be too promising.

This case was fouled up and was going wrong from the very beginning. However, I thought it would be interesting to carry it along to see how it came out. The suspect in this case had excellent connections in spite of the fact he was merely a cheap street thug. All of the dealers in this particular counterfeit note case made sure that enough money was advanced by any distributor so that in the event of a robbery "rip-off" or arrest the people who controlled the distribution would not lose anything.

The conversation at the bar dealt with the delivery of $50,000 in counterfeit currency. This wasn't a problem for Alex, but he wanted the "buy money" in advance. I told him I couldn't possibly do that because the people who controlled the good money would hold me responsible in the event anything went wrong. I told him I would be inclined to gamble and trust him if the genuine money were mine, but that the stakes were too high and I couldn't risk it with someone else's money. I implied that these people would put me in a very tight squeeze if anything happened to their money and if I didn't return with the counterfeit notes. We argued for about an hour and a half, but couldn't come to any terms. I finally told him to forget the whole deal; that I was going back to New York the next morning and maybe I'd come back another time when I had my own money and we could do business on better terms. We parted company and the several agents, who had been covering the activities, and I went to our rooms. I went to bed at about 1:00 AM.

About two hours later, I was awakened by loud a knocking at the door. I asked who it was. The reply was "Alex." I asked him what he wanted and he said, "Let me in! I have something for you!" I wasn't in any position to make a buy at that time. I didn't have the genuine money nor did I have a gun, and the other agents were asleep in their rooms and unavailable to make the arrest. there was also the possibility that he was going to try to rob me of the genuine money he thought I had. I told him I'd meet him in the lobby after I got dressed. He became very agitated and wanted to know if I was crazy or something. He insisted that he had something for me and this was no time to play games. No matter what I told him, he wouldn't go away. I stalled by saying I was getting dressed. He became even more irritated wanting to know why I had to get dressed before opening the door. In the meantime, I was on the house telephone calling the other agents who had rooms nearby. I told them to get into the hallway right away as I was about to let Alex into my room and I didn't know if it was a delivery or a robbery.

I waited a few more minutes then opened the door. Alex was one "mad hombre." He drew back his coat (I thought for sure he was going for a gun) and took a large package of counterfeit hundred dollar bills from his back pockets. While he was still swearing and calling me all kinds of names, I saw the agents approaching down the hall and told Alex, "Wait a second and I'll get the money." I stepped outside and motioned the agents to enter my room. They did and Alex was arrested.

This particular venture had everything go wrong from the very beginning. However it was just one of those cases that are destined to work out no matter how badly things were handled. Frankly, I never expected Alex to return, let alone come to my room to make a delivery and I could see no way he could get the merchandise without payment in advance. I later learned that a little greed goes a long way. He went way overboard to convince the people to give him the money on consignment. He called in old favors and opened old sores about the times he had been a "stand-up guy" keeping his silence on several previous arrests and how his family was not taken care of while he was serving time. He had also told the suppliers that the buyer was related to him and that he knew his relative had all the money necessary to make the purchase. He had gone way out on a limb —with a saw in his hand. He could never explain why it was necessary for him to lie about the buyer being a relative. I guess he was just greedy enough to want to clinch the sale regardless of not having the money in advance.

Q: Is it a good idea to meet the informant other than at the federal office or police station.

A: Most of the time, the informant will tell you where he would like to meet you. On the surface it might be safe to say that an informant should always be met a long way from the official headquarters. However, there are times when there is no danger in the informant meeting the agent in the office. There are many factors that have to be taken into consideration. Do the informant and his friends come from the same city as where the agent's office is located? Would the informant normally have legitimate business in that particular building? Sometimes, the informant has an arrest hanging over him and he would naturally be called to the courthouse on various occasions. It would suffice to say that the informant could best answer this question and he should be asked on the first contact if he has any objection to coming to the agent's office.

In one particular instance, an informant knew he was being followed by some of his associates. Nevertheless, in spite of that fact, he went straight to the federal building in New York City and went to another agency where he had judicial action pending as a result of another arrest. When he left the building, he made a point of seeing his friends on the street and letting them know that this agency wanted him to cooperate with them. He told his friends that agents from that agency were harassing him and he didn't want them coming to his house, so he always came to the federal building whenever they wanted to see him. The associates accepted this explanation and on all the other trips he made to the Federal building he never worried about being followed. This may or may not have been a good idea, but it worked, and the informant went on to make cases for several agencies thereafter.

In another case, the informant was a very high-ranking member of an organized crime group and it would have been sheer folly to have him come to the federal building. Elaborate plans were made to see this man miles and miles away from New York City and its surrounding areas. As time went on, he became more and more careless, even sloppy, about where he would meet the federal agents. He had a business and finally made the back of his store the meeting place for all the agencies he was cooperating with. No amount of caution could convince him that it was dangerous to have meetings on his premises. He was certain that he could talk himself out of any situation and he feared no one. He had an attitude of immortality and his high ranking in his organization and his even larger ego had him convinced that he could continue his double life with impunity.

One day three men went into his place of business and took care of their business — they emptied their handguns into his head and left as quickly as they arrived. Perhaps this was meant to be, but it is a prime example of an informant being his own worst enemy. This man didn't inform because he was a good citizen or a repenter; he was faced with a 15-year sentence for a crime in which he was responsible. His cooperation had reduced the sentence to probation. That was also dangerous and a red flag to his underworld cohorts, but he insisted on "calling his own shots." And eventually it was uncalled shots that ended his life of informing once and for all.

Q: How close should an agent get to an informant personally? Doesn't a certain amount of bonding occur?

A: This is a very difficult question. It depends upon many factors and the informant — why he is informing and what does he expect in return. Sometimes when two people work closely together, they form a mutual professional respect and personal regard for each other. An agent wouldn't want to invite an informant over to his house for dinner, but he may want to share some conversation over a cup of coffee and a sandwich. Sometimes the relationship continues long after the informant has no further material to share with the agent and an agent may take a personal interest in the general welfare of the informant. Of course the agent must have a professional concern for the informant in that he is not placed in jeopardy by the negligence or errors of the agent. Sometimes, an agent can't wait to say good-by to an informant after a case is completed, but there is nothing wrong, with establishing a long-term relationship with an informant. There are certain caveats to be concerned with when dealing with an informant and among them is a caution to be aware of certain barriers that must always be in place. There is a thin line over which you must never step. That line is almost indefinable, but a professional agent will be aware of it and never step over. Many agents and police officers have experienced the professional and personal pain of becoming too familiar with an informant, especially one of the opposite sex.

Q: To what extent should an agent or agency share an informant with another agency?

A: If an informant has knowledge about many crimes other than the one under the jurisdiction of the agency to which he is reporting, it is important that he be seen often. Frequent meetings are maintained in an effort to get the information on other crimes, which could easily be more important than the one he is reporting to you. There is no naivete about cooperation. It is very strongly felt that all agencies should cooperate to the fullest and make information supplied by informants known to the agency having jurisdiction over that particular crime. Unfortunately, this is not always the case. Some agencies only question the informant about what involves their own agency and wink at the other violations that would be of interest to another agency. It is not necessary to make the informant available to the other agency, but the information definitely should be forwarded. If the informant doesn't want to work with the other agency, he should be interviewed in depth and the information turned over to the other agency. If, on the other hand, the informant has no objection to working with the other agency, he should be introduced to one of their agents and be allowed to work for them. If the informant will not work with anyone except the agent handling him, this can be explained to the other agency. Very often the original undercover agent can work for both agencies. This has been done many times in the past when intelligent professional supervisors got together and "cut through the red tape" that inevitably occurs when two law enforcement agencies try to work together.

> We had received information about two men who were attempting to sell counterfeit money. The source of the information was of questionable reliability and during the course of the preliminary investigation we could not uncover any evidence that these men were engaged in any counterfeiting activities. Both men continually bragged about their criminal activity and were feared by many of their fellow "hoods." Both men were about the same age, somewhere in their mid-30s. Rocco was the larger of the two; his partner was called Tonito. No one could remember when either of them had worked at a legitimate job, but they both always seemed to have plenty of "walking-around" money and seemed to meet their obligations.
>
> One night there was a professional boxing match at Madison Square Garden. Rocco and Tonito managed to get tickets for the fight. As usual, they took bets and could be considered as part-time bookmakers. Sometime that evening they met a former fighter who was considered a washed-up, over-the-hill, hanger-on. His nickname was "One-Round Benny" because he never failed to get knocked out in the first round.
>
> During the course of the conversation that evening, Benny mentioned to Rocco that he was anxious to get some counterfeit money. Rocco, spotting an easy mark, said he could get him all the counterfeit money he wanted. Benny said he would contact a few friends and

get enough money to make a sizeable purchase. Rocco and Tonito made arrangements to meet Benny the following evening. Benny was quite happy because he was able to get more money from his friends than he had originally anticipated. The three met at a neighborhood bar and had a conversation and left.

Two days later, Benny's body was found just off the highway approximately 60 miles from New York City. He had been shot at close range in the back of the head and was dumped only a few yards from the roadway. The State Police investigated the case and before long Rocco and Tonito became the principal suspects.

Because the case originated with a discussion about counterfeit money, the State Police investigators called to brief me about the investigation. I informed the investigators that we had recently obtained information that Rocco and Tonito were attempting to get orders for counterfeit money but we could not associate them with any particular note. I requested that I be advised when they were arrested and be allowed to interview them about their alleged counterfeiting activities.

A few days later I received a telephone call from the state police that both men were to be arrested and taken to the local state police headquarters. I arrived at the state police office shortly after the arresting officers who had Rocco and Tonito in custody. I was not present while the homicide investigators interviewed them but when the police were finished, the two men were placed in another interview room where I was allowed to interview them. I pulled up a chair and showed both men my credentials and introduced myself. I told them I was a Treasury Agent interested in counterfeit money, not robbery, murders, or larceny. My job was to suppress counterfeiting. Rocco took the lead and answered most of my questions. He said they had met Benny and he wanted counterfeit money. They told Benny they could get him some and quoted him a price. They made a deal and agreed to meet the next evening. Neither Rocco nor Tonito had a connection for counterfeit money. When Benny showed up with his money they went for a ride and during the ride, they "took him."

I asked if they had any plans to get the counterfeit money and both said "No" That ended the conversation. I wrote a report on my short conversation and gave the state police a copy. Both men eventually pled 'not guilty' and a trial was held charging both with murder. I was very surprised when I was subpoenaed to testify because I had the impression both men had confessed. The District Attorney trying the case said my interview with the prisoners was the most important

> part of the whole prosecution. My actual testimony didn't take long. However, the defense cross-examined me in great detail. No matter of how they approached it, it was always the same. Both men had admitted to me that they had set up a deal for counterfeit money with Benny and that when the deceased came up with the buy money they "took him." Much time was spent on what was meant by they "took him." I stated that I interpreted it to mean that they took Benny's money and possibly his life. I later learned that the jury could not agree on a verdict, so a mistrial was declared. A second trial was held and the jury declared both men guilty of manslaughter in the first degree. They were sentenced to fifteen to 35 years each in the New York State Prison.

While this case did not take any counterfeit money from the streets, it did put away two murderers for a long time. It is a trade-off that should be taken every time. Cooperation between agencies has untold benefits. This case actually occurred just prior to the advent of the Miranda Warning in the early 1960s. But it is indicative of the continued cooperation between agencies and police departments that is very much in evidence today and which is probably even more popular then when this case was being investigated.

Q: Is it a good idea to write down everything an informant tells you?

A: There are times when a law enforcement officer has to take out his notepad and write down the entire interview he has with a witness or possible suspect. However, when talking to an informant, it is a very bad form to whip out a notebook and start writing. That may be intimidating to the informant. Most informants will then be fearful they will be held to everything they say. A better idea is for the undercover agent to have an informal conversation with the informant, possibly in a restaurant or some other neutral location, and just get to know each other. After the conversation has concluded, the officer should return to the office and prepare a memorandum reconstructing the conversation, at least the pertinent details. If there are addresses and telephone numbers that he needs, the agent can obtain them from the informant at a later date, or he can make casual notes without drawing too much attention to that fact. The agent must de-emphasize anything that might draw the informant's attention away from the conversation. Regardless of what an informant tells an officer in their meetings (especially the initial meeting), the officer should act like a priest in a confessional. He shouldn't show any emotion such as surprise or elation. He must maintain a professional image as though he has heard it all before and nothing is a shock to him anymore.

An actual conversation between a rather new agent and an informant went something like this:

Informant: "I know where there's a lot of counterfeit money."
Agent: " Yeah? Like how much?'
Informant: "At least a million dollars"
Agent: "Wow! No kidding? A million dollars? Man, I never saw that much money in my whole life. Let's go and get it. It'll be the biggest case we ever make!"
Informant: "Wait a minute. A lot of heavy people are involved in this."
Agent: Like who?"
Informant: " Pete 'Irish-eyes' White, Horsey 'Gotta Tip' Phillips, and Joe 'Cat' Cataldo."
Agent: "Who are they?'
Informant: "Guys who are all Mafia-connected and heavily involved."
Agent: "Wow! Lemme at em., If you can get me those guys and that money, I'll be on my way! Jeez, I'd give anything to make a case like that!"
Informant: "Well, I can do it, but its gonna cost you …."

We can spend an entire chapter laughing about the mistakes that this agent was making in handling the informant. In the first place, he was too emotional. When he heard the estimate of "a million dollars" he got overexcited and showed his enthusiasm to the informant. When he mentioned that this was probably "the biggest case we'll ever make," he was practically telling the informant to ask for the biggest reward they ever paid. He asked the informant for the names of the people involved, then admitted he never heard of them. He couldn't contain his delight and excitement when the informant mentioned that they were all "Mafia connected. " As the conversation went on, the informant also got carried away with his own importance because of the actions of the agent and it was not long before he was trying to run the whole case. It became necessary to bring in a more experienced agent to work with the informant. It was explained to him that the first agent was relatively new and this case required a more experienced person. It took hours to correct the errors of the first agent. The first agent would have been better served if he had just obtained the facts and reported them to his supervisor before becoming so animatedly excited. Even then he should have tempered his excitement with a little more calm and a lot more restraint. It is interesting to note that this particular informant was merely a big talking braggart and the case he was so wrapped up in proved to be very insignificant. He was paid far more than the information or case were worth and never provided useful information again.

Q: How do you select the right person for a particular undercover case?

A: There are no magic formulas or wands to wave. The only rule of thumb is to try to place the person that is best compatible for the job by virtue of his talents, ability, interests, and confidence level for a particular assignment. There is no such thing as "an undercover agent," only undercover assignments. Some assignments last for a few hours or days; others last for considerable periods of time. It is not unusual for agents in the Secret Service to work undercover cases in the daytime, associating with criminals, informants, pimps and prostitutes and then be assigned to protecting the President of the United States that night. Headquarters in Washington D.C. selects many Secret Service undercover agents by reviewing reports from the offices where the agents have worked, their education, and personnel profile forms specifying any unique qualifications. The criteria is to select a person who would feel comfortable in or be able to adapt to a variety of environments. There are some officers and agents who have a hard time doing undercover work, but are still very important to the success of the case. They may be very skilled at other aspects of the operation such as surveillance or administration details like logistics or planning, and participating in the arrest and interview phase. They may be assigned as a secondary undercover agent in the role of the undercover agent's driver, "bodyguard," or apprentice.

In some agencies undercover personnel are selected from a list of people who have requested the assignment and the opportunity to work undercover. Many counties have special squads of undercover agents drawn from local police departments. These people get an opportunity to work in areas in which they are unknown. In some small towns police officers get very little opportunity to work undercover unless their department joins a larger organization. This plan has worked successfully in many jurisdictions. These days, some agencies have officers and agents who are only in their early 20s and are young-looking enough to work undercover on college campuses and high schools.

In the corporate and industrial world, undercover agents are selected to gather specific information relative to theft, waste, sabotage, or use of illegal substances among many other reasons an employer feels he needs an undercover operative. The undercover agent is selected in the same manner as any other employee. In addition to his ability to conduct undercover investigations he must also be able to complete any labor task assigned to him. For instance, working in a warehouse or manufacturing plant, he may be required to operate a forklift, a crane or a milling machine. Whatever the undercover assignment, the agent must have marketable and proficient skills in the area of his assignment.

As a supervisor you know the particular talents, personalities, and aptitudes of the team working for you. Some individuals are best at working with a particular ethnic group. They seem to instinctively understand the cultural nuances like mannerisms, bravado, language, or speech patterns and even the subtle body language better than most. Some agents just couldn't fit into some subcultures such as very right-wing neo-nazi groups or "outlaw" motorcycle gangs. There are agents who, for certain reasons, can only work the smaller cases. Conversely, there are agents who, because of looks, dress, attitude, etc., can work only the big or major cases. With any group of individuals, each person's particular niche soon becomes apparent to an observant supervisor. There are times when an agent is selected only because he has never been involved in a particular area and would be unknown to the people he would be working with. Sometimes manpower availability will dictate using whatever agent is at hand. In many instances, it is suggested to let the informant select the person he'd like to work with. Generally his suggestion is excellent. He will usually choose someone he is compatible with and feels comfortable working with. He also knows how well a certain person will fit in with the group he is attempting to penetrate. Letting an informant determine who he will be working with in the undercover assignment has another, more esoteric, side benefit. If for any reason the case doesn't succeed, the agent or supervisor won't have to listen to the informant telling them that the case failed because the wrong agent was chosen for the job.

Q: If you trust an informant, how much should you tell him about the case?

A: You have to be very careful about telling an informant about any case. Whether you trust him or not, you should not give him information unless it is important that he needs this information to successfully work the case. He should be informed only on a need to know basis and only when the time is appropriate. To give him any additional information serves no purpose other than to make him knowledgeable and put him in a position to bargain, perhaps with the other side. There was a (non-police) case in which an undercover agent trusted the informant like his best friend. In fact they had known each other for years before the informant came forward with certain sensitive information. He gave the information to the undercover agent who wrote a report detailing the information. Then the undercover agent made a costly, nearly fatal mistake. He let his friend read the report and check it for accuracy. The friend made a copy and left it where it was found by a less scrupulous person who sold a copy to the target of the investigation. Any information given to an informant can, and will, find a way to come back and "bite" the undercover agent. To sum it all up in a manner that is easy to understand and remember— an informant should give information to the police, the police are not supposed to give information to the informant!

Q: What do you think of a hearing aid or a similar indicator of physical impairment as a prop?

A: Normally, a hearing aid shouldn't make anyone too suspicious, unless he is very knowledgeable and knows that a hearing aid could be converted into a transmitter and used as a technical police device. The use of such "props" has been exploited many times in the movies and television to the point that any cautious suspect would be concerned when he saw such a device. The undercover agent would have to be fully prepared to field questions from the suspect about the device such as the extent of the physical impairment, how long has it existed, can the agent function without it, etc. He may also want to examine it and ask technical questions.

Beyond the technical aspects and the questions, assume an agent uses such a prop, he is successful and that particular group learns they have been victimized. It is not difficult to imagine how much success the next undercover agent will have if he decides to employ a similar device. Anything in this category of props is considered as a "one shotter." If used successfully on a case, it should be a long time before it is used again.

Q: At the conclusion of a successful undercover operation, who receives the credit for the case?

A: Like it or not, statistics are a necessary tool in police work as well as in any other business. They are the barometer by which the success of the organization is measured. All police agencies are involved with a battle of the budget and must justify the use of their financial resources. In this sense, statistics are very important. In an undercover case, many people go into the success of the case. The informant, the case agent, the covering agents, the arresting agents, and finally the undercover agent are all a part of the team that put the case together. Regardless of how the credits are distributed, the undercover agent will always be singled out as the person who gets the lion's share of credit. Undercover work captures the imagination of everyone, including the defendants, the judge and jury, the district attorney, the public, and the press. The undercover agent takes the greatest risks and naturally will receive the most credit. There is usually enough backslapping, congratulations, and recognition to go around for everyone and credit should be given to the entire group. To make a successful case, the entire team must function smoothly and know exactly what to do under any set of circumstances and always be in a position to protect the undercover agent at any time during the case. Statistical credit, therefore, should be allotted in such a manner as to reflect the efforts of all participants.

Q: Suppose you are working an undercover counterfeit case and the suspect shows you a genuine article not the contraband as a sample. Should you let him know that you are aware the sample is genuine?

A: Not right away. Nothing would be gained by letting him know that you are an expert in detecting whether items are genuine or counterfeit. It might make him suspicious that you know more than you should. He might then suspect that you are an agent. There's no harm in remarking that the sample looks very good and you hope that the rest that are delivered is of the same high quality. He has a reason for showing you the genuine article. It may be that he cannot get samples and has no intention of delivering the contraband to you. The material that he intends to deliver may be of such poor quality he is afraid that you might not buy them if you saw one of the samples. Showing you genuine samples might put him in a position of asking a much higher price because the merchandise is so good. There was an occasion of note where it became necessary to let the seller know that the samples were genuine.

> I met with the suspect in an upstate motel. He was a legitimate businessman who was 90% legitimate and 10% thief. He was acting as a commission man, a broker, between a group of known thieves and myself. At first he was interested in selling stolen stock certificates as he had a Wall Street background and was very knowledgeable about stocks, bonds, T-bills, etc.
>
> Somewhere along the line, the people he represented told him they could get counterfeit money in any amounts. The switch to discussing counterfeit money was done abruptly, without any indications he was going to talk about it and I immediately became suspicious. This particular suspect and I didn't get along well from the beginning. His asking prices were always too high. He never produced anything of value and I began to suspect that while he was anxious to make a sale, the people behind him were trying to arrange a robbery. However, I told him I was interested in the counterfeit notes and he said that he would have some samples and prices for me the following day. He went into a long speech of how his people had invested a fortune in this scheme and were anxious to make a large sale.
>
> A day or two later, we met again in another motel and he showed me two brand new Federal Reserve notes. He pointed out that each bill bore the same serial number, and therefore were counterfeit. I examined the bills and immediately knew that they were genuine notes. They did bear identical serial numbers, however, I noted that the last digit of each serial number had been removed. These bills

were brand new and originally had consecutive numbers on them. One bill was numbered B80756701C and the other was B80756702C. By erasing the last digit in the number on each bill both bills would read B8075670 C. The extra space between the last number and letter would hardly be noticeable to anyone unfamiliar with money.

I was sure that this man was sincerely convinced that the notes were counterfeit. I agreed that they looked very good and tried to arrive at a price. He wanted something like 35 cents on the dollar in "lots" of $100,000. He wanted the buy money in advance and wanted to complete the sale immediately. We were arguing about the price when I received a telephone call from the covering agents. They advised me that there was a Cadillac full of "hoods" waiting near the entrance of the hotel and that they undoubtedly wanted to rob me if they were convinced that I had any large amount of money. Armed with this information, I went back to negotiating with the suspect in the room. He kept saying that these people had invested a fortune in making these notes and they had done it just for me and that I was obligated to do business with them —their way and as quickly as possible. I pretended to examine the samples and luckily I had two consecutively numbered notes in my own money. While he was talking, I made it appear that it suddenly struck me that there was a swindle brewing. I turned to him and asked, "How much did your people invest in this set up?" He said "a small fortune." I then opened the desk, took out a pencil with an eraser and proceeded to erase the last number on the bills I had in my possession. When I finished, I theatrically threw the bills in his face and said, "What your people invested was exactly 50 cents for an eraser and one minute of their time!" I then grabbed him by the throat and tried to get him to admit that he was part of the swindle. He assured me he wasn't and began to worry that his people were up to something.

He said he'd have a hard time convincing the people that I didn't want the counterfeit money. He felt reasonably sure that this was, in fact, a planned holdup, and being a businessman, he didn't want to become involved. He finally left my room a shaken man and went back to the people in the Cadillac with a story that he didn't trust me and that no deal could be arranged.

The "mob" "hit him up for a good piece of change," supposedly for the trouble they went through. We maintained good relations with the suspect and eventually another agency caught him dealing in stolen stock certificates. He and his associates were arrested during the delivery of over a million dollars worth of stolen stocks.

Information eventually sifted to us that the counterfeiting scheme was just that and there was no intention of delivering counterfeit money. They thought they could pull a robbery on a man in a motel room and because he was engaged in an illegal venture that he probably wouldn't report it to the police.

Q: Would it be proper to let an informant know that another person in the case is an informant and is supplying information on the same case?

A: Most definitely NOT! This topic was strongly addressed previously. An informant should be used for the purpose of obtaining information and should never be in a position where he is getting information from the agency he is working with. If you told him that another person is giving you information as well, he may suppose that you might reveal his cooperation to that other person at some point in time. He might also find an occasion and opportunity that would benefit him to identify that other person to the suspects. Most informants will respect the fact that you will not give them any information and that you are noncommittal about anyone else giving you information.

Q: Is there ever a time when it becomes necessary to drop an informant?

A: I am sure that everyone has had the experience where they feel an informant is not worth working with or that sometime in the past he has double-crossed them and they reach a point where they will not work with him under any circumstances. This is a very rare occurrence and may happen only once or twice in an entire career. An informant shouldn't be dropped for what he has done in the past, but only if the information he is giving is not true or he is merely trying to buy time to forestall a pending judicial action or imprisonment. There is no way of telling if an informant is being truthful with you. You have to listen and evaluate what he tells you and match that with what you already know or can confirm and then arrive at a decision as to whether you can trust him or not. Past performances will play an important part in your decision, but shouldn't be the determining factor.

Our office knew Juan for about 5 years. He was an addict who came around to the office when he was really desperate for money. He invariably came to the office with stories about counterfeit note distribution in his neighborhood, however, he was never able to bring in a counterfeit note or any kind of a sample to show what was being sold in his area. Each time he came to the office he would manage to get a few dollars for expenses and generally nothing ever came of the information that he gave us. It soon became apparent to the agents working with him that he was becoming a nuisance and a "con man" who would invent stories just to get a little pocket money.

One day he called the office and asked to have an agent meet him as he had some valuable information. As Juan was not held in very high regard at this time it is doubtful that any veteran agent would have responded to his request to meet him several miles away. However, the telephone was answered by a relatively new agent who took time out to identify the informant and felt perhaps there was something to his urgent call. Because no one else was available to meet Juan, the agent decided he would meet with him. Juan not only had counterfeiting information, but he also had several samples and a list of names of the people involved and he was also in a position to introduce a Spanish-speaking agent to the group as a potential buyer. Juan had decided to leave the country and was going to try to make a new start in his home country and was letting all caution fall to the wind. His information was good and a counterfeiting conspiracy case was made and a very deceptive note was put out of circulation very early. It was fortunate that the agent trusted his own insticts and handled the matter without relying on past informant performance.

Q: Is there any advantage to having a delivery made in a location away from where the suspect normally operates?

A: Changing cities provides an ideal situation for the undercover agent. Taking the suspect away from his home base reduces his power position and places him in a vulnerable situation. In his hometown he probably knows most of the local police by sight. In the event he sees something he doesn't like, he will likely have contacts who will have no trouble checking it out. In the event of an arrest he can communicate with friends and relatives to arrange bail and release from jail. He can also readily obtain legal aid and advise from his associates and friends. All these advantages are turned to disadvantages when he is arrested in a strange city. It is amazing how often a person is refused help by his associates when he is arrested out of town. Very often, they will even resent the telephone call from the suspect as they fear the police are listening or will be able to trace back to the telephone number dialed long distance and may attempt to tie them into the particular crime. When violators languish in jail, especially in a strange city where there are no visitors and no word reaching them from friends or associates, they soon give some thought to cooperating with the authorities. Psychologically they begin to feel they "have been thrown to the wolves" and they have nothing to gain by keeping quiet. They begin to believe that perhaps some of their own friends gave them up and begin the rationalization for cooperation.

> I was assigned to a city in the Southwest to work with an informant on a counterfeiting case. This particular informant was high in the hierarchy of the underworld in the particular area and an introduction from the man was all that was needed to make a successful case. This particular informant had a spacious home with servants, plenty of money, and all the trappings of a very successful businessman.
>
> That year he gave a Christmas party at his home and invited a lot of people to attend the festivities. I was also invited and during the course of the evening, the informant gave me a casual introduction to the suspect. We managed to establish rapport and become friendly. Before the evening was over, the suspect let it be known that he could get large amounts of counterfeit money. I told him I was going back East and would like to take a couple of thousand dollars with me. He said he could arrange it as he had several thousand in his car. He went out and I met him in the basement of the home where the party was being held. We negotiated a sale with no trouble at all. He then gave me his home telephone number and told me to call him at any time.
>
> After the party was over, I talked to the informant and let him know that a buy had been consummated. The informant made sure to never mention my name in the future, and was laying the groundwork to let it be known that someone else brought me to the party.
>
> A few weeks later, I called the suspect and told him that my people were interested in $150,000 worth of notes and asked him if he could get them. He said it would be no trouble and I could go out there any time to pick them up. I told him my people wanted delivery in New York City and that they would pay the expenses to effect a delivery there. He said that he didn't think he could arrange the delivery in New York. I gave him a telephone number where he could reach me and he said he would call me back.
>
> When he called back he said that he thought he could make the delivery in New York City. He said his girlfriend and another couple wanted to take a trip to New York and he thought he could bring the notes with him and mix business with pleasure. I told him that was fine and promised to get him tickets for shows, nightclubs, etc.
>
> A few days later, the suspect arrived in town, registered at a local hotel, and then called me. My "chauffeur" and I met them the foursome at the hotel. They were all were conversant about the counterfeit

money they had brought and were anxious to swing a deal so they could go out and enjoy themselves.

One of our Chinese agents had arranged with some Chinese friends to borrow the upstairs room in their restaurant in Chinatown. It was very easy to tell the suspects that we were going out for a Chinese dinner and that the owner of the restaurant was the man putting up the money for the counterfeits. The party was delighted and they accepted a lift from my chauffeur to take them down to Chinatown. In the meantime, all was in readiness for them. The outer perimeter covered the street outside the restaurant and also the downstairs portion of the premises. The owner of the restaurant, and several agents posing as part of the syndicate were upstairs preparing for the banquet surprise.

Before coming downtown to meet me, the group of suspects went to a public garage and retrieved the counterfeit money from the back of their rental car. They then accompanied my man on the trip downtown. They arrived on schedule and upon entering the restaurant, were escorted upstairs to meet "the buyers." Needless to say, an arrest was made at our leisure as the suspects were pretty well boxed in.

They were put in a federal detention facility for the night and the next day spent several futile hours trying to get in touch with friends and to arrange bail. For some reason, help wasn't forthcoming and 24 hours after they were arrested, they wanted to make a deal. They made it very clear that the only reason they were cooperating was because they were in a strange town and their friends from back home had apparently abandoned them. Their cooperation was accepted and a deal was worked out. Again, several cases were made and eventually the plant was seized and the manufacturers were arrested.

The point here was that the cooperation was offered solely because they felt they had been abandoned. If the arrest had been made in their hometown, they wouldn't have had any trouble arranging for a bondsman, lawyer, etc. It is interesting to note that aside from the person who checked them into the hotel, every other person they met was a law enforcement official. When the arrest was made and they saw the big picture, they realized how hopeless the situation was and fully cooperated.

The informant in this case also came out perfectly clean. When questioned about me, he said that he only met me for the first time at his home to which I had been brought by a mutual friend. The informant told the suspects that he resented being questioned because, apparently, they had what they thought was a lucrative deal going and he wasn't told about it nor were they going to give him his cut. This was a case where just about everything turned out good for the "good guys."

Q: How about a case where everything doesn't work out for the "good guys?

A: Working undercover is a risky business. As much depends on luck as on anything. Regardless of all the precautions that are taken to ensure an undercover agent's safety, there are always unforeseen events and situations that can't be predicted. We can choose an agent for undercover work in an area that he has never been before. He can be supplied with all the necessary cover, he can work with a reliable, tried and tested informant, and still the case fails, sometimes even before it begins. On some occasions, the reasons for failure are obvious. These failures occur because of a factor that can't be controlled — the human element. There is always the possibility of the agent being recognized by someone whose presence could not have been anticipated in the original planning.

> Maximillian (Max) Gordon was a racketeer of some repute in the New York area. He had been arrested and convicted many times and was considered a "three-time loser" which meant, like the "three strikes law," one more conviction would send him to prison for the remainder of his life. He had a reputation for handling large amounts of many kinds of contraband. He knew he was a target of investigation by both local and federal authorities in the New York area so he was very careful to avoid the next arrest that could mean a life term.
>
> I had recently completed working an undercover case with a very reliable informant. This informant had many contacts in the criminal community and he was anxious to make cases against all of them. He hoped to get enough money from the rewards to leave the area for good and start a new life. The case we had just finished working was a large counterfeiting case and his reward was about $2000. On this particular occasion, he asked me if I knew Max Gordon. I told him I knew his reputation, but that I had never met him and I was positive Max didn't know me. The informant related to me that he had learned that Max was handling counterfeit money and he thought he could make arrangements for me to meet him. We agreed to proceed with a plan to work an undercover operation against Max.
>
> The informant suggested that at precisely 8:00 P.M. on the following Tuesday, I should make it my business to be in a certain midtown bar. He stated that at about that time he would be with Max and several of Max's friends. He knew that at that time Max

and his friends would arrive at the bar for a meeting in a back room with a number of his associates. The plan was for me to sit at the end of the bar near the door to the back room. When Max, his friends, and the informant came in, the informant would recognize me as an old friend he hadn't seen in years. He would then introduce me to Max and the others and invite me into the back room. He would indicate to Max that I was someone who could dispose of any kind of contraband. The informant was sure Max would then offer to sell me either drugs or counterfeit money. Everything was set and in readiness for that night and at about 7:30 P.M. I entered the bar and sat down in the back corner as planned and ordered a drink, exactly according to plan.

A short while later, an obviously drunk man came in. When I got a good look at him, my heart sank as I recognized him as a former sergeant in the Marine Corps who had served under me several years earlier. He came from Missouri and was very much a 'red-neck" and I was at a loss to figure out what he was doing in New York City. I didn't have long to think about that though. I had been hoping in vain that he wouldn't see me, as he was a very loud character even when he was sober, but sure enough once he had surveyed each and every person at the bar he saw me. He immediately recognized me and waved his hand and shouted, "Hi, Captain." At first I paid no attention to him, but his loud shouts were obviously directed at me so I nodded back in recognition. He then staggered over to meand when he got close he said, "Remember me Captain?" I mumbled that he looked familiar. He immediately laughed and shouted, "Isn't it your business to recognize people. You're supposed to be the best hot-damned federal agent in the country. You must be working undercover or something. Yeah, I bet that's it. You are an undercover agent!" At this time, there was great scurrying in the bar as everyone left in a hurry. Suddenly the bar was empty except for the good sergeant and me. There was nothing left to do but drag the drunken, loud mouth, out of the bar and get away from there as fast as I could.

As we were leaving, I saw the informant arrive and enter the bar with Max and his friends, but I made no attempt to contact the informant.

The next day, he called me to say that it had been a good thing that I didn't meet him as we had planned. He said that when they went into the bar the bartender told Max that the place was surrounded with federal agents and there was going to be trouble. The bartender said one of the agents had posed as a drunk and he was sure they were still in the area. The informant said that Max and his

> friends were quite alarmed and left the place immediately. I told the informant that I too had noticed a lot of law in the vicinity and decided not to keep the appointment. I had blown the only opportunity I'd have to make a case against Maximillian Gordon.

I made several mistakes that night. The first one was in not grabbing the sergeant as soon as he entered the bar and explaining to him why he shouldn't be there. The second mistake was in taking a chance by coming early for the appointment and putting myself on display for an extra half hour. Perhaps it was best it ended that way. If I had arrived there on time and been introduced to Max and his friends, the sergeant could have come into the bar and there would have been trouble.

In the long run, nothing was really lost. Shortly thereafter, Max was arrested by the Drug Enforcement Agency (DEA) for the sale of drugs to an undercover agent and subsequently died in prison.

Q: How are the expenses controlled for "buy" money and other costs?
A: Funds used for undercover work are supplied by the agency. The supervisor determines an approximate budget and uses the money as needed. All expenses are justified, recorded and accounted for in a ledger that is open for inspection by higher authority. When working with someone else's money a good rule to follow is: "Handle the money like it belongs to the Mafia."

Q: Should an undercover agent wear a hidden transmitter?
A: This matter may be dictated by circumstances, agency policy, and preferences of the individual agent (or supervisor). A transmitter has advantages: it can provide a recording of all conversations for court purposes and, most importantly, it keeps the covering agents apprised of the progress of the meeting with the suspect and alerts them to possible danger to the undercover agent and of any unforeseen changes in plan. The most serious disadvantage is the possibility of detection of the device. With the sophistication and caution employed by many veteran and security-conscious criminals, there is a risk the undercover agent may have to undergo some type of screening.

> It was not uncommon just 15 or 20 years ago for an undercover agent to take the risk of wearing a body recorder or transmitter only to learn later that it had malfunctioned. There was a case in a large city in which a police detective lieutenant became the suspect in a counterfeiting case. His name surfaced when he passed two counterfeit $20 notes to purchase a tire for his personal car. An agent interviewed him and it was determined that he apparently obtained the bills either

at the bank or in some other transaction. A report was made and it was filed away.

Six months later another man, named Luke, was arrested for passing counterfeit notes. After extensive questioning he stated that a lieutenant in the police department had given him the notes. We checked the records and located the report that had been filed several months earlier. It was the same police lieutenant. We equipped Luke with a body recorder after he agreed to meet with the lieutenant to discuss some more counterfeit money. Our agents and members of the police internal affairs unit covered the meeting.

Luke and the lieutenant met at a restaurant and Luke paid him for the notes he had previously received and they had a long conversation about the counterfeits. After they parted company, Luke returned the recorder and reported his conversation with the lieutenant. However, when we attempted to playback the conversation, the tape recorder didn't work. When we opened it we found that the wire had misfed and we had nothing but a fistful of wire. The internal affairs supervisor sent the material to the manufacturer in an attempt to have the sound restored and the recording enhanced. The lieutenant learned that Luke had been wearing a recording device and at his trial pled guilty. He said that one day while cleaning out his locker he found the counterfeit bills which he had received in an old case. After being questioned about the two notes he had passed, he decided to sell the remaining notes. After the case was completed, I played the recording and I was happy that we didn't have to use it in trial. The recording was full of static and I doubt if a jury would have convicted the lieutenant.Today there are inconspicuous recorders and transmitters that utilize computer chips that are more reliable and powerful and make police work a lot easier by eliminating the potential for malfunction.

Q: How should an agent prepare for an undercover role?

A: Before any undercover case can commence, we must recognize that the person assigned to do the undercover work will have an enormous amount of things on his mind. In order to relieve the tensions, apprehensions, and stress, it always helps to have the supervisor sit down alone with the undercover agent and explain exactly what is expected of him. He should be advised that all undercover cases are not successful and many things can go wrong and through no fault of the agent the case can go completely wrong. If the agent doesn't have any prior experience with undercover work, he should be advised of the pitfalls that are always lurking nearby. It's always possible that someone may recognize the agent especially if the original introduction is made in a public place. The suspect could suddenly turn cold and everyone connected with the case will suddenly leave. Situations like this can't be helped. Before long, the informant will contact the agency and explain why the case suddenly went sour. Usually when the informant advises the agency of the problems, steps can be taken to correct them. Sometimes the suspect simply feels as though he is being followed. The next time a looser surveillance can be maintained on him. If the suspect doesn't feel comfortable with the agent, the agent can be replaced with another agent and the original plans and be completely revised.

When the agent understands the complexity of the case, it should then be arranged for the agent to have a long talk with the informant. The agent is well advised to question the informant about all the suspects in the case. He is to ascertain their modes of dress, their language, their life style, their education and anything else that will give the agent an inside perspective of what to expect from the suspects including the possibility and probability of them being armed. If possible the informant should tell the agent of any special interests, eccentricities, particular concerns and suspicions, habits, and associates of the suspect. If possible, he should learn the method of transportation and identify any vehicles the suspect is likely to use and the probable location where the deal might be completed. If the suspect was previously engaged in other sales by the suspect he should be able to give a good scenario of what can be expected to happen.

After this debriefing, both the agent and the informant should be left alone to work out cover stories and to get to know each other better. This relieves a lot of tension and worry regarding meeting and working with the informant without knowing anything about him.

> Some years ago I was assigned to work in an undercover capacity on a group that was papering the city with counterfeit $10s and $20s. We had an informant who was all set to introduce me to the suspects. At about that same time I received a telephone call from my sister who told me that she and my parents had moved out of Manhattan and into a two-family house on Long Island. She gave me the new address and I promised to visit her shortly.
>
> The informant was from out West somewhere and the next time he came to New York I sat down and had a long chat with him. He gave me the name of the suspect and his address. The address sounded familiar so I immediately checked my sister's address and found it was right next door to where the suspect lived. I explained the situation to the supervisor who arranged to send another agent in my place. The next day I visited my parents and sister in their new house. I told my sister about her neighbors and asked her why she

had decided to move. She stated that she wanted a quiet place for our parents and she liked the idea of living across the street from one of our cousins. She said that most of our relatives lived on Long Island and she chided me for losing contact with our relatives. I then went across the street to visit my cousin.

During our conversation she said that she had lived in the same house for over 20 years and knew everyone in the neighborhood. I asked her about my sister's next door neighbors. She said the Verde family were all O.K. except one brother — everyone called him "Blinky" because he had a problem with his eye. My cousin said that Blinky didn't work and had done been in prison. He also associated with a very bad group of people. Blinky was unmarried and was in his 40s and was always looking for a way to make a fast dollar. I asked my cousin if I could come every day to keep watch on the Verde house from her porch.

After the informant arrived we arranged to have him meet the new undercover agent on the case. He was from Los Angeles and he looked, dressed, and talked like the informant. They got along splendidly. I occupied my time watching the Verde house. I was able to see some of the meetings, get license numbers of cars that stopped at the house, and obtained descriptions of the people who visited. The case ended with the seizure of over a million dollars in counterfeit money. The defendants went to trial, they were convicted, and each received a 15-year sentence.

I hate to think what might have happened if the informant and I hadn't had that talk before he introduced me to Blinky. While he provided me with an enormous amount of related information, giving me the suspect's address saved the case and prevented my family and me from getting into a serious situation.

Q: It has been said that women make good informants. Do women also make good undercover agents?

A: History has provided many instances and names of women working in various and successful undercover capacities. What a male operative can accomplish is not beyond the capabilities of a woman. At least one example of the possible role of a woman in an undercover role has been previously related in the story of the "biker" and his girlfriend making a drug buy. The measure shouldn't be the undercover agent's sex but rather putting the right person in the right job. A male/female team is an excellent choice if circumstances warrant. Many cultures and subcultures will not allow a woman to participate in "business," as it is considered to be the mn's domain. But barriers are quickly falling in all occupations. It is no longer a surprise to see a female trucker or construction worker. If a woman has the willingness, ability, and qualifications the same as her male counterpart, there is no reason why she shouldn't work undercover.

Q: What are the legal considerations of undercover work?
A: The initial reaction to being arrested as the result of an undercover operation is to yell "Entrapment!" The suspect immediately says, "The police entrapped me." What he really means is, "I was found out and caught by the police." On closer examination, as is always common in cases that go to trial, it is found that the defendant had a "mental predisposition to commit the crime." In other words, the defendant would have engaged in the illegal activity whether an undercover agent had been introduced into the case or not.

Statutes defining entrapment as a positive defense are on the books in all state and federal governments. Most of the laws are similar to that of the New York State Penal Law (Chapter 40.05):

> "In any prosecution for an offense, it is an affirmative defense that the defendant engaged in the proscribed conduct because he was induced or encouraged to do so by a public servant, or by a person acting in cooperation with a public servant, seeking to obtain evidence against him for purpose of criminal prosecution, and when the methods used to obtain such evidence were such as to create a substantial risk that the offense would be committed by a person not otherwise disposed to commit it. Inducement or encouragement to commit an offense means active inducement or encouragement. Conduct merely affording a person an opportunity to commit an offense does not constitute entrapment."

An undercover agent shouldn't become overly concerned with the intricacies of the law. The primary thing to remember is that the agent may provide the opportunity, but not the original idea. When a suspect asks the undercover agent what he does for a living, a good reply is to say, "I buy and sell." The suspect then will ask, "Buy and sell what?" "I buy low and sell high." It is best to leave it to the suspect's imagination to use the words "counterfeit," "phony money," "bogus bills," etc. The same advice pertains to any undercover enterprise, drugs, computer equipment, etc.

An argument can be made for a charge of entrapment in some "decoy" situations such as a "passed-out drunk" on a park bench with money hanging out of his pocket. The line of argument is that a passerby wouldn't have given the "drunk" a second thought, but the sight of the money was a temptation that led to "boosting" it from his pocket. In instances where a warehouse has been set up for the purchase of stolen merchandise, the argument can again be made that the individual selling the material was merely taking advantage of an opportunity to make money by selling whatever he could. These are arguments for the courtroom and should not restrict the police from initiating operations that will lead to the arrest of criminal practitioners. An effective counter-argument is that the police were merely affording the thief or black marketeer the opportunity to engage in his preconceived illegal activity.

Police and other law enforcement officers are highly trained in all laws and court decisions that affect the limitations and range of undercover operations. In the non-law enforcement arena, surreptitious or clandestine investigations are commonly undertaken by a private investigator at the direction of a senior corporate executive. The undercover investigation usually involves the placement of an agent on the payroll of a commercial business for a specific purpose such as determining internal theft, drug dealing, etc. The investigator must be trained in undercover assignments but he must also be familiar with laws pertaining to his role. He must know about entrapment, of course, but he should also be trained in the areas of labor law, criminal law and procedures, controlled substances, and a whole range of legal categories similar to, perhaps exceeding, that of a police officer. He must also realize that he is working undercover in a non-law enforcement capacity and his liability for errors and omissions is not under the protective umbrella of peace officer status. As a private investigator, his duty is to the entity that hired him. He is not obligated by law or sworn to make an arrest. Nevertheless, to make a successful case he must follow procedures prescribed by law.

Q: When do you consider a case closed?

A: There are many ways to close a case, depending on the type of crime. In street crimes, the local police department often closes the case following an arrest. Some departments close the case when there are no more productive investigative leads to pursue. Other times a case is closed when the main suspect dies or is sent to prison for a long term. Closing cases is not a problem because just as soon as a potential lead emerges the case can be reopened just as quickly as it was closed.

> In New York City we had a Special Agent-in-Charge who wouldn't let you close a case until all potential leads had been followed and the suspect had been interviewed. I wasn't happy about going to a suspect and asking him if he was a counterfeiter. My first attempt was a complete disaster. I went to the man's house, showed him my

credentials, and asked him if he was a counterfeiter. His answer was "No!" I thanked him and left. When I reported back all the agent-in-charge would say was, "You'll learn. You'll learn."

On subsequent similar cases I changed my approach and many of them worked! I would identify myself and show my credentials and ask the man if he had any enemies. The man would answer, "I guess we all have enemies." I would then ask him if he ever handled counterfeit money. The answer was always, "No." He would then ask why we had singled him out. My answer was, "We keep getting calls that you are involved in passing or distributing counterfeit money." They usually gave me the names and addresses of the people who might be calling our office. I never had a man admit outright that he was involved with counterfeit money. But before our conversation was over, I usually had a notebook full of notes and very good intelligence that was useful in other matters.

One day I asked a suspect all the usual questions. All his replies were negative. Then he said, "I know who gave you my name. It's got to be "Crazy Mike." He lives around the corner, he is crazy as a coot and he writes to everyone including the police, the FBI, and even the President. He's crazy and he's gonna get into trouble yet. I don't trust that guy."

I obtained all the information I could on "Crazy Mike."I made enquiries in the neighborhood and everyone agreed that he was a bomb ready to explode. I checked with our headquarters in Washington D.C. and they verified that he had, in fact, been writing the president and had made a threat against his life. We worked with his family and eventually they had the man committed to a mental institution. When the agent-in charge read the report he said, "It takes time, but you'll learn."

Summary

New agents and officers always have questions. Veterans will have some answers and solutions, but when dealing with something as unpredictable as the human element, questions will continue to be an important consideration. A trainer/educator won't always have the answer. All we can do is to address those questions that are most commonly asked by those who have an interest and expect to work undercover. The answers provided here are the result of many years of working undercover and have been proven by the test of time and experience. When working in areas such as undercover, one should always expect the unexpected, but if some doubts can be eliminated the undercover agent can go forward with an increased attitude of confidence.

Final Summary

8

Of all the tools available to law enforcement personnel, nothing quite captures the imagination or evokes the excitement, danger, and intrigue as does working undercover. Perhaps it is the allusion to "daring-do" or respect for the courage and resourcefulness of the undercover operative, but the mere mention of undercover work in a case causes a jury to listen a little more attentively, the press to be more interested, and the public to be eager to learn more. Undercover is the non-military equivalent of covert human intelligence gathering. It actually places an operative in the camp of those who would commit an otherwise unsolvable or undetectable crime.

Historically, since there have been opposing factions, the concept of undercover has been part and parcel of each sides inventory of weapons. Some may call it "spying," others call it "entrapment" but to law enforcement personnel who are working to stem the flow of drugs or other contraband, undercover work is called "effective." Since the days when English Parliament member, Sir Robert Peel launched a successful campaign to establish a jurisdictional police force to quell the chaos of an unruly society where crimes went unreported, undetected, and unsolved, undercover has been embraced as a means to gather evidence, produce witnesses to testify in court, and to deter certain unlawful activities.

The principles of undercover work are simple enough: infiltrate the target criminal group, obtain the evidence, effect an arrest, and testify in court. But getting from A (infiltration of the group or introduction to the suspect) to Z (incarceration of the lawbreaker) requires many critical steps.

The initiation of the undercover case most often originates with an indispensable and sometimes disparaged partner — the informant. Often wrongly referred to as a "squeal," a "stool," or a "whistle-blower," an informant provides information about a wrongful act or a continuing series of acts, which, if left unchecked would result in great financial loss or human life. A secondary role of the informant, but of no less importance, is his unique positioning to introduce or expedite the introduction of an undercover agent into the sphere of the person or group responsible for the illegal acts.

Working with an informant is very sensitive simply because of his positioning or relationship to the suspect. Anyone can be an informant — a housewife, the corner newspaper salesman, pimps and prostitutes, high-level business executives, anyone who has information and wishes to provide that knowledge to an appropriate law enforcement agency. As varied as the personality, life style, and background of the informant, so to are the reasons or motivations they have for providing the information. Some informants come forward for the most basic of reasons — the prospect of a monetary reward. They will "shop around" until they find an agent or agency willing to pay market price for something that only they can provide — knowledge of an illegal activity and the prospect of introducing an undercover agent to the participants of the activity. Other people inform for personal reasons. They want revenge upon a former colleague, they have concern for a family member, or perhaps they are attempting to make a deal to satisfy a pending legal action of their own.

Whenever an agent prepares a complaint or warrant based upon information received from an informant, he must articulate the reliability of the informant and the likely accuracy of the information. This may be achieved by citing the informant's past involvement in cases that resulted in the seizure of contraband, the suppression of the illegal activity and/or the arrest of a suspect. If the informant has no past history of providing information, his reliability can be established by independent verification such as documentation of activity as described by the informant and other factors that can be investigated. The only informant and information that does not have to be explained to a court in terms of reliability is that received from a fellow law enforcement agent. Courts have recognized that information received from a law enforcement officer is considered reliable solely because it originates with a sworn police officer.

Cooperation between officers and agencies is a very necessary part of the equation against the proliferation of contraband and the livelihood of the criminals. The sharing of information and informants is a very necessary part of law enforcement. There should be no secrets or professional reservations about sharing relevant information that may be of official interest to another agency. If, however, an informant does not wish to be identified to another agency, his concern should be respected. It is very possible to share information while protecting the identity of the informant.

Shielding the informant's identity is of utmost importance and concern to the agent and the agency conducting the undercover work. The life of the informant and/or his family could be dependent upon his identity never being disclosed. One of the most famous informants of all time, whose identity has never been revealed is "Deep Throat", the individual working in the inner circles of the White House who provided the *Washington Post* reporters with a daily flow of "insider" information regarding the Nixon-Watergate scandal and subsequent coverup.

Even though potentially having to testify in a court is only a small part of the necessity of an informant, in some rare instances it is better to have the cases dismissed rather than disclose the identity of an informant. The role of the undercover agent includes making observations, engaging in activities with the suspect, and testifying in court. In the absence of other witnesses or by refusing to place the informant in jeopardy, it is the responsibility of the undercover agent to testify fully and establish credibility for his courtroom testimony. The agent must never lie or mislead the court to protect an informant. His credibility will be impeached and the case lost.

Doing "more of what works and less of what doesn't" is a postulate to be followed in any enterprise but in a business like undercover work, where there aren't step-by-step instructions to the human variables, the best teacher is experience. An interchange of ideas and thoughts combined with actual application in real situations produces successful undercover operatives. Less-experienced agents should listen and learn from seasoned agents. It is a reckless, perhaps dangerous, pursuit to fail to learn from every undercover operation. Whether it is a first time undercover assignment or the latest in a long line of many years of dealing with unsavory elements in their own environment, the undercover agent will gain a certain bit of knowledge that will serve him well on future assignments. At the conclusion of the case, it is imperative that an in-depth debriefing be held to examine the circumstances of the case. The factors that led to success should be noted and retained for future reference while examining and discarding those that either failed to produce results or contributed a risk of exposure to either the informant or the undercover agent.

The one factor that cannot be predicted and controlled is the human involvement. An informant, though a very helpful and important part of the operation, might not always be fully trustworthy or because of some human foible may cause an inadvertent misstep resulting in exposure or suspicion on the part of the suspect. The informant will be cooperating for any number of reasons and his motivation may not always be clear but an undercover agent must determine, to the extent possible, the informant's incentive. Understanding why an informant is involving himself will provide the undercover agent with information that he can factor in and plan around if necessary and make whatever adjustments he feels are prudent. The suspect may make demands that are beyond the reach of reason, creating undue pressure and risk to the undercover agent. An individual in an undercover capacity will feel emotions of misgivings and apprehension that if left unchecked will lead to self-doubt and possible loss of confidence. An undercover agent must project an image of strength and control. He has to have confidence in his own ability, the reliability of the informant and most importantly his support team. The undercover agent's first commandment should be to arrange particulars and details as much in his favor as possible. He should attempt to control the selection of location for meetings, the method of exchanging money for contraband, and any other consideration that will push the odds of success more into his control. Often there are situations that cannot be controlled by the undercover agent and he must either make allowances for them by countering with alternate plans or being flexible enough to arrange mitigating circumstances. When dealing with such variables as human involvement, nothing should be taken for granted or assumed. The only thing that can be taken for granted and assumed is that something unforeseen will occur and only with good luck and/or quick thinking will the undercover agent be able to overcome it.

Knowing that he is being placed in a potentially dangerous position, the undercover agent must be mentally prepared for any contingency. That includes suspicion by the suspect and his associates, possible exposure, and physical harm. It is usually the agent's option, depending upon the circumstances of the case and the people he is dealing with, to carry a concealed weapon and/or a body transmitter. The agent will experience anxiety and fear, as he knows he will be working alone. That fear can be healthy and turned to the agent's advantage. Sometimes he will have a partner posing as a secondary "buyer" and a covering team may be in the vicinity, but the usual condition places the undercover agent alone in an environment that one miscalculation or mistake could mean serious trouble. His mental attitude uses his fear and anxiety to make him more alert to everything that is happening around him and forces him to be able to cope with most any evolving situation. The agent will have mentally addressed the possibility of facing guns pointed at him in anger and mistrust. One undercover agent said he goes into every undercover situation accepting that he might be hurt but his "mental set" is such that he also knows he can minimize his pain and that he will also be able to overcome his wounds. He recognizes that the mental approach is extremely important when facing potentially serious injury. His attitude is that the suspect will not have the same mental approach, therefore he will be able to prevail. Fear is a natural emotion for this type of work but it is also a great motivator.

Product knowledge is a prerequisite for any good salesman. The same stipulation must be placed on an undercover agent because what is an undercover agent if not a good salesman? Whether it is counterfeit clothing, luggage, or money, drugs, pirated computer software, or widgets, the undercover agent must be able to appreciate and know what he is buying. Without recognizing or being able to distinguish the quality of the product he is buying, the undercover agent will not be able to determine the value of his purchase. Overpaying for the goods and "throwing" money will most likely tip off the suspect. He will either become suspicious and withdraw from further negotiations or plan on "ripping-off" the undercover agent or "setting" him up for injury.

Physical preparation for doing undercover work is as important as the mental. It begins with meeting with the informant and discussing as many aspects of the suspect and his operation as the informant may know. This includes everything from clothing, habits, place of residence, employment, etc. to food and drink preferences. The undercover agent should dress and act accordingly but must not role-play beyond his assumed identity. That is, he should never present himself as a former prison inmate if he has no knowledge of the prison system, meaning from the prisoner's point of view. The same is to be said for any role he takes. The undercover agent must have an insider's knowledge of whatever occupation he alludes to and must be prepared to answer any and all questions regarding his assumed identity. When preparing an undercover identification such as a driver's license, organization and union cards, or business cards the agent should choose a name that sounds like his real name and possibly one with the same initials. This makes for easier response and signature writing and in the instance someone recognizes him and calls him by his real name, the agent can readily say that the name was misunderstood.

The undercover agent's car and wallet must be carefully searched to remove any papers or articles that would arouse the suspect's suspicions. It may be desirable to place certain documents in the car or wallet to mislead the suspect if he decides to search the undercover agent. These documents could include letters from a parole board, newspaper articles, etc. It might even be necessary to establish an employment work place and references.

The search for better methods and more efficient ways to combat crime are never ending. Technology has made more sophisticated equipment available to investigative agencies. Computers are making information instantly available (though at the same time providing the criminal with more sophisticated ways to "beat the system"). Colleges and universities are doing their part by providing degrees and training in the criminal justice and administration of justice systems including courses in the latest investigative techniques. Police academies are providing realistic training about the policies and procedures of law enforcement and orientation to the legal requirements of their position. Foundations are offering grants for research into crime and ways to combat it. Police organizations have pooled their assets to make a stronger assault against the criminal. Several units and task forces are being formed by city, state, and federal governments to form a concentrated effort to fight organized crime, drug smuggling, and proliferation of contraband. These are some of the positive sides of the ledger, on the opposite side we have apathy on the part of the public who are not interested in suppressing crime until it hits close to home. There is also, in some cases, apathy on the part of the police officer himself, both the old timer and the newest recruit who are satisfied to hold down a job for the sake of the paycheck and could care less about detection and prevention of crime. The pendulum swings only so far in one direction and must change its position and inexorably head in the opposite direction. There appears to be a new popular interest in crime deterrence and police agencies are attempting to identify and remove those officers who are just "marking time."

The first line of defense for those caught as a result of the hard work and courage of a few undercover agents is to cry "foul." The perennial plea is to proclaim innocence through entrapment. The defense of entrapment has been liberalized but the interpretation has also been broadened to give law enforcement wider latitude in the scope of their investigations. If the concept of the criminal activity does not originate with the officer and if it can be articulated that the defendant had a mental predisposition to carry out the crime with or without the officers involvement, there is no entrapment defense. It has been shown in most undercover cases that the officer was merely a conduit for the illegal purposes of the criminal, thus there is no entrapment.

With all the new innovations in criminal investigations nothing has really changed in the basic concept of the work. Like the infantry soldier in all the past wars, the police officer is the final bastion in the war against crime. In order to solve a case, a suspect must be identified, arrested, and convicted. In order to convict a person there must be witnesses to testify. It is the policeman whose job it is to find the witness and produce him in court. In some cases it is the policeman himself who either has witnessed the crime or becomes a witness because he has worked undercover and can give first-hand testimony. This is the supreme effort any officer can make in the battle against crime, short of giving his life, which on occasions he is forced to do.

Much has been discussed about undercover work in this book. There is no doubt it is one of the more successful ways to fight crime. We have discussed that it is not an exact science but a specialized art that cannot be learned by reading books and sitting in classrooms. The principles can be learned from texts and lectures but experience is the mother of all teachers. Over the years, certain techniques have been tried and discarded, others have been tried and retained. As the underworld becomes familiar with certain methods and procedures they are reevaluated and new techniques have to be innovated to stay one step ahead of the criminal.

Undercover work has been used to some successful degree through the years. Its popularity continues to grow. Evolution of procedures has led us to newer forms of undercover operations. The trend today is toward "sting" operations where police establish a "store-front" operation, providing a place where criminals can bring the contraband to a seemingly legitimate outlet. This provides an opportunity to videotape and record the transactions without placing an undercover agent at the mercy and whims of a suspect. Arrests are made on a wholesale scale at a later date and at the convenience of the police. Sting operations have been proven as very effective tools but there will always be a need for "trench warfare"... the lone operative walking a tightrope in a clandestine role, meeting, and "roping" the "coniackers. "

Glossary

Beef A violation; a criminal matter; "working off a beef" is when a criminal becomes an informant in another case to receive favorable consideration in his own case.

Blow away Shoot or kill.

Blow off Disregard; pay no attention.

Bogus bills or bogus Counterfeit money or an imitation article.

Bringing heat Focusing police or law enforcement attention on a particular individual, group or activity.

Bust Arrest.

Buy/Bust An arrest of the suspect immediately after exchange of contraband and money.

Buy Making a purchase of contraband; usually in an undercover capacity.

Carrying heat Carrying a concealed weapon.

Coiner One who makes counterfeit coins.

"Coniacker" One who deals in counterfeit money or coins.

Connected Having ties to organized crime figures; an associate of the Mafia, the "Mob" or the "Syndicate."

Contraband A product or substance whose mere possession is illegal.

Counterfeit Not the real thing; an imitation.

Entrapment When the concept of the illegal activity originates with the law enforcement agent and the suspect is arrested as a result.

Flash roll A large roll of cash usually of smaller denominations covered with one or two large denomination bills. A visual trick to deceive another into believing the holder has a large amount of cash.

Front A façade; a person acting as a surrogate for another person or organization; the point person.

Front money Money paid in advance of receiving the contraband.

Funny money Counterfeit money.

G-man Government agent.

Going sideways Double dealing; leading the undercover agent into a possible trap.

Going to the hole A law enforcement officer, primarily a patrol officer, finding a quiet, undisturbed place to sleep while on duty.

Good-faith money Money given or put up by a buyer to show his "good will" or intention to continue the bargain.

Green stuff Counterfeit money.

Heat A slang term for police or law enforcement; refers to the closeness or interest of police in a certain person or activity.

Heater A slang term for a gun.

Heavy; Heavy weight; Heavy hitter An influential or very involved person.

Informant Literally one who gives information; usually a conduit through which an undercover agent gains access or an introduction to a suspect or group.

Junkie Lending of money at exorbitant or usurious and extortionate rates..

Loanshark An addicted drug abuser or narcotic user.

Mental A person experiencing mental problems; someone considered not normal or average.

Mental case A mentally ill person; may be considered out of touch with reality.

Plant Place where counterfeit money is made; *see* Source.

Plant connection Principal salesman of counterfeit money; has ties to the source or plant.

Plant man Maker of counterfeit money.

Plates Metal plates used to print counterfeit money.

Police junkie A "groupie;"a police "wannabe;" obsessed with police matters and officers; having a need to be involved with police business; usually a female admirer of police officers.

Psycho An obviously demented person; someone experiencing episodes of mental illness; a possible threat.

Queer Counterfeit; "funny money."

Rip-off A robbery or theft; taking the property of another without his consent or through trickery, fraud, or force.

Roll-over A defendant decides to cooperate; changes sides.

Roping An old-time term for working undercover.

Roscoe; "Brother Roscoe" An old-time slang term for a gun usually a revolver or pistol.

SA Special Agent.

SAIC Special Agent-in-Charge.

Scam A fraud; a convincing act to gain the confidence of an intended victim or a ruse, a form of trickery to separate a person from his money or property.

Set-up A plan or activity enticing the victim into a trap or a vulnerable position.

Source Person responsible for the making and/or distribution of contraband.

Stand-up guy Someone who will take full blame and not implicate others.

Sting A planned police operation affording an opportunity for a criminal to conduct his illegal enterprise; a "confidence" game. The word was popularized by the press after the success of the movies by the same name.

Strung out A drug user needing a "hit," a "booster shot," or a "fix;" beginning to feel the side effects or withdrawal symptoms of using drugs; under a great deal of stress.

Talk-the-talk Popular jargon/slang; having the ability to converse on a peer level with a particular culture/subculture.

The Man Police, law enforcement agents, authority figures; occasionally used to describe a racketeer who controls the plant or source of the contraband; the main person involved with the criminal enterprise; the top decision maker.

T-Man Treasury Agent.

Wannabe "Want to be," i.e., person who has a great ambition in being involved with police work, yet, for some reason is not qualified to be considered for employment.

APPENDIX A
Corporate/Industrial Undercover

The emphasis of this book has been on law enforcement undercover work with a special focus on U.S. Secret Service cases. However, undercover work is not the sole province of governmental agencies. Industry and the corporate environment also have their reasons for utilizing the unique talents of an undercover agent. We have referred to numerous items from non-law enforcement and private and business sectors that are counterfeited and sold as contraband. But purchasing contraband and pursuing the manufacturers and distributors are not the only areas of interest to an industrial undercover operative. The following list contains some of the topics that may be brought to the attention of the investigator. While this list may not include all the subjects of concern, it incorporates many factors that an industrial undercover agent might have to develop further. It contains areas a corporate executive will seek to have resolved and most probably will be the motivation for employing the undercover agent.[1]

Controlled Substances:

- talk of drugs/alcohol
- sale, possession, or use of drugs
- alcohol consumption
- working under the influence of drugs/alcohol

Misconduct:

- theft
- talk of theft

[1] These lists have been complied with the special assistance of Ms. Barbara Greer-Petzold of Advance Career College/American Academy of Police Science, Los Angeles, CA.

- unauthorized use of company property (telephones, computers, copiers, fax machines)
- vandalism, graffiti, or sabotage/misuse of company property
- falsification of company records (times cards, production records, etc.)
- tardiness/absenteeism
- gambling/loansharking
- arguing/fighting/threats on employees/extortion
- pilfering (stealing from storage or warehousing)
- idling
- eating/smoking in unauthorized areas
- insubordination
- disgruntled employee/violence indicators
- unauthorized breaks

Management Issues:

- lack of supervision
- favoritism/discrimination
- sexual/employee harassment
- unnecessary overtime
- fraternization (management/employee)
- profanity
- quality control and customer service
- training
- quality of supervision
- effects of policy, systems, or procedure changes
- confidentiality issues

Miscellaneous:

- questionable activity
- talk of criminal activity
- past criminal history (not noted on job application)
- injuries (genuine and alleged)
- poor custodial maintenance resulting in health and safety hazards

Security Issues:

- weapons possession (knives, guns, etc.)
- fences/enclosures
- vehicle/equipment security
- hazardous conditions
- proprietary information and classified documents
- employee and visitor screening

APPENDIX B
U.S. Secret Service Investigations

The U. S. Secret Service continues to suppress the counterfeiting of currency and securities of the United States and of foreign governments. The Service is also responsible for investigating the fraud and forgery of U. S. checks, bonds, and other obligations. In 1984, Congress passed legislation expanding Secret Service investigative jurisdiction to include fraud related to false identification documents and devices; fraud and related activities involving credit and debit cards; investigative authority relating to computer fraud; and, at the direction of the Secretary of the Treasury, authorization to investigate fraud associated with the electronic funds transfer system of the U. S. Treasury. In 1990, Congress further expanded the Service's jurisdiction regarding criminal violations against federally insured financial institutions to include savings and loan investigations.

During the first year on the job, a special agent receives five months of formal classroom and simulation training. The remaining seven months are spent in an on-the-job training program.

Special agents begin general investigative training at the Federal Law Enforcement Training Center in Glynco, Georgia. They continue to receive comprehensive and specialized protective and investigative training at Secret Service facilities in the Washington D. C. area. The special agent training curriculum consists of protective techniques, investigative procedures, criminal law, rules of evidence, surveillance techniques, undercover operations, interviewing techniques, defensive measures, and emergency medicine. Special emphasis is placed on the jurisdictional areas of counterfeiting, forgery, financial crimes, and physical protection.

Throughout their careers, special agents regularly participate in advanced training programs that enhance their ability to effectively accomplish the Secret Service mission.

Because of the magnitude of its responsibilities, the Secret Service relies heavily on the support of outside organizations and individuals. State, county, and local law enforcement organizations are valued partners of the Service in every phase of its investigative and protective operations.

Ordinary citizens also assist the Service in various ways: by learning about counterfeiting and forgery; by taking steps to protect themselves from these crimes; and by reporting any suspicious activity to their local police or Secret Service office. The support of all Americans is important to the success of the dual investigative and protective missions of the Secret Service.[1]

[1] From U.S. Secret Service information brochures.